FATHERS

Enjoy reading this
book — share
in the lives of others.

Love,

Alan

2015. 12.

Fathers

A LITERARY ANTHOLOGY

Edited by
André Gérard

Patremoir Press
#18 2649 Quebec St.
Vancouver, B.C.
V5T 3A6
604 872 8255
grenpipiens@gmail.com

As much as possible, the spelling, typography and the layout of the pieces in this anthology try to respect the original British, Canadian and American sources. Permissions are listed on pages 426-429.

LIBRARY AND ARCHIVES CATALOGUING ON PUBLICATION

Fathers : a literary anthology / edited by André Gérard.

ISBN 978-0-9865554-0-4

1. Fathers—Literary collections. 2. English literature—20th century. 3. American literature—20th century. 4. Canadian literature (English)—20th century. I. Gérard, André, 1953-

PR1111.F37F37 2011   820.8'035251   c2011-900064-4

Edited by André Gérard
Frogs by Susan Pearson (susanpearson.ca)
Cover sketch, "Creative Hands" by Jane Wolsak
Cover photograph, "Generations" by Thomas Coles
   (jthomasphotographic.com)
Design and layout by Vancouver Desktop Publishing Centre
   (self-publish.ca)
Printed in Canada by Friesens

For family and friends,
for Gunner, Tess, and Aron,
and for Bill Messenger.

Patremoir (pa-tre-mwär): book, essay, poem, play, or film built around memories of the author's father.

If I'm not here you can still talk to me. You can talk to me and I'll talk to you. You'll see.

—Cormac McCarthy, *The Road*

CONTENTS

INTRODUCTION

All fathers except mine are invisible in daytime; daytime is ruled by mothers, and fathers come out at night. Darkness brings home fathers, with their real, unspeakable power. There is more to fathers than meets the eye.

—Margaret Atwood, *Cat's Eye*

But first, a word about mothers. Nothing can be said about fathers without first saying a word about mothers. Fathers and mothers are inextricably, intimately linked. In the natural, procreative course of things there is no mother without a father and, conversely, no father without a mother. In the essays and poems that follow, the idea of mother closely shadows the idea of father, and in many instances what can be said of one parent can be said of the other. However, where either parent could be invoked, the word *father* is used for simplicity's sake and, of course, because this is an anthology about fathers.

A further word about mothers. It could be said that until recently the subject of fathers preoccupied essayists far more than the subject of mothers. This may be because, in patriarchal societies, fathers were valued more than mothers. It may also be that children, and particularly sons, have taken their mothers for granted. More likely, though, as Atwood observes, it is because children often have a hard time seeing and understanding their fathers clearly. As such father essays are tools crafted to elucidate, to liberate. And so, on to fathers and all that they entail, including mothers.

Since the beginnings of Western Literature, children have been looking to understand their fathers, trying to gather father stories, attempting to make sense of their own lives by putting together the pieces of their fathers' lives. It is often overlooked that the *Odyssey* is almost as much the story of Telemachus trying to learn about his father as it is an account of Odysseus' personal trials. The goddess Athena in her wisdom sends Telemachus off to Pylos and Sparta to seek out news of his father. Only by coming to terms with his father can Telemachus become an adult and claim the kingdom that is rightfully his.

As Telemachus learns, "It's a wise child who knows its own father," and it's a rare child indeed who hasn't been troubled by trying to make sense of its father, in the flesh or in the spirit. We don't, it would seem, have to be Hamlets to be troubled by the ghosts of our fathers, living or dead. With the possible exception of *mother*, *father* is the most burdened word in our language, containing within it a bewildering profusion of emotions, experiences, understandings, and misunderstandings. Fathers, as Atwood's quotation suggests, are often Grendelian figures, figures of darkness and myth, figures to be fought and feared. The mother, in her ready availability, and with her nurturing warmth, is usually more accessible to us. The father, however—even today—is often more remote, more absent, and more authoritarian,—and to judge by the following essays our interactions with him, whether physical or psychic, are often difficult.

Perhaps because of the problematic nature of father-child interactions, the father essay does not appear until the end of the 19th century. Confronting fathers directly and publicly is not, and never has been, easy: the patriarch should judge and not be judged. To write about the father is to sit in judgement upon him, and for most cultures this was a taboo too strong to be overcome. The Greeks, despite their searingly perceptive stories about father-child interactions, did not attempt to do so—nor did the Romans, the Italians of the Renaissance, the Elizabethans, or even the Romantics. Paradoxically—but not surprisingly, given the rigid paternalism of the age and the attendant psychological pressures—the father essay, like radical feminism, is a product of the Victorian era.

In 1907, six years after the death of Queen Victoria, Edmund Gosse published his memoir *Father and Son*. As he acknowledges in his concluding sentence, the book was an attempt to throw off his father's yoke and "to fashion his inner life for himself." It was an act of revolt: it was an act of courage. In Victorian England the boundary between the personal and the public world was a formidable one, and Dickens' portrayal of Wemmick in *Great Expectations* is an all too accurate caricature of how sharply those worlds were kept apart. To break down that boundary and to publicly reveal elements of your deepest private self was shocking. To speak intimately and publicly about the father was heretical. Small wonder that *Father and Son* was first published anonymously.

In writing *Father and Son*, Gosse was likely influenced by Puritan biographies of the father such as Increase Mather's *The Life and Death of That Reverend Man of God, Mr. Richard Mather* (1670) and Cotton Mather's *Parentator* (1724). Such biographies were Puritan 'plain style' documents of religious instruction, doctrinal pieces which portrayed the father as a religious *exemplum* rather than as an individual. Gosse was familiar with the writings of Cotton Mather, and in an essay titled "American Folk-song," Gosse refers to the Reverend Cotton Mather as a "surly watch-dog of old times." Most likely, too, he was aware that for over 38 years Cotton Mather served as minister and assistant to his father at Boston's prestigious Old North Church. As Gosse struggled to break free of the influences of his father and his father's religion, Cotton Mather would have provided a powerful cautionary figure.

Though *Father and Son* almost certainly owes a further debt to John Stuart Mill's frankness in speaking of his own father in his *Autobiography* (1873), Gosse's importance in breaking down taboos cannot be overstated. In "The Art of Biography" Virginia Woolf credits him as the first writer who "dared to say that his own father was a fallible human being," thereby opening the way for Lytton

Strachey, Harold Nicolson and the "new biographers." Certainly, *Eminent Victorians* and *Some People* owe a lot to Gosse. Nicolson himself stated that *Father and Son* is not "a conventional biography; still less is it an autobiography. It is something entirely original; it is a triumphant experiment in a new formula." In confronting the memory of the fanatical monomaniac who was his father and by relating the details of his suffocating childhood, Sir Edmund made it "possible to tell the truth about the dead," and to publicly and honestly attempt to explore father-child relationships.

Just over one hundred years after *Father and Son's* publication, the writings in this anthology—along with such recent powerful and moving father tributes as Paul Auster's *The Invention of Solitude*, Li-Young Lee's *Winged Seed*, Art Spiegelman's *Maus*, and Miriam Toews' *Swing Low*—show the great debt we owe Edmund Gosse. Although she meant to be disparaging, Virginia Woolf spoke truer than she knew when she said: "[w]here Boswell left us that profound and moving masterpiece, *The Life of Johnson*, Gosse left us the *Father and Son*." *Father and Son*, in turn, has engendered and continues to engender a rich, varied, and rewarding progeny. Mary Gordon, too, was right when she wondered if she wasn't writing "some non-fiction genre whose proper name hasn't yet been found?"

Edmund Gosse is the father of the "patremoir."

The essays and poems in this anthology are brave, personal attempts to come to terms with fathers, and the variety of responses is as overwhelming as is the intensity. Some of the portrayals are breathtakingly unfair—Sylvia Plath's vitriolic demonization of the father she barely knew—while others are so lovingly affectionate, think Broyard's or Day's—as to make one wonder about the darker side of the man. Not surprisingly, given the welter of complex feelings fathers arouse, this anthology is a feast for Freudians. When writing about fathers, Wordsworth's phrase "The Child is father of the Man," should more properly be rewritten as, "The child is father of the father"; and much can be read in the details of that often painful, often messy birth.

More subtle analysts may want to puzzle out how daughters differ from sons in writing about their fathers. Certainly, sons should be expected to have a more complex relationship since they are usually fated to step into the father role themselves, and so their connection to their fathers may, in that regard, be more ambivalent and more poignant. E. B. White's essay speaks to that. Daughters, though, may have Electra issues to deal with, since for them the father becomes the archetype of the opposite sex. Bliss Broyard's essay, loving and delightful as it is, hints at a daughter dilemma every bit as challenging as the son's. Incest, real or imagined, can further complicate and darken the father-daughter relationship. The essays in this anthology would suggest that daughters and sons can be equally doomed, equally blessed.

For many, the response to the father is complicated by the fact that, for a while at least, the father was often a god who could do no wrong, a giant who cast light so bright and shadow so dark that true sight was never possible. Mary Gordon examines this problem, and Franz Kafka and E.E. Cummings—to name but a few of many others—illustrate it. Even though we often try to make them so, fathers are never of a piece. This is a consequence both of fact and of multiple, superimposed perceptions. The young, vital, god-like father of our infancy metamorphoses into the dying old man of our maturity. Our age shapes our response to our fathers, and the father of our childhood is not the father of our teens, still less of our maturity. The temporal variations in father-child interactions create a distortion, a haze, through which fathers can only be guessed at.

Images of the father are further distorted in the fun house mirror of the child's personality, a personality with strengths and weaknesses and shapes and sizes of its own. Because of temperament—because of confidence, insecurity, courage, timidity, trust, or doubt—for one child a father is a romanticized god, for another a demonized monster with neither view particularly true to an outside observer. Mary Gordon and Sylvia Plath, united in losing their fathers at an early age, made very different men of their respective fathers. Plath's exaggerated portrait is a tantrum of hysterical proportions, while in Gordon's ruefully wistful reappraisal of her disreputable father we see the courage of mature acceptance and generous love. The fathers in these writings reflect their children's needs and emotions.

Clearly, the feelings engendered by a father need bear little correspondence to the man he actually was. Very often the father isn't much more than a receptacle, a mould into which we can project our deepest fears and desires. Pity the poor scapegoat father recast and caricatured in the distortions of the child. Our fathers are what we make of them, and what we make of them depends on who we are; to push the tautology even further, who we are often depends on what we've made of our father. Our fathers absorb us as we absorb them.

Pity, then, poor Herman Kafka. He seems to have been no worse, no more insensitive than the average man, and yet as projected by the consciousness of his hypersensitive son, he assumes Brobdingnagian proportions of coarseness and wilful perversity. In his biography of his father, Lord Randolph Churchill, Winston Churchill, on the other hand, manages to make of his father a visionary paragon, a patriotic Solomon, as misunderstood as he was brilliant, when a truer portrait would have been that of a deranged, deluded, and disturbingly monomaniacal syphilitic. It would seem that in thinking about and trying to understand our fathers, too often we know not what we do, and we should cry out to our fathers to forgive us the injustices we do them.

We live in a confessional age, an age of Oprah and of Letterman, an age whose public revelations make even Jean-Jacques Rousseau seem inhibited, close-mouthed, and reserved. The rush to confession, the rush to wallow publicly in the most private recesses of the self, has spewed forth a host of undigested father essays and raw revelations. Disturbingly similar and boringly repetitious as such essays often are, their constant lamentations and imprecations underscore how painful the subject of fathers can even be, if we abstract the elegiac pain, the simple pain of loss.

Not only do our fathers engender us, they bring us face to face with our own mortality. For much of our lives they stand between us and death. Their death and dissolution, though, presages our own, and for many people the fascination with the father is an expression of our fascination with death. Every father, unless like Bruce Chatwin we have the bad luck to predecease our father, is a pioneer in the world of death, and the older we become the more inclined we are to see them as such. We pore over the details of our father's dying in order to plan our own. We glean and hoard the fragments of their passing in a desperate attempt to cheat death. It is not necessarily concern for our fathers that prompts us to urge them to "rage, rage against the dying of the light." If the father can be reconstituted, if the father can outlive his dying, perhaps immortality or meaning can be conferred upon our own lives.

Perhaps it is rarely possible to be a father without inflicting pain and disappointment on a child; or, more probably, pain and conflict are spurs to writing, and those who write about their fathers are predominantly the grieving, the wounded, and the angry. For all their pain, for all their anger, writings about the father can be an uplifting, moving, stimulating, and insightful form of literature. The pieces in this anthology emphatically demonstrate that poetry and prose about fathers deserve to be sifted free from the mountains of Hallmark saccharine and the hate-filled vomitings which so often obscure and deface the genre. And there can be no denying that father writing is a genre.

Finally, a word about the filters used to select the pieces in this anthology. This anthology makes no claims to being scholarly or exhaustive. Its primary purpose is to gather together good pieces of writing on the common theme of fathers. Quality took precedent over content and that is why much of recent male literature about fathers (*pace* Robert Bly) is not included here. Also, an effort was made to select pieces that were complete within themselves, pieces that were originally written as essays or, in the case of Clarence Day and Churchill, stories that verge on essay form. An excerpt was chosen only when the piece excerpted was felt to be of such high standard (Roth, Dillard), insight (Kafka), or historic importance (Gosse), that it would have been shameful not to include it.

The fame of a writer was also a factor in selecting pieces. Fame may seem to be an undemocratic and reprehensible filter to use in compiling an anthology, yet there is often pleasure in learning more about people we already know something of. In the case of famous writers, there is also the pleasure, if desired, of relating their fatherly explorations to other public aspects of their life. There can also be some literary benefit to knowing a child's thoughts about its father. "Metamorphoses" becomes even more moving after reading Kafka's "Letter," and those who have not yet read Miriam Toews' *A Complicated Kindness* would do well to read a copy to see how lovingly, comically, and wondrously a writer can transmute elements of a father into fiction.

Multiple and subjective as these filters are, this anthology's objective will have been fulfilled if it succeeds in helping readers gain deeper understanding of their relationships with their own fathers. Like Aeneas carrying Anchises from Troy on his back, we all carry our fathers with us. Reading the following essays and poems, seeing how others have handled the load, might make that burden a little lighter and us a little stronger.

—*André Gérard*

Note:

Several readers of the publisher's proof of *Fathers* have taken issue with the lack of attributions for quotations. For the most part, attributions were deliberately omitted so as not to burden this book with too much scholarly apparatus and, with one exception, all quotations should be easily traceable with the help of Google.

DORIS LESSING

There was never any doubt as to which essay would open this anthology. Not only do the opening words of "My Father" provide a wise and poetic explanation of why fathers loom so large in our imaginations, but Doris Lessing's comment that "[w]riting this article is difficult because it has to be 'true'" bravely raises the problem of how we can arrive at the truth when contemplating a subject as complex and as emotionally fraught as a father. The truth is what you make it, and this adage is never truer than when thinking and writing about fathers. Lessing's truth about her father is a marvel of fairness and balance; but if the scale is tipped on the side of love, most children will understand. This essay, after all, is a belated attempt to be there for her father.

MY FATHER

We use our parents like recurring dreams, to be entered into when needed; they are always there for love or for hate; but it occurs to me that I was not always there for my father. I've written about him before, but novels, stories, don't have to be "true." Writing this article is difficult because it has to be "true." I knew him when his best years were over.

There are photographs of him. The largest is of an officer in the 1914-18 war. A new uniform—buttoned, badged, strapped, tabbed—confines a handsome, dark young man who holds himself stiffly to confront what he certainly thought of as his duty. His eyes are steady, serious, and responsible, and show no signs of what he became later. A photograph at sixteen is of a dark, introspective youth with the same intent eyes. But it is his mouth you notice—a heavily-jutting upper lip contradicts the rest of a regular face. His moustache was to hide it:

"Had to do something—a damned fleshy mouth. Always made me uncomfortable, that mouth of mine."

Earlier a baby (eyes already alert) appears in a lace waterfall that cascades from the pillowy bosom of a fat, plain woman to her feet. It is the face of a head cook. "Lord, but my mother was a practical female—almost as bad as you!" as he used to say, or throw at my mother in moments of exasperation. Beside her stands, or droops, arms dangling, his father, the source of the dark, arresting eyes, but otherwise masked by a long beard.

The birth certificate says: Born 3rd August, 1886, Walton Villa, Creffield Road, S. Mary at the Wall, R.S.D. Name, Alfred Cook. Name and surname of Father: Alfred Cook Tayler. Name and maiden name of Mother: Caroline May Batley. Rank or Profession: Bank Clerk. Colchester, Essex.

They were very poor. Clothes and boots were a problem. They "made their own amusements." Books were mostly the Bible and *The Pilgrim's Progress*. Every Saturday night they bathed in a hipbath in front of the kitchen fire. No servants. Church three times on Sundays. "Lord, when I think of those Sundays! I dreaded them all week, like a nightmare coming at you full tilt and no escape." But he rabbited with ferrets along the lanes and fields, bird-nested, stole fruit, picked nuts and mushrooms, paid visits to the blacksmith and the mill, and rode a farmer's carthorse.

They ate economically, but when he got diabetes in his forties and subsisted on lean meat and lettuce leaves, he remembered suet puddings, treacle puddings, raisin and currant puddings, steak and kidney puddings, bread and butter pudding, "batter cooked in the gravy with the meat," potato cake, plum cake, butter cake, porridge with treacle, fruit tarts and pies, brawn, pig's trotters and pig's cheek and home-smoked ham and sausages. And "lashings of fresh butter and cream and eggs." He wondered if this diet had produced the diabetes, but said it was worth it.

There was an elder brother described by my father as: "Too damned clever by half. One of those quick, clever brains. Now I've always had a slow brain, but I get there in the end, damn it!"

The brothers went to a local school, and the elder did well, but my father was beaten for being slow. They both became bank clerks in, I think, the Westminster Bank, and one must have found it congenial, for he became a manager, the "rich brother," who had cars and even a yacht. But my father did not like it, though he was conscientious. For instance, he changed his writing, letter by letter, because a senior criticised it. I never saw his unregenerate hand, but the one he created was elegant, spiky, careful. Did this mean he created a new personality for himself, hiding one he did not like, as he hid his "damned fleshy mouth"? I don't know.

Nor do I know when he left home to live in Luton or why. He found family life too narrow? A safe guess—he found everything too narrow. His mother was too down-to-earth? He had to get away from his clever elder brother?

Being a young man in Luton was the best part of his life. It ended in 1914, so he had a decade of happiness. His reminiscences of it were all of pleasure, the delight of physical movement, of dancing in particular. All his girls were "a beautiful dancer, light as a feather." He played billiards and Ping-Pong (both for his country); he swam, boated, played cricket and football, went to picnics and horse races, sang at musical evenings. One family of a mother and two daughters treated him "like a son only better. I didn't know whether I was in love with the mother or the daughters, but oh I did love going there; we had such good times." He was engaged to one daughter, then, for a time, to the other. An engagement was broken off because she was rude to a waiter. "I could not marry a woman who allowed herself to insult someone who was defenceless." He used to say to my wryly smiling mother: "Just as well I didn't marry either of *them*; they would never have stuck it out the way you have, old girl."

Just before he died he told me he had dreamed he was standing in a kitchen on a very high mountain holding X in his arms. "Ah, yes, that's what I've missed in my life. Now don't you let yourself be cheated out of life by the old dears. They take all the colour out of everything if you let them."

But in that decade—"I'd walk 10, 15 miles to a dance two or three times a week and think nothing of it. Then I'd dance every dance and walk home again over the fields. Sometimes it was moonlight, but I liked the snow best, all crisp and fresh. I loved walking back and getting into my digs just as the sun was rising. My little dog was so happy to see me, and I'd feed her, and make I myself porridge and tea, then I'd wash and shave and go off to work."

The boy who was beaten at school, who went too much to church, who carried the fear of poverty all his life, but who nevertheless was filled with the memories of country pleasures; the young bank clerk who worked such long hours for so little money, but who danced, sang, played, flirted—this naturally vigorous, sensuous being was killed in 1914, 1915, 1916. I think the best of my father died in that war, that his spirit was crippled by it. The people I've met, particularly the women, who knew him young, speak of his high spirits, his energy, his enjoyment of life. Also of his kindness, his compassion, and—a word that keeps recurring—his wisdom. "Even when he was just a boy he understood things that you'd think even an old man would find it easy to condemn." I do not think these people would have easily recognised the ill, irritable, abstracted, hypochondriac man I knew.

He "joined up" as an ordinary soldier out of a characteristically quirky scruple: it wasn't right to enjoy officers' privileges when the Tommies had such a bad time. But he could not stick the communal latrines, the obligatory drinking, the collective visits to brothels, the jokes about girls. So next time he was offered a commission he took it.

His childhood and young man's memories, kept fluid, were

added to, grew, as living memories do. But his war memories were congealed in stories that he told again and again, with the same words and gestures, in stereotyped phrases. They were anonymous, general, as if they had come out of a communal war memoir. He met a German in no-man's-land, but both slowly lowered their rifles and smiled and walked away. The Tommies were the salt of the earth, the British fighting men the best in the world. He had never known such comradeship. A certain brutal officer was shot in a sortie by his men, but the other officers, recognising rough justice, said nothing. He had known men intimately who saw the Angels at Mons. He wished he could force all the generals on both sides into the trenches for just one day, to see what the common soldiers endured—*that* would have ended the war at once.

There was an undercurrent of memories, dreams, and emotions much deeper, more personal. This dark region in him, fate-ruled, where nothing was true but horror, was expressed inarticulately, in brief, bitter exclamations or phrases of rage, incredulity, betrayal. The men who went to fight in that war believed it when they said it was to end war. My father believed it. And he was never able to reconcile his belief in his country with his anger at the cynicism of its leaders. And the anger, the sense of betrayal, strengthened as he grew old and ill.

But in 1914 he was naive, the German atrocities in Belgium inflamed him, and he enlisted out of idealism, although he knew he would have a hard time. He knew because a fortuneteller told him. (He could be described as uncritically superstitious or as psychically gifted.) He would be in great danger twice, yet not die—he was being protected by a famous soldier who was his ancestor. "And sure enough, later I heard from the Little Aunties that the church records showed we were descended the backstairs way from the Duke of Wellington, or was it Marlborough? Damn it, I forget. But one of them would be beside me all through the war, she said." (He was romantic, not only about this solicitous ghost, but also about being a descendant of the Huguenots, on the strength of the "e" in Tayler; and about "the wild blood" in his veins from a great uncle who, sent unjustly to prison for smuggling, came out of a ten-year sentence and earned it, very efficiently, along the coasts of Cornwall until he died.)

The luckiest thing that ever happened to my father, he said, was getting his leg shattered by shrapnel ten days before Passchendaele. His whole company was killed. He knew he was going to be wounded because of the fortuneteller, who had said he would know. "I did not understand what she meant, but both times in the trenches, first when my appendix burst and I nearly died, and then just before Passchendaele, I felt for some days as if a thick, black velvet pall was settled over me. I can't tell you what it was like. Oh, it was awful, awful, and the second time it was so bad I wrote to the old people and told them I was going to be killed."

His leg was cut off at mid-thigh, he was shell-shocked, he was very ill for many months, with a prolonged depression afterwards. "You should always remember that sometimes people are all seething underneath. You don't know what terrible things people have to fight against. You should look at a person's eyes, that's how you tell . . . When I was like that, after I lost my leg, I went to a nice doctor man and said I was going mad, but he said, don't worry, everyone locks up things like that. You don't know—horrible, horrible, awful things. I was afraid of myself, of what I used to dream. I wasn't myself at all."

In the Royal Free Hospital was my mother, Sister McVeagh. He married his nurse which, as they both said often enough (though in different tones of voice), was just as well. That was 1919. He could not face being a bank clerk in England, he said, not after the trenches. Besides, England was too narrow and conventional. Besides, the civilians did not know what the soldiers had suffered, they didn't want to know, and now it wasn't done even to remember

"The Great Unmentionable." He went off to the Imperial Bank of Persia, in which country I was born.

The house was beautiful, with great stone-floored high-ceilinged rooms whose windows showed ranges of snow-streaked mountains. The gardens were full of roses, jasmine, pomegranates, walnuts. Kermanshah he spoke of with liking, but soon they went to Teheran, populous with "Embassy people," and my gregarious mother created a lively social life about which he was irritable even in recollection.

Irritableness—that note was first struck here, about Persia. He did not like, he said, "the graft and the corruption." But here it is time to try and describe something difficult—how a man's good qualities can also be his bad ones, or if not bad, a danger to him.

My father was honourable—he always knew exactly what that word meant. He had integrity. His "one does not do that sort of thing," his "no, it is *not* right," sounded throughout my childhood and were final for all of us. I am sure it was true he wanted to leave Persia because of "the corruption." But it was also because he was already unconsciously longing for something freer, because as a bank official he could not let go into the dream-logged personality that was waiting for him. And later in Rhodesia, too, what was best in him was also what prevented him from shaking away the shadows: it was always in the name of honesty or decency that he refused to take this step or that out of the slow decay of the family's fortunes.

In 1925 there was leave from Persia. That year in London there was an Empire Exhibition, and on the Southern Rhodesian stand some very fine maize cobs and a poster saying that fortunes could be made on maize at 25/- a bag. So on an impulse, turning his back forever on England, washing his hands of the corruption of the East, my father collected all his capital, £800, I think, while my mother packed curtains from Liberty's, clothes from Harrods, visiting cards, a piano, Persian rugs, a governess, and two small children.

Soon, there was my father in a cigar-shaped house of thatch and mud on the top of a kopje that overlooked in all directions a great system of mountains, rivers, valleys, while overhead the sky arched from horizon to empty horizon. This was a couple of hundred miles south from the Zambesi, a hundred or so west from Mozambique, in the district of Banket, so called because certain of its reefs were of the same formation as those called *banket* on the Rand. Lomagundi—gold country, tobacco country, maize country—wild, almost empty. (The Africans had been turned off it into reserves.) Our neighbours were four, five, seven miles off. In front of the house . . . no neighbours, nothing; no farms, just wild bush with two rivers but no fences to the mountains seven miles away. And beyond these mountains and bush again to the Portuguese border, over which "our boys" used to escape when wanted by the police for pass or other offences.

And then? There was bad luck. For instance, the price of maize dropped from 12/- to 9/- a bag. The seasons were bad, prices bad, crops failed. This was the sort of thing that made it impossible for him ever to "get off the farm," which, he agreed with my mother, was what he most wanted to do.

It was an absurd country, he said. A man could "own" a farm for years that was totally mortgaged to the Government and run from the Land Bank, meanwhile employing half-a-hundred Africans at 12/- a month and none of them knew how to do a day's work. Why, two farm labourers from Europe could do in a day what twenty of these ignorant black savages would take a week to do. (Yet he was proud that he had a name as a just employer, that he gave "a square deal.") Things got worse. A fortuneteller had told him that her heart ached when she saw the misery ahead for my father: this was the misery.

But it was my mother who suffered. After a period of neurotic illness, which was a protest against her situation, she became brave and resourceful. But she never saw that her husband was not living in a real world, that he had made a captive of her common sense. We were always about to "get off the farm." A miracle would do it—a sweepstake, a goldmine, a legacy. And then? What a question! We would go to England where life would be normal with people coming in for musical evenings and nice supper parties at the Trocadero after a show. Poor woman, for the twenty years we were on the farm, she waited for when life would begin for her and for her children, for she never understood that what was a calamity for her was for them a blessing.

Meanwhile my father sank towards his death (at 61). Everything changed in him. He had been a dandy and fastidious, now he hated to change out of shabby khaki. He had been sociable, now he was misanthropic. His body's disorders—soon diabetes and all kinds of stomach ailments—dominated him. He was brave about his wooden leg, and even went down mine shafts and climbed trees with it, but he walked clumsily and it irked him badly. He greyed fast, and slept more in the day, but would be awake half the night pondering about . . .

It could be gold divining. For ten years he experimented on private theories to do with the attractions and repulsions of metals. His whole soul went into it but his theories were wrong or he was *unlucky*—after all, if he had found a mine he would have had to leave the farm. It could be the relation between the minerals of the earth and of the moon; his decision to make infusions of all the plants on the farm and drink them himself in the interests of science; the criminal folly of the British Government in not realising that the Germans and the Russians were conspiring as Anti-Christ to . . . the inevitability of war because no one would listen to Churchill, but it would be all right because God (by then he was a British Israelite) had destined Britain to rule the world; a prophecy said 10 million dead would surround Jerusalem—how would the corpses be cleared away?; people who wished to abolish flogging should be flogged; the natives understood nothing but a good beating; hanging must not be abolished because the Old Testament said "an eye for an eye and a tooth for a tooth . . ."

Yet, as this side of him darkened, so that it seemed all his thoughts were of violence, illness, war, still no one dared to make an unkind comment in his presence or to gossip. Criticism of people, particularly of women, made him more and more uncomfortable till at last he burst out with: "It's all very well, but no one has the right to say that about another person."

In Africa, when the sun goes down, the stars spring up, all of them in their expected places, glittering and moving. In the rainy season, the sky flashed and thundered. In the dry season, the great dark hollow of night was lit by veld fires; the mountains burned through September and October in chains of red fire. Every night my father took out his chair to watch the sky and the mountains, smoking, silent, a thin shabby fly-away figure under the stars. "Makes you think—there are so many worlds up there, wouldn't really matter if we did blow ourselves up—plenty more where we came from."

The Second World War, so long foreseen by him, was a bad time. His son was in the Navy and in danger, and his daughter a sorrow to him. He became very ill. More and more often it was necessary to drive him into Salisbury with him in a coma, or in danger of one, on the back seat. My mother moved him into a pretty little suburban house in town near the hospitals, where he took to his bed and a couple of years later died. For the most part he was unconscious under drugs. When awake he talked obsessively (a tongue licking a nagging sore place) about "the old war." Or he remembered his youth. "I've been dreaming—Lord, to see those horses come lickety-split down the course with their necks stretched out and the sun on their coats and everyone shouting . . . I've been dreaming how I walked along the river in the mist as the sun was rising . . . Lord, lord, lord, what a time that was, what good times we all had then, before the old war."

PATRICK LANE

"I circle my father's death for a means to get close. I remember my Uncle Jack pushing my head into my father's coffin. The taste of lipstick and powder will stay on my lips forever. Kiss him, he cried, Kiss your father goodbye." So Patrick Lane *in his memoir,* There is a Season. *There is a cruel courage in how Lane dwells on the memory of his murdered father, in how he sings his song of grief and his own failures as a father dim against the elegiac grief of his own hurt heart. Even so, "Father" would not deserve inclusion in this anthology, would not stand out from dozens of equally worthy poems by dozens of equally worthy poets, if it were not for* There is a Season. *"Father" is a pale, forced intimation of the peace in violence which Lane eventually achieved in his 2004 memoir. In a similar breathtaking, breath-giving vein as Derek Jarman's* Modern Nature *(1991),* There is a Season *turns to nature and gardens for healing from the hurtful, painful wonder of life. In this savage, soothing memoir, Lane fulfills the promise he made in another early father poem, "Fathers and Sons," and reaches "down into the heavy earth" to sing his father "back into the day," and himself free of the poisons of drugs and alcohol.*

FATHER

My father with his bright burst heart, the bullet
exploding in him like some gift the wind had given him,
fell from the sky he'd climbed to, the blood
rushing into him from his startled flesh
so that I imagine his heart a broken sail,
the centre suddenly torn and the strong wind rushing
through him, his blood taking him nowhere
at last, his body a whole vessel.

Who will I be,
I who am now as old as his death,
I who have never been a father to my own
lost children, who have left them
to shift in their worlds, their faces shining
in the bewilderment of their lives?

I have turned in my flesh,
rising to the night and the light of the candles
and stood among shadows that are only the stunned
wandering of moths, their burning wings thin sails
in the flickering light. It is here in the shadows
I try to imagine myself young again, a man
who can lift his father from the sky,
take him down and hold him in my arms,
hold him against my mouth,
and with one free hand, stroke his wet red hair
away from his forehead and tell him it is all
right, that I have him, that the bullet
that streamed through the air toward him
was only the wind.

It did not want his death,
was only a bit of wind in the wrong place
tearing him apart. I want then the whole sails of his heart
beating against my chest. I want him smiling
up at me and saying something I can hear at last
instead of this silence, the sound of his voice,
my own children far away rocking in their lives,
his body next to mine, both of us still alive
and not falling, not falling,
the hurt heart dead at last.

ANGELA CARTER

Even the sunniest of fathers hides patches of darkness. In this exuberant essay, an essay sparkling with a positive, hyperbolic energy worthy of Joyce Cary's Gulley Jimson, Angela Carter's loving portrait hides those patches well—almost as well as, and perhaps for the same reason that her father hid his membership in the Scottish Conservative Party. Nonetheless, Carter is too great an artist, too honest an explorer of the sexual darkness in fairy tales, not to unsettle us with hints about what might lie on the other side of the "curious abyss." Sugar daddies, after all, have more to do with sex than with sugar. The description of her father "chirruping down the street, accompanied by an ever-increasing procession of cats" makes him a Pied Piper figure, a piper of cats rather than of rats, but still, clearly, a Pied Piper. There is also Carter's identification with Cordelia, an identification which many daughters would hesitate to make. Finally, and most disturbingly, there is the striking resemblance between this portrait of Carter's father and that of Uncle Perry, the mythic, surrogate father in her final novel, Wise Children *(1991). It's a wise child who knows her own father, and in* Wise Children, *the heroine, irrepressibly vital and transgressive in her old age, completes her knowledge of Uncle Perry with an incestuous encounter. In her novels or her essays, Angela Carter is never less than subversive.*

SUGAR DADDY

Iwould say my father did not prepare me well for patriarchy; himself confronted, on his marriage with my mother, with a mother-in-law who was the living embodiment of peasant matriarchy, he had no choice but to capitulate, and did so. Further, I was the child of his mid-forties, when he was just the age to be knocked sideways by the arrival of a baby daughter. He was putty in my hands throughout my childhood and still claims to be so, although now I am middle-aged myself while he, not though you'd notice, is somewhat older than the present century.

I was born in 1940, the week that Dunkirk fell. I think neither of my parents was immune to the symbolism of this, of bringing a little girl-child into the world at a time when the Nazi invasion of England seemed imminent, into the midst of death and approaching dark. Perhaps I seemed particularly vulnerable and precious and that helps to explain the over-protectiveness they felt about me, later on. Be that as it may, no child, however inauspicious the circumstances, could have been made more welcome. I did not get a birthday card from him a couple of years ago; when I querulously rang him up about it, he said: 'I'd never forget the day you came ashore.' (The card came in the second post.) His turn of phrase went straight to my heart, an organ which has inherited much of his Highland sentimentality.

He is a Highland man, the perhaps atypical product of an under-developed, colonialized country in the last years of Queen Victoria, of oatcakes, tatties and the Church of Scotland, of four years' active service in World War One, of the hurly-burly of Fleet Street in the twenties. His siblings, who never left the native village, were weird beyond belief. To that native village he competently removed himself ten years ago.

He has done, I realize, what every Sicilian in New York, what every Cypriot in Camden Town wants to do, to complete the immigrant's journey, to accomplish the perfect symmetry, from A to B and back again. Just his luck, when he returned, that all was as it had been before and he could, in a manner of speaking, take up his life where it left off when he moved south seventy years ago. He went south; and made a career; and married an Englishwoman; and lived in London; and fathered children, in an enormous parenthesis of which he retains only sunny memories. He has 'gone home', as immigrants do; he established, in his seventh decade, that 'home' has an existential significance for him which is not part of the story of his children's independent lives. My father lives now in his granite house filled with the souvenirs of a long and, I think, happy life. (Some of them bizarre; that framed certificate from an American tramp, naming my father a 'Knight of the Road', for example.)

He has a curious, quite unEnglish, ability to live life in, as it were, the *third person*, to see his life objectively, as a not unfortunate one, and to live up to that notion. Those granite townships on the edge of the steel-grey North Sea forge a flinty sense of self. Don't think, from all this, he isn't a volatile man. He laughs easily, cries easily, and to his example I attribute my conviction that tears, in a man, are a sign of inner strength.

He is still capable of surprising me. He recently prepared an electric bed for my boyfriend, which is the sort of thing a doting father in a Scots ballad might have done had the technology been available at the time. We knew he'd put us in separate rooms—my father is a Victorian, by birth—but not that he'd plug the metal base of Mark's bed into the electric-light fitment. Mark noticed how the bed throbbed when he put his hand on it and disconnected every plug in sight. We ate breakfast, next morning, as if nothing untoward had happened, and I should say, in the context of my father's house, it had not. He is an enthusiastic handyman, with a special fascination with electricity, whose work my mother once described as combining the theory of Heath Robinson with the practice of Mr Pooter.

All the same, the Freudian overtones are inescapable. However unconsciously, as if *that* were an excuse, he'd prepared a potentially lethal bed for his daughter's lover. But let me not dot the *i*'s and cross the *t*'s. His final act of low, emotional cunning (another Highland characteristic) is to have lived so long that everything is forgiven, even his habit of referring to the present incumbent by my first husband's name, enough to give anybody a temporary feeling.

He is a man of immense, nay, imposing physical presence, yet I tend to remember him in undignified circumstances.

One of my first memories is how I bust his nose. (I was, perhaps, three years old. Maybe four.) It was on a set of swings in a public park. He'd climbed up Pooterishly to adjust the chains from which the swings hung. I thought he was taking too long and set the swing on which I sat in motion. He wasn't badly hurt but there was a lot of blood. I was not punished for my part in this accident. They were a bit put out because I wanted to stay and play when they went home to wash off the blood.

They. That is my father and my mother. Impossible for me to summon one up out of the past without the other.

Shortly after this, he nearly drowned me, or so my mother claimed. He took me for a walk one autumn afternoon and stopped by the pond on Wandsworth Common and I played a game of throwing leaves into the water until I forgot to let go of one. He was in after me in a flash, in spite of the peril to his gents' natty suiting (ever the dandy, my old man) and wheeled me dripping in my pushchair home to the terrible but short-lived recriminations of my mother. Short-lived because both guilt and remorse are emotions alien to my father. Therefore the just apportioning of blame is not one of his specialities, and though my mother tried it on from time to time, he always thought he could buy us off with treats and so he could and that is why my brother and I don't sulk, much. Whereas she—

She has been dead for more than a decade, now, and I've had ample time to appreciate my father's individual flavour, which is a fine and gamy one, but, as parents, they were far more than the sum of their individual parts. I'm not sure they understood their instinctive solidarity against us, because my mother often tried to make us take sides. Us. As their child, the product of their parenting, I cannot dissociate myself from my brother, although we did not share a childhood for he is twelve years older than I and was sent off, with his gas mask, his packed lunch and his name tag, as an evacuee, a little hostage to fortune, at about the time they must have realized another one was on the way.

I can only think of my parents as a peculiarly complex unit in which neither bulks larger than the other, although they were very different kinds of people and I often used to wonder how they got on, since they seemed to have so little in common, until I realized that was *why* they got on, that not having much in common means you've always got something interesting to talk about. And their children, far from being the *raison d'être* of their marriage, of their ongoing argument, of that endless, quietly murmuring conversation I used to hear, at night, softly, dreamily, the other side of the bed-room wall, were, in some sense, a sideshow. Source of pleasure, source of grief; not the glue that held them together. And neither of us more important than the other, either.

Not that I suspected this when I was growing up. My transition from little girl to ravaged anorexic took them by surprise and I thought they wanted my blood. I didn't know what they wanted of me, nor did I know what I wanted for myself. In those years of ludicrously overprotected adolescence, I often had the feeling of being 'pawns in their game'. . . in *their* game, note . . . and perhaps I indeed served an instrumental function, at that time, rather than being loved for myself.

All this is so much water under the bridge. Yet those were the only years I can remember when my mother would try to invoke my father's wrath against me, threaten me with his fury for coming home late and so on. Though, as far as the 'and so on' was concerned, chance would have been a fine thing. My adolescent rebellion was considerably hampered by the fact that I could find nobody to rebel with. I now recall this period with intense embarrassment, because my parents' concern to protect me from predatory boys was only equalled by the enthusiasm with which the boys I did indeed occasionally meet protected themselves against me.

IT WAS a difficult time, terminated, inevitably, by my early marriage as soon as I finally bumped into somebody who would go to Godard movies with me and on CND marches and even have sexual intercourse with me, although he insisted we should be engaged first. Neither of my parents were exactly overjoyed when I got married, although they grudgingly did all the necessary. My father was particularly pissed off because he'd marked me out for a career on Fleet Street. It took me twenty years more of living, and an involvement with the women's movement, to appreciate he was unusual in wanting this for his baby girl. Although he was a journalist himself, I don't think he was projecting his own ambitions on me, either, even if to be a child is to be, to some degree, the projective fantasy of its parents. No. I suspect that, if he ever had any projective fantasies about me, I sufficiently fulfilled them by being born. All he'd wanted for me was a steady, enjoyable job that, perhaps, guaranteed me sufficient income to ensure I wouldn't too hastily marry some nitwit (a favourite word of his) who would displace him altogether from my affections. So, since from a child I'd been good with words, he apprenticed me to a suburban weekly newspaper when I was eighteen, intending me to make my traditional way up from there. From all this, given my natural perversity, it must be obvious why I was so hell-bent on getting married—not, and both my parents were utterly adamant about this, that getting married meant I'd give up my job.

In fact, it *did* mean that because soon my new husband moved away from London. 'I suppose you'll have to go with him,' said my mother doubtfully. Anxious to end my status as their child, there was no other option and so I changed direction although, as it turns out, I *am* a journalist, at least some of the time.

As far as projective fantasies go, sometimes it seems the old man is only concerned that I don't end up in the workhouse. Apart from that, anything goes. My brother and I remain, I think, his most constant source of pleasure—always, perhaps, a more positive joy to our father than to our mother, who, a more introspective person, got less pure entertainment value from us, partly, like all mothers, for reasons within her own not untroubled soul. As for my father, few souls are less troubled. He can be simply pleased with us, pleased that we exist, and, from the vantage point of his wondrously serene and hale old age, he contemplates our lives almost as if they were books he can dip into whenever he wants.

As for the books I write myself, my 'dirty books', he said the other day: 'I was a wee bitty shocked, at first, but I soon got used to it.' He introduces me in the third person: 'This young woman . . . ' In his culture, it is, of course, a matter of principle to express pride in one's children. It occurs to me that this, too, is not a particularly English sentiment.

Himself, he is a rich source of anecdote. He has partitioned off a little room in the attic of his house, constructed the walls out of cardboard boxes, and there he lies, on a camp-bed, listening to the World Service on a portable radio with his cap on. When he lived in London, he used to wear a trilby to bed but, a formal man, he exchanged it for a cap as soon as he moved. There are two perfectly good bedrooms in his house, with electric blankets and everything, as I well know, but these bedrooms always used to belong to his siblings, now deceased. He moves downstairs into one of these when the temperature in the attic drops too low for even his iron constitution, but he always shifts back up again, to his own place, when the ice melts. He has a ferocious enthusiasm for his own private space. My mother attributed this to a youth spent in the trenches, where no privacy was to be had. His war was the War to end Wars. He was too old for conscription in the one after that.

When he leaves this house for any length of time, he fixes up a whole lot of burglar traps, basins of water balanced on the tops of doors, tripwires, bags of flour suspended by strings, so that we worry in case he forgets where he's left what and ends up hoist with his own petard.

He has a special relationship with cats. He talks to them in a soft chirruping language they find irresistible. When we all lived in London and he worked on the night news desk of a press agency, he would come home on the last tube and walk, chirruping, down the street, accompanied by an ever-increasing procession of cats, to whom he would say good night at the front door. On those rare occasions, in my late teens, when I'd managed to persuade a man to walk me home, the arrival of my father and his cats always caused consternation, not least because my father was immensely tall and strong.

He is the stuff of which sitcoms are made.

His everyday discourse, which is conducted in the stately prose of a thirties *Times* leader, is enlivened with a number of stock phrases of a slightly eccentric, period quality. For example. On a wild night: 'Pity the troops on a night like this.' On a cold day:

Cold, bleak, gloomy and glum.

Cold as the hairs on a polar bear's—

The last word of the couplet is supposed to be drowned by the cries of outrage. My mother always turned up trumps on this one, interposing: 'Father!' on an ascending scale.

At random: 'Thank God for the Navy, who guard our shores.' On entering a room: 'Enter the fairy, singing and dancing.' Sometimes, in a particularly cheerful mood, he'll add to this formula: 'Enter the fairy, singing and dancing and waving her wooden leg.'

Infinitely endearing, infinitely irritating, irascible, comic, tough, sentimental, ribald old man, with his face of a borderline eagle and his bearing of a Scots guard, who, in my imagination as when I was a child, drips chocolates from his pockets as, a cat dancing in front of him, he strides down the road bowed down with gifts, crying: 'Here comes the Marquess of Carrabas!' The very words, 'my father', always make me smile.

But why, when he was so devilish handsome—oh, that photograph in battledress!—did he never marry until his middle thirties?

Until he saw my mother, playing tennis with a girlfriend on Clapham Common, and that was it. The die was cast. He gave her his card, proof of his honourable intentions. She took him home to meet her mother. Then he must have felt as though he were going over the top, again.

In 1967 or 1968, forty years on, my mother wrote to me: 'He really loves me (I think).' At that time, she was a semi-invalid and he tended her, with more dash than efficiency, and yet remorselessly, cooking, washing up, washing her smalls, hoovering, as if that is just what he'd retired from work to do, up to his elbows in soapsuds after a lifetime of telephones and anxiety. He'd bring her dinner on a tray with always a slightly soiled tray-cloth. She thought the dirty cloth spoiled the entire gesture. And yet, and yet . . . was she, after all those years, still keeping him on the hook? For herself, she always applauded his ability to spirit taxis up as from the air at crowded railway stations and also the dexterous way he'd kick his own backside, a feat he continued to perform until well into his eighties.

Now, very little of all this has to do with the stern, fearful face of the Father in patriarchy, although the Calvinist north is virtually synonymous with that ideology. Indeed, a short-tempered man, his rages were phenomenal; but they were over in the lightning flash they resembled, and then we all had ice-cream. And there was no fear. So that, now, for me, when fear steps in the door, then love and respect fly out the window.

I do not think my father has ever asked awkward questions about life, or the world, or anything much, except when he was a boy reporter and asking awkward questions was part of the job. He would regard himself as a law-and-order man, a law-abiding man, a man with a due sense of respect for authority. So far, so in tune with his background and his sense of decorum. And yet somewhere behind all this lurks a strangely free, anarchic spirit. Doorknobs fall from doors the minute he puts his hand on them. Things fall apart. There is a sense that anything might happen. He is a law-and-order man help-lessly tuned in to misrule.

AND SOMEWHERE in all this must lie an ambivalent attitude to the authority to which he claims to defer. Now, my father is not, I repeat, an introspective man. Nor one prone to intellectual analysis; he's always got by on his wits so never felt the need of the latter. But he has his version of the famous story, about one of the Christmas truces during World War One, which was *his* war, although, when he talks about it, I do not recognize Vera Brittain's war, or Siegfried Sassoon's war, or anything but a nightmarish adventure, for, as I say, he feels no fear. The soldiers, bored with fighting, remembering happier times, put up white flags, moved slowly forward, showed photographs, exchanged gifts—a packet of cigarettes for a little brown loaf . . . and then, he says, 'Some fool of a first lieutenant fired a shot.'

When he tells his story, he doesn't know what it *means*, he doesn't know what the story shows he really felt about the bloody officers, nor why I'm proud of him for feeling that; nor why I'm proud of him for giving the German private his cigarettes and remembering so warmly the little loaf of bread, and proud of him for his still undi-minished anger at the nitwit of a boy whom they were all forced to obey just when the ranks were in a mood to pack it in and go home.

Of course, the old man thinks that, if the rank and file *had* packed it in and gone home in 1915, the Tsar would still rule Russia and the Kaiser Germany, and the sun would never have set on the British Empire. He is a man of grand simplicities. He still grieves over my mother's 'leftish' views; indeed, he grieves over mine, though not enough to spoil his dinner. He seems, rather, to regard them as, in some way, genetically linked. I have inherited her nose, after all; so why not my mother's voting patterns?

She never forgave him for believing Chamberlain. She'd often bring it up, at moments of stress, as proof of his gullibility. 'And what's more, you came home from the office and said: "There ain't gonna be a war."'

SEE HOW she has crept into the narrative, again. He wrote to me last year: 'Your mammy was not only very beautiful but also very clever.' (Always in dialect, always 'mammy'.) Not that she did anything with it. Another husband might have encouraged her to work, or study, although in the 1930s, that would have been exceptional enough in this first-generation middle-class family to have projected us into another dimension of existence altogether. As it was, he, born a Victorian and a sentimentalist, was content to adore, and that, in itself, is sufficiently exceptional, dammit, although it was not good for her moral fibre. She, similarly, trapped by historic circumstances, did not even know, I think, that her own vague discontent, manifested by sick headaches and complicated later on by genuine ill-health, might have had something to do with being a 'wife', a role for which she was in some respects ill suited, as my father's tribute ought to indicate, since beauty and cleverness are usually more valued in mistresses than they are in wives. For her sixtieth birthday, he gave her a huge bottle of Chanel No. 5.

For what it's worth, I've never been in the least attracted to older men—nor they to me, for that matter. Why *is* that? Possibly something in my manner hints I will expect, nay, demand, behaviour I deem appropriate to a father figure, that is, that he kicks his own backside from time to time, and brings me tea in bed, and weeps at the inevitability of loss; and these are usually young men's talents.

Don't think, from all this, it's been all roses. We've had our ups and downs, the old man and I, for he was born a Victorian. Though it occurs to me his unstated but self-evident idea that I should earn my own living, have a career, in fact, may have originated in his experience of the first wave of feminism, that hit in his teens and twenties, with some of whose products he worked, by one of whose products we were doctored. (Our family doctor, Helen Gray, was eighty when she retired twenty years ago, and must have been one of the first women doctors.)

Nevertheless, his Victorianness, for want of a better word, means he feels duty bound to come the heavy father, from time to time, always with a histrionic overemphasis: 'You just watch out for yourself, that's all.' 'Watching out for yourself' has some obscure kind of sexual meaning, which he hesitates to spell out. As advice he gave me when I was a girl (I could paraphrase this advice as 'Kneecap them'), if this advice would be more or less what I'd arm my own daughters with now, it ill accorded with the mood of the sixties. Nor was it much help in those days when almost the entire male sex seemed in a conspiracy to deprive me of the opportunity to get within sufficient distance. The old man dowered me with too much self-esteem.

But how can a girl have *too much* self-esteem?

Nevertheless, not all roses. He is, you see, a foreigner; what's more, a Highland man, who struck further into the heartland of England than Charles Edward Stuart's army ever did, and then buggered off, leaving his children behind to carve niches in the alien soil. Oh, he'd hotly deny this version of his life; it is my own romantic interpretation of his life, obviously. He's all for the Act of Union. He sees no difference at all between the English and the Scots, except, once my mother was gone, he saw no reason to remain among the English. And his always unacknowledged foreignness, the extroversion of his manners, the stateliness of his demeanour, his fearlessness, guiltlessness, his inability to feel embarrassment, the formality of his discourse, above all, his utter ignorance of and complete estrangement from the English systems of social class, make him a being I puzzle over and wonder at.

It is that last thing—for, in England, he seemed genuinely classless—that may have helped me always feel a stranger, here myself.

He is of perfectly good petty-bourgeois stock; his grandfather owned a shoe shop although, in those days, that meant being able to make the things as well as sell them, and repair them, too, so my grandfather was either a shopkeeper or a cobbler, depending on how you looked at it. The distinction between entrepreneur and skilled artisan may have appeared less fine, in those days, in that town beside the North Sea which still looks as if it could provide a good turnout for a witch burning.

THERE ARE all manner of stories about my paternal grandfather, whom I never met; he was the village atheist, who left a fiver in his will to every minister in the place, just in case. I never met my Gaelic-speaking grandmother, either. (She died, as it happens of toothache, shortly before I was born.) From all these stories I know they both possessed in full measure that peculiar Highland ability, much perplexing to early tourists, which means that the meanest, grubbing crofter can, if necessary, draw himself up to his full height and welcome a visitor into his stinking hovel as if its miserable tenant were a prince inviting a foreign potentate into a palace. This is the courtly grace of the authentic savage. The women do it with especially sly elegance. Lowering a steaming bowl on to a filthy tablecloth, my father's sister used to say: 'Now, take some delicious kale soup.' And it was the water in which the cabbage had been boiled.

It's possible to suspect they're having you on, and so they may be; yet this formality always puts the visitor, no matter what his or her status, in the role of supplicant. Your humiliation is what spares you. When a Highlander grovels, then, oh, then is the time to keep your hand on your wallet. One learns to fear an apology most.

These are the strategies of underdevelopment and they are worlds away from those which my mother's family learned to use to contend with the savage urban class struggle in Battersea, in the 1900s. Some of my mother's family learned to manipulate cynically the English class system and helped me and my brother out. All of them knew, how can I put it, that a good table with clean linen meant self-respect and to love Shakespeare was a kind of class revenge. (Perhaps that is why those soiled tray-cloths upset my mother so; she had no quarrel with his taste in literature.) For my father, the grand gesture was the thing. He entered Harrods like a Jacobite army invading Manchester. He would arrive at my school 'to sort things out' like the wrath of God.

This effortless sense of natural dignity, or his own unquestioned worth, is of his essence; there are noble savages in his heredity and I look at him, sometimes, to quote Mayakovsky, 'like an Eskimo looking at a train.'

For I know so little about him, although I know so much. Much of his life was conducted in my absence, on terms of which I am necessarily ignorant, for he was older than I am now when I was born, although his life has shaped my life. This is the curious abyss that divides the closest kin, that the tender curiosity appropriate to lovers is inappropriate, here, where the bond is involuntary, so that the most important things stay undiscovered. If I am short-tempered, volatile as he is, there is enough of my mother's troubled soul in me to render his very transparency, his psychic good health, endlessly mysterious. He is my father and I love him as Cordelia did, 'according to my natural bond'. What the nature of that 'natural bond' might be, I do not know, and besides, I have a theoretical objection to the notion of a 'natural bond'.

But, at the end of *King Lear*, one has a very fair notion of the strength of that bond, whatever it is, whether it is the construct of culture rather than nature, even if we might all be better off without it. And I do think my father gives me far more joy than Cordelia ever got from Lear.

SHARON OLDS

The Greeks understood how frightening the father could be, and in their mythology, the Titan Kronos castrated his own father before he became the ogre who ate his children alive. Visceral as she so often is, in the following poem Sharon Olds puts the Roman mask on Kronos to highlight the father's darkness and to distance him from the timely distortions which swath the primal darkness of the Greek original. The ravages of time are minimized to bring out the raw psychological savagery with which a father can devour and damage his children. The drunken father, lolling oblivious on the sofa, rapes the tender vulnerability of childhood with sickening gusto. The emphasis is deliberately sexual, deliberately male. Though all the children are being eaten—are being swallowed up by the darkness of the father—what Olds dwells on is the brother's arm, the brother's head, and the brother's genitals. Even when seemingly passive, fathers can be monstrous, and all the more so because they teach the same perversions to their sons. The greatest horror, though, and one familiar to many a father, lies in the fact "he knew what he was doing and he could not / stop himself."

SATURN

He lay on the couch night after night,
mouth open, the darkness of the room
filling his mouth, and no one knew
my father was eating his children. He seemed to
rest so quietly, vast body
inert on the sofa, big hand
fallen away from the glass.
What could be more passive than a man
passed out every night—and yet as he lay
on his back, snoring, our lives slowly
disappeared down the hole of his life.
My brother's arm went in up to the shoulder
and he bit it off, and sucked at the wound
as one sucks at the sockets of lobster. He took
my brother's head between his lips
and snapped it like a cherry off the stem. You would have
    seen
only a large, handsome man
heavily asleep, unconscious. And yet
somewhere in his head his soil-colored eyes
were open, the circles of the whites glittering
as he crunched the torso of his child between his jaws,
crushed the bones like the soft shells of crabs
and the delicacies of the genitals
rolled back along his tongue. In the nerves of his gums and
bowels he knew what he was doing and he could not
stop himself, like orgasm, his
boy's feet crackling like two raw fish
between his teeth. This is what he wanted,
to take that life into his mouth
and show what a man could do—show his son
what a man's life was.

ALAN BENNETT

This moving piece comes from Alan Bennett's Untold Stories *(2005), a collection of reminiscences and essays which he describes as a "compendium" in the nostalgic tradition of Christmas annuals. More poignantly, it is also a book of pre-posthumous pieces. Bennett wrote them after he was diagnosed with cancer and told he had only a fifty-fifty chance of recovery—and this particular piece is imbued with the clarity, gentle honesty, and wry humour that some courageous people are capable of summoning when confronted with the possibility of imminent death. With love and sympathetic understanding, Bennett transcends the barriers of reserve and misunderstanding which often separate children from their fathers. Writing in* The New Yorker, *John Lahr called Bennett the "laureate of loss and littleness"; if to be laureate is to celebrate your subject, then in his conferring of dignity and resolution upon loss and littleness, Bennett is truly deserving of the title. His father is great in his littleness. Bennett celebrates him in the spare, simple details, the honest reserve, the felicity of style, and the intimations of stories left untold.*

excerpt from *UNTOLD STORIES*

My father wore a suit every day of his life. He had two, 'my suit' and 'my other suit', 'my suit' being the one he wore every day, 'my other suit' his best. On the rare occasions when he invested in a new suit the suits moved up a place, 'my other suit' becoming 'my suit', the new suit becoming 'my other suit', with the old one just used for painting in or working in the shop. They were three-piece suits, generally navy, and he always wore black shoes and a collar and tie. This makes him seem formal or dressed like an accountant but he didn't give that impression because he never managed to be smart, his waistcoat ('weskit' as he pronounced it) generally unbuttoned and showing his braces, his sleeves rolled up, and when he was still butchering the suit would smell of meat, with the trousers and particularly the turn-ups greasy from the floor. He never had an overcoat, just a series of fawn or dark green gabardine raincoats, and he always wore a dark green trilby hat.

About clothes Dad must always have been conservative. There are photographs of him as a young man, sitting on the sands in a deck-chair in the 1920s, and he is in his three-piece suit, with dicky-bow and flycollar and even a bowler hat, his only concession to the holiday spirit bare feet. Retirement, which often sanctions some sartorial indulgence, didn't alter this state of affairs, the regime of suit and other suit maintained as before. Or almost.

After he had learned to drive my parents would sometimes collect me off the train at Lancaster. Meeting them there one day in 1970, I came across the bridge to see my mother waiting at the barrier with a stranger, someone got up in a grey check sports coat, two-tone cardigan, brown trousers and what I suppose would be called loafers. I was deeply shocked. It was Dad in leisurewear, the only relic of the man he had always been his green trilby hat.

'What do you think of your Dad's new get-up?' Mam enquired as we were driving home. Not much was the truth of it but I didn't let on, and as Dad didn't say much either I took it to have been Mam's idea, confirmed when the experiment turned out to be short-lived; the sports coat and brown trousers soon demoted to the status of gardening clothes, and we were back on the regime of 'my suit' and 'my other suit'.

Dad's brief excursion into leisurewear wasn't an isolated occurrence but part of a process (Mam would have liked it to have been a programme) called 'branching out'. The aim of 'branching out' was to be more like other people, or like what Mam imagined other people to be, an idea she derived in the first instance from women's magazines and latterly from television. The world of coffee mornings, flower arrangement, fork lunches and having people round for drinks was never one my parents had been part of. Now that Mam was well again and Dad could drive, Mam's modest social ambitions, long dormant, started to revive and she began to entertain the possibility of 'being a bit more like other folks'. The possibility was all it was, though, and much to Dad's relief, all that it remained.

'It's your Dad,' Mam would complain. 'He won't mix. I'd like to, only he won't.'

And there was no sense in explaining to her that these occasions she read about in *Homes and Gardens* were not all that they were cracked up to be, or if it came to the point she'd be nonplussed in company. Other people did it, why couldn't we?

Drink would have helped but both my parents were teetotallers, though more from taste than conviction. Indeed alcohol had, for Mam at least, a certain romance, partly again to be put down to the cocktail parties she had read about in women's magazines. She had never been to, still less given, a cocktail party, which explains why she could never get the pronunciation of the actual word right, invariably laying the stress on the final syllable, cock*tail*. What a cock*tail* was I am sure she had no idea. Russell Harty used to tell how when he was at Oxford he had invited Vivien Leigh round for drinks and she had asked for pink gin. Only having the plain stuff Russell sent a friend out to the nearest off-licence for a bottle of the pink variety. Mam would not have understood there was a joke here, and had she ever got round to giving a cocktail party she would probably have tried to buy a bottle of cocktails.

The nearest my parents came to alcohol was at Holy Communion and they utterly overestimated its effects. However bad the weather, Dad never drove to church because Mam thought the sacrament might make him incapable on the return journey.

They did, however, gather that sherry was a generally acceptable drink, so once they were settled down in the village they invested in a bottle, as a first move in the 'branching out' campaign.

'Your Dad and me are going to start to mix,' Mam wrote. 'We've got some sherry in and we've got some peanuts too.'

Never having tasted the mysterious beverage, though, they lacked any notion of when it was appropriate and treated it as a round-the-clock facility. Thus the vicar, calling with the Free Will offering envelope, was startled to be offered a sweet sherry at 10 o'clock in the morning. They, of course, stuck to tea; or, when they were trying to fit in, Ribena.

'Well,' said Mam resignedly, 'it doesn't do for us. Our Kathleen used to put it in the trifle and it always rifted up on me.'

On another occasion when they had actually been asked out to drinks and gone in great trepidation Mam rang up in some excitement.

'Your Dad and me have found an alcoholic drink that we really like. It's called bitter lemon.'

Nor was it merely the drink at cocktail parties my mother found mysterious, but the food that was on offer there too—cocktail snacks, bits of cheese and pineapple, sausages-on-sticks, food that nowadays would come under the generic term of nibbles. Now sausages were not unknown in our house: my father had been a butcher after all, we took them in our stride. But a sausage had only to be hoisted onto a stick to become for my mother an emblem of impossible sophistication.

With these notions it's hardly surprising they never made the social round or lived the kind of model life my mother used to read about in magazines. They put it down, as they did most of their imagined shortcomings, to their not having been educated, education to them a passport to everything they lacked: self-confidence, social ease and above all the ability to be like other people. Every family has a secret and the secret is that it's not like other families. My mother imagined that every family in the kingdom except us sat down together to a cooked breakfast, that when the man of the house had gone off to work and the children to school there was an ordered programme of washing, cleaning, baking and other housewifely tasks, interspersed with coffee mornings and (higher up the social scale) cocktail parties. What my parents never really understood was that most families just rubbed along anyhow.

A kind of yearning underlay both their lives. Before they moved to the village, my father's dream was of a smallholding (always referred to as such). He saw himself keeping hens, a goat, and growing his own potatoes; an idyll of self-sufficiency.

I was in Holland not long ago, where along every railway line and on any spare bit of urban land were hundreds of neat plots, which were not allotments so much as enclosed gardens, each with a hut, a pavilion almost, outside which the largely elderly owners were sunbathing (some of them virtually naked). Dad would never have gone in for that, but I think, though less cheek by jowl, this was just what he meant by a smallholding. It was a dream, of course, of a generation older than his, a vision of the soldiers who survived the First World War, with Surrey, Essex and Kent full of rundown chicken farms, the sad relics of those days.

Dad had no social ambitions, such aspirations as he did have confined to playing his violin better. He read a good deal, though there was never a bookshelf in the living room and all the books in the house were kept in my room, Mam's view being that books not so much furnished a room as untidied it. What books they had of their own were kept in the sideboard, most of them even at this late stage in their lives to do with self-improvement: *How to Improve Your Memory Power, In Tune With the Infinite, Relax Your Way to Health!* After Dad died my brother and I went to collect his belongings from the hospital—his bus pass, a few toffees he'd had in his pocket, and in his wallet a cutting from a newspaper: 'Cure Bronchitis in a Week! Deep Breathing the Only Answer'.

'We're neither of us anything in the mixing line. We were when we were first married, but you lose the knack.'
'Anyway, I don't see what God has to do with mixing. Too much God and it puts the tin hat on it.'

This is an exchange from *Say Something Happened,* a TV play of mine about an oldish couple visited by a young social worker who is worried by their isolation. It never got to the social worker stage with Mam and Dad, but certainly they kept to themselves more and more as they got older and as Mam's depressions became more frequent. Besides, everything was social. They stopped going to church because all too often they got roped in after the service to take part in a discussion group.

'It was a talk on the Third World,' Dad wrote to me. 'Well, your Mam and me don't even know where the Third World is. Next week it's Buddhism. We're going to give it a miss.'

Small talk, Buddhism, sausages-on-sticks, like the second name he did not want Gordon to have, they were for other people, not for them.

With Mam, though, the dream of sociability persisted. When, after Dad died, she went to live with my brother, I was clearing out the kitchen cupboard, and there behind an old bottle of Goodall's Vanilla Essence and a half-empty packet of Be-Ro Self-Raising Flour I came across a sad little tube of cocktail sticks.

Put simply and as they themselves would have put it, both my parents were shy, a shortcoming they thought of as an affliction while at the same time enshrining it as a virtue. Better to be shy, however awkward it made you feel, than be too full of yourself and always shoving yourself forward.

It may have been shyness that drew my parents together in the first place; my mother was shy as her sisters were not and my father was the least outgoing of his brothers. The early morning wedding at St Bartholomew's, Armley, was a ceremony for a couple shy of ceremony, so it's not surprising if in the years that followed a premium was put on shy and it became our badge.

Half of Dad's morality came out of his shyness, reinforcing as it did the modesty of his expectations while resigning him to the superior enterprise and good fortune of others.

'Your Dad won't push himself forward,' Mam would say, 'that's his trouble.' That it was her trouble too was not the point; she was a woman, after all. Thus he seldom got angry and, too shy to tell anybody off, just 'felt sickened'. Regularly cheated or done down in business, he never became hardened to it or came by a philosophy to cope, other than doing imitations of the people he disliked, longing to give them 'Joe Fitton's remedy'* or just being funny generally. But he chafed against a temperament that made him much liked by everyone except himself and it's not surprising that, suppressing his real feelings, he was a martyr to stomach trouble, a complaint, along with the shyness, he has bequeathed to me.

Shynesss (which will keep cropping up in this book) is a soft word, foggy and woollen, and it throws its blanket over all sorts of behaviour. It covers a middle-aged son or neurasthenic daughter living at home with an elderly mother, through to some socially crippled and potentially dangerous creature incapable of human response; shy a spectrum that stretches from the wallflower to the psychopath. 'A bit of a loner' is how the tabloids put it after some shrinking wreck has ventured to approach or make off with a child

---

* *During the war Dad was a warden in the ARP, his companion on patrol a neighbour, Joe Fitton. Somebody aroused Joe's ire (a persistent failure to draw their blackout curtains, perhaps), and one night, having had to ring the bell and remonstrate yet again, Joe burst out, 'I'd like to give them a right kick up the arse.' This wasn't like Joe at all and turned into a family joke—and a useful one too, as Dad never swore, so to give somebody a kick up the arse became euphemistically known as 'Joe Fitton's remedy'. With Dad it even became a verb: 'I'd like to Joe Fitton him.'*

or exposed himself in a park, 'shy' thought altogether too kindly a description. Because 'soft' comes near it, and 'timid', too, but without the compassion or understanding implicit in shy. That he or she is shy is an excuse or an extenuation that is made by others (mothers in particular) but seldom by the persons concerned. Because if you are shy then you're generally too shy to say so, 'I'm shy' a pretty bold thing to come out with.

Sheltering under shy, it was a long time before I understood that the self-effacing and the self-promoting, shy and its opposite, share a basic assumption, shy and forward the same. Everybody is looking at me, thinks the shy person (and I wish they weren't). Everybody is looking at me, thinks the self-confident (and quite right too). I learned this lesson in time to be able to point it out, probably rather sententiously, to my parents, but it was too late for them, and the other lesson I had learned, that to be shy was to be a bit of a bore, they knew already, to their cost. I assured them, falsely, that everybody felt much as they did but that social ease was something that could and should be faked.

'Well, you can do that,' Dad would say, 'you've been educated,' adding how often he felt he had nothing to contribute. 'I'm boring, I think. I can't understand why anybody likes us. I wonder sometimes whether they do, really.'

I found this heartbreaking because it wasn't said with an eye to being told the opposite. It was genuinely how they thought of themselves.

Left out of this account are all their jokes and fun, the pleasure they got out of life and their sheer silliness. After retirement they both put on weight, and coming in one day I found them sitting side by side on the sofa. 'Here were are,' said Dad, 'Fat Pig One and Fat Pig Two.'

Dad had always been shy about sex, never talking about it directly and disapproving of any reference to it by us as children or even of Mam's occasional 'cheeky' remark. I was used to this and respected it, except that I was not immune to some of the modish stuff talked about mental illness in the seventies and at some point on one of the long drives to and from the hospital I heard myself asking my father if he touched my mother enough. He was too embarrassed to reply, 'Nay, Alan' all that he'd commit himself to, the implication being what business was it of mine. And he was quite right. Who was I to ask what amount of touching went on, who at that time had touched and was touching virtually no one at all? It might have been better, more acceptable as a question, had I said hugging rather than touching, but hugging as a manifestation of (often unfeeling) affection had not yet achieved the currency it did in the eighties and nineties when it often served to demonstrate that other loveless construct, caring. The thought of myself putting the question at all makes me wince in retrospect, but how should I ask about hugging when I knew, as he did, that none of our family were great huggers, though no less affectionate for that.

Dad would have been shy to have been seen embracing Mam, but when I put to him the unnecessary question about touching he could, unthinkably, have retorted that, though it was nothing to do with me, at seventy he still was actually touching Mam when and where it mattered. This emerged a year or two later, in 1974, when he was lying in Intensive Care in the same Airedale hospital recovering, as we were assured, from a heart attack. Mam had only just been discharged from the same hospital and was at home coming round after yet another bout of depression. Dazed by her own illness and stunned by his, she lay in bed talking about Dad, sometimes, as was not uncommon when she was poorly, taking me for him. Out of the blue she suddenly said,

'He does very well, you know, your Dad.'

'Yes,' I said, taking this for a general statement.

'No. I mean for a fellow of seventy-one.'

Again I did not twig.

'Why?'

'Well, you know when we were in Leeds he had to have that little operation to do with his water. Well, most fellers can't carry on much after that. But it didn't make any difference to your Dad. He does very well.'

Had I known it, the pity was all in the tense, since his doing, however well, was now almost done, and he died a few days later.

'It was only on Tuesday he drove us over to Morecambe,' said Mam. 'It was miserable all day, only it fined up at tea time so we thought we'd have a run-out. Will it be all the driving to the hospital that's done it?'

I said I didn't think so, though I did.

'We went up to the West End by the golf course. I wanted a bit of a walk on the sands but we'd only been going a minute when he said, "Nay, Mam, you'll have to stop. I can't go no further." It must have been coming on then.'

I knew exactly the place where they would have been walking. It was up towards Bare, the suburb of Morecambe always thought 'a bit more select'. We had walked on the same sands often, particularly during the war, when all our seaside holidays seemed to be taken at Morecambe. For Dad they were scarcely a holiday at all, as with no one to stand in for him at the Co-op he never managed more than a couple of days, a break so short it was always overshadowed by the grief-stricken leave-taking with which it invariably concluded. The sadness of these partings ought to have been comic, though it never seemed so. Having seen him off on the train the three of us would walk on the empty evening sands as the sun set across the bay, and Mam wept and wept. For what? They were only to be separated four or five days at the most, and Dad wasn't going back to the front but to dreary old Leeds, which seldom even ran to an air raid. It was love, I suppose, and the loneliness of a week with her two uncomforting boys.

So that these sands, where once she had wept so bitterly and grieved so needlessly, should now be the setting for their last walk together seems, if not fitting, then at least symmetrical, the disproportionate grief then finding its appropriate object forty years later, the equation complete.

Afterwards I came to think I might have been in some degree responsible, and that Dad's death was my doing if not my fault. Already written in 1974, though not filmed, was my second TV play, *Sunset Across the Bay,* where I had included a scene in which a retired couple say farewell to their son, who is going off to Australia. I set the goodbye on that same stretch of Morecambe sand before, in a later scene, killing off the father with a stroke in a seafront lavatory. The couple in the play have retired to Morecambe from Leeds and were not unlike my parents, except that whereas in the play their lives are lonely and unhappy and their expectations from retirement unfulfilled, Mam and Dad's retirement, even with Mam's depression, was one of the happiest times of their lives. We made the film that autumn, by which time Dad was three months dead, his first heart attack one Saturday morning in August 1974, the second a week later killing him.

Anyone who writes will be familiar with the element of involuntary prediction that informs the imagination; one writes about something, and if it does not exactly happen a version of it does. Sometimes, when one is writing about oneself, for instance, there is an objective explanation; it was only after writing a play that dealt, albeit farcically, with sexual inhibition that my own sex life picked up, the play a form of crude psychotherapy, 'getting it out of your system' (or 'off your chest') another way of putting it.

That by writing a play about the death of a father I brought on the death of my own is perhaps fanciful, though the thought certainly occurred. But there were other, less notional ways, too, in which I may have contributed to his dying.

The heart attack had not been without warning, but all attention, Dad's included, had been so concentrated on Mam's situation and her recurring depressions that his own failing health went unconsidered, at any rate by me, and he, typically, said nothing on the phone. Or did he? Maybe I didn't want to hear.

I had been taking the journey north less often than previously because I was acting in *Habeas Corpus* in the West End, the only way to get home to drive up on the Sunday and back on the Monday, so if I was neglecting my duties there was some excuse. Still, it was an excuse, and the truth was I was reluctant to be away from London even for a night because I was having a nice time, and what was more, knew it. I was 'living' as one of the characters in another play describes it, the play being *Intensive Care*, in which a father has a heart attack and his son sits at his hospital bedside in order to be with him when he dies, but at the crucial moment is not with his father but in bed with a nurse. I am not I and he is not he, but I could see where that play, written six years later, came from.

I had always been a late starter and aged forty, and in the nick of time as it seemed to me then, I had caught up with that sexual revolution which, so Philip Larkin (who was not a reliable witness) claimed, had begun a decade earlier. While sexual intercourse did not quite begin in 1974 it was certainly the year when sex was available pretty much for the asking . . . or maybe I had just learned the right way to ask. Whatever the reason, I suddenly seemed to be leading the kind of life I was told everybody else had been leading for years. I had at last, as they say, got it together. It was at this point my father died and I was summarily banished from London, where such things were possible, to live with my mother in Yorkshire, where they were not.

It was not quite as sudden as that, as a week intervened between his first attack and the second. I went up straight away to find him in Intensive Care, tired but said to be on the mend. *Habeas Corpus* had only half a dozen performances left so I was going back to London to finish the run, and also to resume my suddenly eventful existence, at least for as long as I was allowed to. On my way I called at the hospital to say goodbye and to tell him that I'd see him in a week's time. He was propped up in bed, his pyjama jacket open, the electrodes that monitored his heart attached to his chest. I don't think he ever sunbathed in his life or even wore an open-necked shirt and the line of his collar was sharp, his worn red face and neck like a helmet above the creamy whiteness of his chest.

We never kissed much in our family; I kissed my mother often but I don't ever recall kissing my father since I was a boy. Even when we were children Dad would make a joke of kissing, pulling a face and sticking his cheek out to indicate the exact spot on which this distasteful task had to be carried out. Seeing him less often than I did, my brother would shake hands, but I can't recall ever doing that either. Which is not to say that we were remote from each other, and indeed I felt much closer to him grown up than I ever did as a child when, smart and a show-off, I often felt myself an embarrassment and not the child he would have wanted.

So I sat for a while at his bedside and then stood up to say goodbye. And uniquely in my adulthood, kissed him on the cheek. Seeing the kiss coming he shifted slightly, and I saw a look of distant alarm in his eyes, on account not just of the kiss but of what it portended. I was kissing him, he clearly thought, because I did not expect to see him again. He knew it for what it was and so did I, because somebody had once done the same to me.[*] It was the kiss of death.

If I could wipe away that kiss and the memory of it I would do, though trusting in the doctor's prognosis I had no thought that Dad was likely to die. I fear what made me kiss him was again the fashionable nonsense

---

[*] See 'A Common Assault', p. 560.

about families being healthier for touching and showing affection, the same modish stuff that had made me ask him if he touched my mother. And it was something similar that made me ask after his death if I might see his body. It was death as the last taboo, death as much a part of life as birth, all the up-to-the-minute Sunday papers stuff. Less forgivably there was some notion that being a writer demanded an unflinching eye, to look on death part of the job. Besides, I was forty and the death of the father was one of the great formative experiences; I had a duty to make the most of it.

He had died on the Saturday morning when I was already on the train north, so when I saw his body on the Monday at Airedale Hospital he had been dead two days. The mortuary was somewhere at the back of the hospital; not a facility I suppose they wanted to make a show of, it was near the boiler room and the back doors of the kitchens. I was put into a curtained room (called the viewing room) where Dad lay under a terrible purple pall. There were two attendants, one of whom pulled back the shroud. It was a shocking sight. His face had shrunk and his teeth no longer fitted so that his mouth was set in a snarl, a look about as uncharacteristic of him as I could ever have imagined. It was the first time in his life (except that it wasn't in his life) that he can have looked fierce. I noticed that the attendants were looking at me, more interested in my reactions than in the corpse which to them must have been commonplace. Noting that at seventy-one he still had scarcely a grey hair, I nodded and they wheeled him out.

Back in London for a couple of days I mentioned my father's death to Miss Shepherd, the tramp on the street who, a few months before, had moved her van into my garden. She did not trouble to express any sympathy, never altogether crediting the misfortune of anyone but herself. Nor in this case.

'Yes. I knew he must have died. I saw him a few days ago. He was hovering over the convent at the top of the street. I think it was to warn you against the dangers of Communism.'

This vision was only slightly more implausible than its purported purpose. I could think of many reasons why my father might have been hovering around at the top of the street ('Try and be more patient with your Mam' for instance) but the Red Menace would have come very low down on the list.

MICHAEL ONDAATJE

In The Man-Eater of Punanai, *Christopher Ondaatje, Michael's brother, writes that "if you don't come to terms with the ghost of your father, it will never let you be your own man." In* "Letters & Other Worlds," *though, Michael is not so much wrestling with ghosts as he is trying to reconcile poetry and prose, past and present. To come to terms with memories of his father, Ondaatje seeks an equilibrium between mind and matter, fact and metaphor; a balance between sobriety and intoxication, life and death. The poetry of the first two stanzas and the last five lines brackets a deliberately inadequate prose report of details of Mervyn Ondaatje's life, details so spare that we have to turn to the father quest of Christopher's* The Man-Eater of Punanai *or to the mythic magic of Michael's* Running in the Family *to fully appreciate Mervyn's deranged obsession with trains and the extremes of his squalid, hallucinatory drinking bouts. Ultimately, Michael Ondaatje creates his father as a "devious and defensive" man, a father who weakly tried to shield his children from his darker worlds. "Letters & Other Worlds" sifts the wreckage of his father's life for "the logic of his love." Michael imaginatively enters into his father to become "the blood searching in his head without metaphor." While imagination allows him to reconcile the irreconcilable, there is a damaged sadness in the forced forgiveness of this reconciliation as Ondaatje collects and invents fragments of "lost history" to call up & possess the ghost.*

LETTERS & OTHER WORLDS

'for there was no more darkness for him and, no doubt
like Adam before the fall, he could see in the dark'

My father's body was a globe of fear
    His body was a town we never knew
    He hid that he had been where we were going
    His letters were a room he seldom lived in
    In them the logic of his love could grow

    My father's body was a town of fear
    He was the only witness to its fear dance
    He hid where he had been that we might lose him
    His letters were a room his body scared

He came to death with his mind drowning.
On the last day he enclosed himself
in a room with two bottles of gin, later
fell the length of his body
so that brain blood moved
to new compartments
that never knew the wash of fluid
and he died in minutes of a new equilibrium.

His early life was a terrifying comedy
and my mother divorced him again and again.
He would rush into tunnels magnetized
by the white eye of trains
and once, gaining instant fame,
managed to stop a Perahara in Ceylon
—the whole procession of elephants dancers

local dignitaries—by falling
dead drunk onto the street.
As a semi-official, and semi-white at that,
the act was seen as a crucial
turning point in the Home Rule Movement
and led to Ceylon's independence in 1948.

   (My mother had done her share too—
   her driving so bad
   she was stoned by villagers
   whenever her car was recognized)

For 14 years of marriage
each of them claimed he or she
was the injured party.
Once on the Colombo docks
saying goodbye to a recently married couple
my father, jealous
at my mother's articulate emotion,
dove into the waters of the harbour
and swam after the ship waving farewell.
My mother pretending no affiliation
mingled with the crowd back to the hotel.

Once again he made the papers
though this time my mother
with a note to the editor
corrected the report—saying he was drunk
rather than broken hearted at the parting of friends.
The married couple received both editions
of *The Ceylon Times* when their ship reached Aden.

And then in his last years
he was the silent drinker,
the man who once a week
disappeared into his room with bottles
and stayed there until he was drunk
and until he was sober.

There speeches, head dreams, apologies,
the gentle letters, were composed.
With the clarity of architects
he would write of the row of blue flowers
his new wife had planted,
the plans for electricity in the house,
how my half-sister fell near a snake
and it had awakened and not touched her.
Letters in a clear hand of the most complete empathy
his heart widening and widening and widening
to all manner of change in his children and friends
while he himself edged
into the terrible acute hatred
of his own privacy
till he balanced and fell
the length of his body
the blood screaming in
the empty reservoir of bones
the blood searching in his head without metaphor

WINSTON CHURCHILL

While this piece was selected by Joseph Epstein for the Norton Book of Personal Essays *(1997), its dream device makes it almost more of a short story than an essay, a Chaucer child rather than one of Montaigne's descendants. Story or essay, this piece impresses with the son's need for parental approbation, even when the father is long dead and the son is an elderly man of 72. It says a lot about the power of fathers that a man as venerable and venerated as Winston Churchill, past and future Prime Minister and the living embodiment of his nation, should still be wrestling with his father's ghost more than 50 years after his death. Admittedly, Churchill had a lot to wrestle with: his father was always very grudging with admiration, approval and attention, and in one harrowing letter, written in 1894, he excoriated the young Churchill for academic failure. Part of his lengthy tirade read, "I no longer attach the slightest weight to anything you may say about your own achievements and exploits." Fathers can possess and obsess us through neglect and injustice as easily as through love.*

THE DREAM

One foggy afternoon in November 1947 I was painting in my studio at the cottage down the hill at Chartwell. Someone had sent me a portrait of my father which had been painted for one of the Belfast Conservative Clubs about the time of his visit to Ulster in the Home Rule crisis of 1886. The canvas had been badly torn, and though I am very shy of painting human faces I thought I would try to make a copy of it.

My easel was under a strong daylight lamp, which is necessary for indoor painting in the British winter. On the right of it stood the portrait I was copying, and behind me was a large looking glass, so that one could frequently study the painting in reverse. I must have painted for an hour and a half, and was deeply concentrated on my subject. I was drawing my father's face, gazing at the portrait, and frequently turning round right-handed to check progress in the mirror. Thus I was intensely absorbed, and my mind was freed from all other thoughts except the impressions of that loved and honoured face now on the canvas, now on the picture, now in the mirror.

I was just trying to give the twirl to his moustache when I suddenly felt an odd sensation. I turned round with my palette in my hand, and there, sitting in my red leather upright armchair, was my father. He looked just as I had seen him in his prime, and as I had read about him in his brief year of triumph. He was small and slim, with the big moustache I was just painting, and all his bright, captivating, jaunty air. His eyes twinkled and shone. He was evidently in the best of tempers. He was engaged in filling his amber cigarette-holder with a little pad of cotton-wool before putting in the cigarette. This was in order to stop the nicotine, which used to be thought deleterious. He was so exactly like my memories of him in his most charming moods that I could hardly believe my eyes. I felt no alarm, but I thought I would stand where I was and go no nearer.

"Papa!" I said.

"What are you doing, Winston?"

"I am trying to copy your portrait, the one you had done when you went over to Ulster in 1886."

"I should never have thought it," he said.

"I only do it for amusement," I replied.

"Yes, I am sure you could never earn your living that way."

There was a pause.

"Tell me," he asked, "what year is it?"

"Nineteen forty-seven."

"Of the Christian era, I presume?"

"Yes, that all goes on. At least, they still count that way."

"I don't remember anything after ninety-four. I was very confused that year . . . So more than fifty years have passed. A lot must have happened."

"It has indeed, Papa."

"Tell me about it."

"I really don't know where to begin," I said.

"Does the Monarchy go on?" he asked.

"Yes, stronger than in the days of Queen Victoria."

"Who is King?"

"King George the Sixth."

"What! Two more Georges?"

"But, Papa, you remember the death of the Duke of Clarence."

"Quite true; that settled the name. They must have been clever to keep the Throne."

"They took the advice of the Ministers who had majorities in the House of Commons."

"That all goes on still? I suppose they still use the Closure and the Guillotine?"

"Yes, indeed."

"Does the Carlton Club go on?"

"Yes, they are going to rebuild it."

"I thought it would have lasted longer; the structure seemed quite solid. What about the Turf Club?"

"It's OK."

"How do you mean, OK?"

"It's an American expression, Papa. Nowadays they use initials for all sorts of things, like they used to say RSPCA and HMG."

"What does it mean?"

"It means all right."

"What about racing? Does that go on?"

"You mean horse-racing?"

"Of course," he said. "What other should there be?"

"It all goes on."

"What, the Oaks, the Derby, the Leger?"

"They have never missed a year."

"And the Primrose League?"

"They have never had more members."

He seemed to be pleased at this.

"I always believed in Dizzy, that old Jew. He saw into the future. He had to bring the British working man into the centre of the picture." And here he glanced at my canvas.

"Perhaps I am trespassing on your art?" he said, with that curious, quizzical smile of his, which at once disarmed and disconcerted.

Palette in hand, I made a slight bow.

"And the Church of England?"

"You made a very fine speech about it in eighty-four," I quoted, "'And, standing out like a lighthouse over a stormy ocean, it marks the entrance to a port wherein the millions and masses of those who at times are wearied with the woes of the world and tired of the trials of existence may seek for, and may find, that peace which passeth all understanding.'"

"What a memory you have got! But you always had one. I remember Dr Welldon telling me how you recited the twelve hundred lines of Macaulay without a single mistake."

After a pause. "You are still a Protestant?" he said.

"Episcopalian."

"Do the bishops still sit in the House of Lords?"

"They do indeed, and make a lot of speeches."

"Are they better than they used to be?"

"I never heard the ones they made in the old days."

"What party is in power now? Liberals or Tories?"

"Neither, Papa. We have a Socialist Government, with a very large majority. They have been in office for two years, and will probably stay for two more. You know we have changed the Septennial Act to five years."

"Socialist!" he exclaimed. "But I thought you said we still have a Monarchy."

"The Socialists are quite in favour of the Monarchy, and make generous provisions for it."

"You mean in regard to Royal grants, the Civil List, and so forth? How can they get those through the Commons?"

"Of course they have a few rebels, but the old Republicanism of Dilke and Labby is dead as mutton. The Labour men and the trade unions look upon the Monarchy not only as a national but a nationalised institution. They even go to the parties at Buckingham Palace. Those who have very extreme principles wear sweaters."

"How very sensible. I am glad all that dressing up has been done away with."

"I am sorry, Papa," I said, "I like the glitter of the past."

"What does the form matter if the facts remain? After all, Lord Salisbury was once so absent-minded as to go to a levée in uniform with carpet slippers. What happened to old Lord Salisbury?"

"Lord Salisbury leads the Conservative party in the House of Lords."

"What!" he said. "He must be a Methuselah!"

"No. It is his grandson."

"Ah, and Arthur Balfour? Did he ever become Prime Minister?"

"Oh, yes. He was Prime Minister, and came an awful electoral cropper. Afterwards he was Foreign Secretary and held other high posts. He was well in the eighties when he died."

"Did he make a great mark?"

"Well, Ramsay MacDonald, the Prime Minister of the first Socialist Government, which was in office at his death, said he 'saw a great deal of life from afar.'"

"How true! But who was Ramsay MacDonald?"

"He was the leader of the first and second Labour-Socialist Governments, in a minority."

"The first Socialist Government? There has been more than one?"

"Yes, several. But this is the first that had a majority."

"What have they done?"

"Not much. They have nationalised the mines and railways and a few other services, paying full compensation. You know, Papa, though stupid, they are quite respectable, and increasingly bourgeois. They are not nearly so fierce as the old Radicals, though of course they are wedded to economic fallacies."

"What is the franchise?"

"Universal," I replied. "Even the women have votes."

"Good gracious!" he exclaimed.

"They are a strong prop to the Tories."

"Arthur was always in favour of Female Suffrage."

"It did not turn out as badly as I thought," I said.

"You don't allow them in the House of Commons?" he inquired.

"Oh, yes. Some of them have even been Ministers. There are not many of them. They have found their level."

"So Female Suffrage has not made much difference?"

"Well, it has made politicians more mealy-mouthed than in your day. And public meetings are much less fun. You can't say the things you used to."

"What happened to Ireland? Did they get Home Rule?"

"The South got it, but Ulster stayed with us."

"Are the South a republic?"

"No one knows what they are. They are neither in nor out of the Empire. But they are much more friendly to us than they used to be. They have built up a cultured Roman Catholic system in the South. There has been no anarchy or confusion. They are getting more happy and prosperous. The bitter past is fading."

"Ah," he said, "how vexed the Tories were with me when I observed that there was no English statesman who had not had his hour of Home Rule." Then, after a pause, "What about the Home Rule meaning 'Rome Rule'?"

"It certainly does, but they like it. And the Catholic Church has now become a great champion of individual liberty."

"You must be living in a very happy age. A Golden Age, it seems."

His eye wandered round the studio, which is entirely panelled with scores of my pictures. I followed his travelling eye as it rested now on this one and on that. After a while: "Do you live in this cottage?"

"No," I said, "I have a house up on the hill, but you cannot see it for the fog."

"How do you get a living?" he asked. "Not, surely, by these?" indicating the pictures.

"No, indeed, Papa. I write books and articles for the Press."

"Ah, a reporter. There is nothing discreditable in that. I myself wrote articles for the *Daily Graphic* when I went to South Africa. And well I was paid for them. A hundred pounds an article!"

Before I could reply: "What has happened to Blenheim? Blandford [his brother] always said it could only become a museum for Oxford."

"The Duke and Duchess of Marlborough are still living there."

He paused again for a while, and then: "I always said, 'Trust the people.' Tory democracy alone could link the past with the future."

"They are only living in a wing of the Palace," I said. "The rest is occupied by MI5."

"What does that mean?"

"A Government department formed in the war."

"War?" he said, sitting up with a startled air. "War, do you say? Has there been a war?"

"We have had nothing else but wars since democracy took charge."

"You mean real wars, not just frontier expeditions? Wars where tens of thousands of men lose their lives?"

"Yes, indeed, Papa," I said. "That's what has happened all the time. Wars and rumours of war ever since you died."

"Tell me about them."

"Well, first there was the Boer War."

"Ah, I would have stopped that. I never agreed with 'Avenge Majuba'. Never avenge anything, especially if you have the power to do so. I always mistrusted Joe."

"You mean Mr Chamberlain?"

"Yes. There is only one Joe, or only one I ever heard of. A Radical turned Jingo is an ugly and dangerous thing. But what happened in the Boer War?"

"We conquered the Transvaal and the Orange Free State."

"England should never have done that. To strike down two independent republics must have lowered our whole position in the world. It must have stirred up all sorts of things. I am sure the Boers made a good fight. When I was there I saw lots of them. Men of the wild, with rifles, on horseback. It must have taken a lot of soldiers. How many? Forty thousand?"

"No, over a quarter of a million."

"Good God! What a shocking drain on the Exchequer!"

"It was," I said. "The Income Tax went up to one and three-pence." He was visibly disturbed. So I said that they got it down to eightpence afterwards.

"Who was the General who beat the Boers?" he asked.

"Lord Roberts," I answered.

"I always believed in him. I appointed him Commander-in-Chief in India when I was Secretary of State. That was the year I annexed Burma. The place was in utter anarchy. They were just butchering one another. We had to step in, and very soon there was an ordered, civilised Government under the vigilant control of the House of Commons." There was a sort of glare in his eyes as he said "House of Commons".

"I have always been a strong supporter of the House of Commons, Papa. I am still very much in favour of it."

"You had better be, Winston, because the will of the people must prevail. Give me a fair arrangement of the constituencies, a wide franchise, and free elections—say what you like, and one part of Britain will correct and balance the other."

"Yes, you brought me up to that."

"I never brought you up to anything. I was not going to talk politics with a boy like you ever. Bottom of the school! Never passed any examinations, except into the Cavalry! Wrote me stilted letters. I could not see how you would make your living on the little I could leave you and Jack, and that only after your mother. I once thought of the Bar for you but you were not clever enough. Then I thought you might go to South Africa. But of course you were very young, and I loved you dearly. Old people are always very impatient with young ones. Fathers always expect their sons to have their virtues without their faults. You were very fond of playing soldiers, so I settled for the Army. I hope you had a successful military career."

"I was a Major in the Yeomanry."

He did not seem impressed.

"However, here you are. You must be over seventy. You have a roof over your head. You seem to have plenty of time on your hands to mess about with paints. You have evidently been able to keep yourself going. Married?"

"Forty years."

"Children?"

"Four."

"Grandchildren?"

"Four."

"I am so glad. But tell me more about these other wars."

"They were the wars of nations, caused by demagogues and tyrants."

"Did we win?"

"Yes, we won all our wars. All our enemies were beaten down. We even made them surrender unconditionally."

"No one should be made to do that. Great people forget sufferings, but not humiliations."

"Well, that was the way it happened, Papa."

"How did we stand after it all? Are we still at the summit of the world, as we were under Queen Victoria?"

"No, the world grew much bigger all around us."

"Which is the leading world-power?"

"The United States."

"I don't mind that. You are half American yourself. Your mother was the most beautiful woman ever born. The Jeromes were a deep-rooted American family."

"I have always," I said, "worked for friendship with the United States, and indeed throughout the English-speaking world."

"English-speaking world," he repeated, weighing the phrase. "You mean, with Canada, Australia and New Zealand, and all that?"

"Yes, all that."

"Are they still loyal?"

"They are our brothers."

"And India, is that all right? And Burma?"

"Alas! They have gone down the drain."

He gave a groan. So far he had not attempted to light the cigarette he had fixed in the amber holder. He now took his matchbox from his watch-chain, which was the same as I was wearing. For the first time I felt a sense of awe. I rubbed my brush in the paint on the palette to make sure that everything was real. All the same I shivered. To relieve his consternation I said:

"But perhaps they will come back and join the English-speaking world. Also, we are trying to make a world organisation in which we and America will be quite important."

But he remained sunk in gloom, and huddled back in the chair. Presently: "About these wars, the ones after the Boer War, I mean. What happened to the great States of Europe? Is Russia still the danger?"

"We are all very worried about her."

"We always were in my day, and in Dizzy's before me. Is there still a Tsar?"

"Yes, but he is not a Romanoff. It's another family. He is much more powerful, and much more despotic."

"What of Germany? What of France?"

"They are both shattered. Their only hope is to rise together."

"I remember," he said, "taking you through the Place de la Concorde when you were only nine years old, and you asked me about the Strasbourg monument. You wanted to know why this one was covered in flowers and crape. I told you about the lost provinces of France. What flag flies in Strasbourg now?"

"The Tricolor flies there."

"Ah, so they won. They had their revanche. That must have been a great triumph for them."

"It cost them their life blood," I said.

"But wars like these must have cost a million lives. They must have been as bloody as the American Civil War."

"Papa," I said, "in each of them about thirty million men were killed in battle. In the last one seven million were murdered in cold blood, mainly by the Germans. They made human slaughter-pens like the Chicago stockyards. Europe is a ruin. Many of her cities have been blown to pieces by bombs. Ten capitals in Eastern Europe are in Russian hands. They are Communists now, you know—Karl Marx and all that. It may well be that an even worse war is drawing near. A war of the East against the West. A war of liberal civilisation against the Mongol hordes. Far gone are the days of Queen Victoria and a settled world order. But, having gone through so much, we do not despair."

He seemed stupefied, and fumbled with his matchbox for what seemed a minute or more. Then he said:

"Winston, you have told me a terrible tale. I would never have believed that such things could happen. I am glad I did not live to see them. As I listened to you unfolding these fearful facts you seemed to know a great deal about them. I never expected that you would develop so far and so fully. Of course you are too old now to think about such things, but when I hear you talk I really wonder you didn't go into politics. You might have done a lot to help. You might even have made a name for yourself."

He gave me a benignant smile. He then took the match to light his cigarette and struck it. There was a tiny flash. He vanished. The chair was empty. The illusion had passed. I rubbed my brush again in my paint, and turned to finish the moustache. But so vivid had my fancy been that I felt too tired to go on. Also my cigar had gone out, and the ash had fallen among all the paints.

MICHAEL LONGLEY

The soldier-father is a common literary trope. In this anthology, he can be glimpsed in Cofer, Chatwin, and Lessing. Dressed in civvies, he also stands in the dwindling light of "Sauvez Vous, Les Enfants," and he lurks, too, in the ever-present shadow of Odysseus. In "Wounds," Longley's achievement is to domesticate the soldier-father, to render him as inextricable from "the violence which lurks under the apparently peaceful surface of our civilization," from the quotidian of carpet-slippers, blaring television, and uncleared supper dishes. In other father poems, Longley's obsequies remember the dismembered elements and memories of the father: "the shrapnel shards that sliced your testicle," the bayoneting of "a tubby German / Who pleaded and wiggled." In the two stanzas of "Wounds," two macabre memories from WWI are juxtaposed against two atrocities from the Irish civil war. "Wounds" is a Heart of Darkness *poem. "Wilder than Gurkhas," it sites "The horror, the horror!" in the "whited sepulchre" of urban detail and civilian life. The narrative "I" throws the packet of Woodbines in with the lucifer and the Sacred Heart of Jesus, in part because "wild" Woodbines (popular with soldiers in both world wars) contributed to the father's real-life cancer and, in part, because despite all of technology and all of our spiritual yearnings we are still bound to savagery and the wildness of the woods. In the face of institutional paralysis and a spinning moral compass, the only hope seems to lie in the last rites of poetic incantation. Memories of the father build the empathy needed to understand and perhaps move past the predicament of the shivering boy.*

WOUNDS

Here are two pictures from my father's head—
I have kept them like secrets until now:
First, the Ulster Division at the Somme
Going over the top with 'Fuck the Pope!'
'No Surrender!': a boy about to die,
Screaming 'Give 'em one for the Shankill!'
'Wilder than Gurkhas' were my father's words
Of admiration and bewilderment.
Next comes the London-Scottish padre
Resettling kilts with his swagger-stick,
With a stylish backhand and a prayer.
Over a landscape of dead buttocks
My father followed him for fifty years.
At last, a belated casualty,
He said—lead traces flaring till they hurt—
'I am dying for King and Country, slowly.'
I touched his hand, his thin head I touched.

Now, with military honours of a kind,
With his badges, his medals like rainbows,
His spinning compass, I bury beside him
Three teenage soldiers, bellies full of
Bullets and Irish beer, their flies undone.
A packet of Woodbines I throw in,
A lucifer, the Sacred Heart of Jesus
Paralysed as heavy guns put out
The night-light in a nursery for ever;
Also a bus-conductor's uniform—
He collapsed beside his carpet-slippers
Without a murmur, shot through the head

By a shivering boy who wandered in
Before they could turn the television down
Or tidy away the supper dishes.
To the children, to a bewildered wife,
I think 'Sorry Missus' was what he said.

MICHAEL IGNATIEFF

Although "August in My Father's House" reaches far beyond the exiled, isolated fabric of Michael Ignatieff's father to present the fuller weave of family, the house is still seen as the father's. "In my father's house every object is a hook which catches my thoughts as they pass," says Ignatieff; and so, too, do his spare, lyrical words stir up and catch memories for the reader. Gentle and intimate as the essay is, it also snarls and bristles with painful insights, insights such as, "[victimhood] is a natural temptation for sons of powerful fathers," and "there is nothing more common, more natural than for fathers and sons to be strangers to each other." "August in My Father's House" is a good introduction to the treasures to be found in Ignatieff's novel, Scar Tissue *and in his non-fiction chronicle,* The Russian Album. Scar Tissue, *incidentally, should be compulsory reading for anyone with a family member who suffers from Alzheimer's or senility. It should be read alongside of Miriam Toew's* Swing Low; *both are moving, clear-eyed, emotionally troubling, yet ultimately therapeutic accounts of what Alzheimer-afflicted families undergo.*

AUGUST IN MY FATHER'S HOUSE

It is after midnight. They are all in bed except me. I have been waiting for the rain to come. A shutter bangs against the kitchen wall and a rivulet of sand trickles from the adobe wall in the long room where I sit. The lamp above my head twirls in the draught. Through the poplars, the forks of light plunge into the flanks of the mountains and for an instant the ribbed gullies stand out like skeletons under a sheet.

Upstairs I can hear my mother and father turn heavily in their sleep. Downstairs our baby calls from the bottom of a dream. What can his dreams be about? I smooth his blanket. His lips pucker, his eyes quiver beneath their lashes.

I have been married seven years. She is asleep next door, the little roof of a book perched on her chest. The light by the bed is still on. Her shoulders against the sheet are dark apricot. She does not stir as I pass.

At the window, the air is charged and liquid. The giant poplars creak and moan in the darkness. It is the mid-August storm, the one which contains the first intimation of autumn, the one whose promise of deliverance from the heat is almost always withheld. The roof tiles are splashed for an instant, and there is a patter among the trumpet vines. I wait, but it passes. The storm disappears up the valley and the first night sounds return, the cicadas, the owl in the poplars, the rustle of the mulberry leaves, the scrabble of mice in the eaves. I lean back against the wall. The old house holds the heat of the day in its stones like perfume in a discarded shawl. I have come here most summers since I was fifteen.

When I was fifteen, I wanted to be a man of few words, to be small and muscular with fine bones, to play slide guitar like Elmore James. I wanted to be fearless. I am thirty-seven. The page is white and cool to the touch. My hands smell of lemons. I still cling to impossible wishes. There is still time.

The house was once a village wash-house. At one end of the pillared gallery, there is a stone pool—now drained—where women used to wash clothes in the winter. At the bottom of the garden under the lyre-shaped cherry tree, there is the summer pool where the sheets were drubbed and slopped between their knuckles and the slanted stones. That was when the village raised silkworms for the Lyons trade a hundred years ago. When that trade died, the village died and the washing pool was covered over with brambles.

THE HOUSE became a shepherd's shelter. He was a retarded boy, crazed by his father's beatings, by the miserable winter pastures, by the cracked opacity of his world. One night in the smoke-blackened kitchen, he and his father were silently drinking. When the father got up to lock away the animals, the son rose behind him and smashed his skull into the door-jamb. After they took the boy away and buried the father, the house fell into ruin, marked in village memory by the stain of parricide.

When we came to look at the place that evening twenty-two years ago, my father sent me up the back wall to check the state of the roof tiles. The grass and brambles were waist-high in the doorway. A tractor was rusting in the gallery and a dusty rabbit skin hung from a roof beam. One push, we thought, and the old adobe walls would collapse into dust. But the beam took my weight and there were only a few places where the moonlight was slicing through to the dirt floor below. The tiles were covered with lichen and I could feel their warmth through the soles of my feet. When I jumped down, I could see they had both made up their mind to buy it.

IT IS my mother's favourite hour. Dinner has been cleared away from the table under the mulberry tree, and she is sitting at the table with a wineglass in her hand watching the light dwindling away behind the purple leaves of the Japanese maple. I sit down beside her. She is easy to be with, less easy to talk to. The light is falling quickly, the heat it bears is ebbing away. After a time she says, 'I never expected anything like this . . . the stone wall that Roger built for us, the lavender hedges, the bees, the house. It's all turned out so well.'

Her voice is mournful, far away.

A Toronto schoolmaster's daughter, squint-eyed and agile, next-to-youngest of four, she rode her bicycle up and down the front steps of her father's school, the tomboy in a family of intellectuals. I have a photograph of her at the age of ten, in boy's skates with her stick planted on the ice of the rink at her father's school. She is staring fiercely into the camera in the manner of the hockey idols of the twenties, men with slick side-partings and names like Butch Bouchard.

It is nearly dark and the lights have come on across the valley. She twirls her wineglass between her fingers and I sit beside her to keep her company, to help the next words come. Then she says, out of nowhere, 'When I was seven, my father said, "Who remembers the opening of the *Aeneid*?" as he stood at the end of the table carving the Sunday joint. "Anyone?" They were all better scholars than me, but I *knew*. "*Arma virumque cano...*" Everyone cheered—Leo, the cook, Margaret, Charity, George, even Mother. My father slowly put down the knife and fork and just stared at me. I wasn't supposed to be the clever one.'

There is some hurt this story is trying to name, a tomboy's grief at never being taken seriously, never being listened to, which has lasted to this moment next to me in the darkness. But her emotions are a secret river. She has her pride, her gaiety and her elusiveness. She will not put a name to the grievance, and silence falls between us. It is dark and we both feel the chill of evening. She gets up, drains her glass and then says, 'Mother always said, "Never make a fuss." That was the family rule. Good night.' I brush her cheek with a kiss. We will not make a fuss.

She was a painter once, and her paintings have become my memory for many of the scenes of my childhood; playing with a crab in a bucket on a rock in Antigonish, Nova Scotia, and watching her painting at the easel a few paces away, her back, her knees and her upraised arm making a triangle of concentration, her brush poised, still and expectant before the canvas, her face rapt with the pleasure of the next stroke.

When I was six she painted my portrait. It was an embarrassment at the time: my friends came to point and laugh because I looked so solemn. But I see now the gift she was handing me across the gulf which divides us from the vision of others: a glimpse of the child I was in my mother's eye, the child I have kept within me. She doesn't paint any more. For a time, marriage and children allowed her a room of her own. But then it was swallowed up or renounced, I don't know which. She says only, 'Either I do it well, or I do not do it at all'.

SHE whispers, 'Have you seen my glasses?'

'Your glasses don't matter. You can do the shopping without them.'

'I know they don't matter. But if he finds out . . . '

'Tell him to . . . ' But now I'm the one who is whispering.

When I find her glasses by the night-table where she put them down before going to sleep, the lenses are fogged and smudged with fingerprints. A schoolgirl's glasses.

She says, 'I know. I know. It runs in the family.'

'What? Forgetting?'

'No.' She gives me a hard stare. 'Dirty glasses. My father's pupils used to say that he washed his in mashed potatoes.'

She owns only one pair. She could hide a second pair in a jar by the stove so she wouldn't be caught out. But she won't defend herself.

I take her into town and buy her a chain so that she can wear them around her neck and not lose them. She submits gaily but in the car on the way back home, she shakes her fist at the windscreen: 'I swore I'd never wear one of these goddamned things.'

When we lived in the suburbs of Ottawa in the fifties, she used to come out and play baseball with the kids in the street on summer evenings. She could hit. In my mind's eye, I see the other boys' mouths opening wide as they follow the flight of the ball from her bat and I see them returning to her face and to her wincing with pleasure as the ball pounds on to the aluminium roof of the Admiral's garage. She puts the bat down with a smile and returns to make supper, leaving us playing in the street under her amused gaze from the kitchen window.

When the Yankees played the Dodgers in the World Series, she wrote to the teacher to say I was sick and the two of us sat on her bed and watched Don Larsen pitch his perfect game and Yogi Berra race to the mound throwing his mask and mitt into the air. We saw Sandy Amaros racing across centre field chasing a high fly ball which he took with a leap at the warning track. In life, the ball hits the turf. In memory, its arc returns unendingly to the perfection of the glove.

THE *notaire* arrives as dusk falls. We sit down for business under the mulberry tree. When my mother and father bought the house and fields twenty-two years ago, the *notaire* was a rotund Balzacian figure who observed with amused contempt while the peasants from whom we were purchasing the property passed a single pair of wire-rim glasses round the table so that each in turn could pore over the documents of sale. The new *notaire* is a sparrow of a woman, my age, a widow with two young sons and a motorcycle helmet on the back seat of her car.

We pore over deeds of sale and cadastral surveys of the fields: one planted in clover once and now overgrown with mint and high grass. The goat is staked there under the walnut tree and eats a perfect circle for his breakfast. Framed between the poplars in front of the house is the lavender field. Once a year in the first week of August, the farmer comes with a machine which straddles the purple rows and advances with a scrabbling, grinding sound, tossing aside bound and fragrant bunches. We watch from the terrace as the field is stripped of its purple and is left a bare, spiky green. The butterflies and bees retreat ahead of the mechanical jaws and, at the end of the day, are found in a desperate, glittering swarm on the last uncut row, fighting for the sweetness of the last plants like refugees crowded into an encircled city.

Then there is the orchard behind the house. It was once full of plums, but the trees were old and wormy and, one by one, they were dropping their branches, tired old men letting go of their burdens. Father called in the bulldozer, but when it came, we all went indoors and clapped our hands over our ears so that we wouldn't have to listen to the grinding of steel on the bark and the snapping of the tap roots. In a quarter of an hour, the planting of generations had been laid waste. But it had to be done. The field is bare now, but olive saplings are beginning to rise among the weeds.

The deeds of sale are all in order. My mother runs a finger over the old papers and stops at her name: *'née à Buckleberry Bradford, Angleterre, le 2 février 1916, épouse sans profession,'* and at his *'né à Saint Petersbourg, Russie, le 16 décembre, 1913, profession diplomate.'*

'"Épouse sans profession" sounds sad, doesn't it?' she says.

They are transferring the title of the property to me and my brother. 'Just once more,' she asks, 'tell me why we have to.'

'Because,' I reply, 'it is cheaper than doing it afterwards.'

Sometimes on the airless August nights, I lie in bed and imagine what it would be like to sell the house, turn it over to strangers and never come back. I find myself thinking of hotel rooms somewhere else: the echo of the empty *armoire*, the neon blinking through the shutters, the crisp anonymity of the towels and sheets. I remember the Hôtel Alesia in Paris, eating brie and cherries together on a hot June afternoon; the Hotel San Cassiano in Venice and its vast *letto matrimoniale*. I remember the next morning lying in bed watching her comb her hair at the dressing-table by the open window. A curl of smoke is rising from the ashtray and the swoop of her brush flickers in the facets of the mirrors. Through the window comes the sound of lapping water and the chug of a barge. We have the whole day ahead of us. I think of all the writing I might do in hotel rooms. Words come easily in hotels: the coils spring free from the weight of home.

In my father's house every object is a hook which catches my thoughts as they pass: the barometers which he taps daily and which only he seems to understand; the dark *armoire* they bought from the crooked *antiquaire* in Île sur Sogue; the Iroquois mask made of straw; the Russian bear on a string; the thermometer marked *gel de raisin, Moscou 1812* at the cold end and *Senegal* at the hot end. My thoughts, cornered by these objects, circle at bay and spiral back-wards to the moods of adolescence.

'OLD AGE is not for cowards.' My father looks at me angrily, as if I cannot possibly understand. 'I have no illusions. It is not going to get any better. I know what she goes through. Don't think I don't. You wake up some mornings and you don't know where the hell you are. Just like a child. Everything is in the fog. Some days it lifts. Some days it doesn't.'

He paces slowly at the other end of the long room, at the distance where truth is possible between us. It is late. Everyone else has gone to bed. We are drinking *tisane*, a nightly ritual usually passed in si-lence. There are thirty-four years between us: two wars and a revo-lution. There is also his success: what he gave me makes it difficult for us to understand each other. He gave me safety. My earliest memory is rain pounding on the roof of the Buick on the New Jersey Turnpike. I am three, sitting between them on the front seat, with the chrome dashboard in front of me at eye level and the black knobs of the radio winking at me. The wipers above my head are scraping across the bubbling sheet of water pouring down the windscreen. We are all together side by side, sharing the pleasure of being trapped by the storm, forced to pull off the road. I am quite safe. They made the world safe for me from the beginning.

He was never safe. His memory begins at a window in St Petersburg on a February morning in 1917. A sea of flags, ragged uniforms and hats surges below him, bayonets glinting like slivers of glass in the early morning sunlight. The tide is surging past their house; soon it will break through the doors, forcing them to run and hide. He remembers the flight south in the summer of 1917, corpses in a hospital train at a siding, a man's body bumping along a dusty road in Kislovodsk, tied by one leg behind a horse. I see it all as newsreel. He was there, with the large eyes of a six-year-old.

As he gets older, his memory scours the past looking for something to hold on to, for something to cling to in the slide of time. Tonight, pacing at the end of the room while I sit drinking the tea he has made for both of us, it is Manya who is in his mind, his nurse-maid, the presence at the very beginning of his life, a starched white uniform, warm hands, the soft liquid syllables of a story at bedtime heard at the edge of sleep. She followed them south into exile. She was the centre of his world, and one morning she was no longer there.

'I woke up and she was gone. Sent away in the night. Perhaps they couldn't afford her. Perhaps they thought we were too close. I don't know.'

Across seventy years, his voice still carries the hurt of that separation, a child's helpless despair. He was her life. She was his childhood.

I try to think about him historically, to find the son within the father, the boy within the man. His moods—the dark self-absorption—have always had the legitimacy of his dispossession. Exile is a set of emotional permissions we are all bound to respect.

He is still pacing at the other end of the room. He says suddenly, 'I don't expect to live long.'

I say: 'It's not up to you, is it?'

He stokes the prospect of his death like a fire in the grate. Ahead of me the prospect beckons and glows, sucking the oxygen from the room. He says he is not afraid of dying, and, in so far as I can, I believe him. But that is not the point. In his voice, there is a child's anger at not being understood, an old man's fear of being abandoned. He does not want a son's pity or his sorrow, yet his voice carries a plea for both. A silence falls between us. I hear myself saying that he is in good health, which is true and entirely beside the point. He says good night, stoops briefly as he passes through the archway, and disappears into his room.

On some beach of my early childhood—Montauk Point? Milocer?—he is walking ahead of me, in those white plastic bathing shoes of his, following the lines of the water's edge, head down, bending now and again and turning to show me what he has found. We decide together which finds go into the pocket of his bathing-suit. We keep a green stone with a white marble vein in it. He takes it to a jeweller to have it set as a ring for her. In some jewellery box back home, it is probably still there.

I don't believe in the natural force of blood ties. There is nothing more common, more natural than for fathers and sons to be strangers to each other. It was only on those silent beach walks together, our voices lost in the surf, our footprints erased by the tide, our treasure accumulated mile by mile, that we found an attachment which we cannot untie.

There was a period in my twenties when that attachment foundered on my embrace of victimhood. It is a natural temptation for sons of powerful fathers. I was elated with destructiveness, righteous for truth. They had sent me away to school when I was eleven, and I wanted to know why. We had ceased to be a family in the flesh, and became one by air mail and transatlantic telephone. Once a year, for a month, in this house, we tried to become a real family again. Such is the story which the victim writes. I wanted to know why. I see his hands covering his face.

Why did I cling to the grievance? The truth is I loved going away from home, sitting alone in a Super Constellation shuddering and shaking high above Greenland on the way back to school, watching the polar flames from the engines against the empty cobalt sky. I won a first-team tie in football. I listened to Foster Hewitt's play by play of Hockey Night in Canada on the radio under my mattress after lights out in the dorm. I was caned for a pillow-fight, a wild and joyful midnight explosion of feathers, the only true uprising that I have ever taken part in. After such an uprising, the punishment—twelve stripes with a bamboo cane—was an honour.

I read *King Lear* in Gallimore's English class. He frogmarched us through every scene, battering us with his nasal southern Ontario intonations: until I fell in love, for the first time, with the power of words.

I went to my first dances and breathed in that intoxicating scent of hairspray, sweat, powder and the gardenia of girls' corsages, that promise of lush revelations in the dark. I became an adult in a tiny tent on a camping ground north of Toronto. The gravel was excruciating on my knees and elbows. The girl was very determined. She guided my hands in the dark. Afterwards she slapped my face, like a caress.

I did what I wanted. Because I was at school, I didn't have to bring her home; I could keep sex a secret. But I clung to the grievance of banishment.

I clung to another grievance too, but this one as much my making as his. I said to him, You have crushed her. She used to paint. Not any more. She has wishes for you and for me, but none for herself. Not any more.

He never forgave me for that, for the absolution I had given myself in blaming him. I see his hands covering his face.

'Truth is good, but not all truth is good to say.'

MY SON is sitting on his grandfather's knee, working over his grandfather's hands with his gums. I notice that my father's signet ring, a carving in amber of Socrates set in a gold oval—one of the survivors of exile and the pawnshop—is missing from the little finger of his left hand. In its place there is a small university ring which seems to pinch. He notices me looking at it.

'I gave it to your brother. You'll get the watch.'

The tops of his hands are strong and sunburned, but the palms are gullied and clenched with arthritis. He no longer wields the axe.

He is tender and wary with his grandson, this messenger of life and his mortality. He strokes the child's chest absently, as if relearning a long-forgotten gesture. My son turns in his lap, and with infantile de liberation removes his grandfather's spectacles. They exchange a blue glance across seventy years. 'In the year 2000,' my father says, 'he will be sixteen.'

When I come through the beaded curtain with my breakfast, my mother is whirling the baby around slowly beneath the mulberry tree, cheek to cheek, holding his arm out against hers in the old style and crooning, 'Come to me, my melancholy baby.' My son has a wild look of pleasure on his face.

'You dance well,' I say.

She whirls slowly to a stop and hands him to me: 'No, I lead too much.'

She whispers in the baby's ear, 'Crazy old granny, crazy old granny.' She is not crazy. She is afraid. Her memory is her pride, her refuge. The captions of *New Yorker* cartoons not seen for forty years; lyrics of Noël Coward and Gerty Lawrence songs from the London of the thirties; the name of the little girl with Shirley Temple curls at the desk next to hers at Bishop Strachan School for Girls; the code-names of all the French agents she helped to parachute into France during the war: her memory is a crammed shoebox of treasures from a full life. It is what happened five minutes ago that is slipping away—the pot on the stove, the sprinkler in the garden, what she just said.

The memory which frightens her, which portends the losses still to come, is of the last time she saw her mother. They spent a week together, and as they were leaving, her mother turned to my father and said, 'You're Russian, aren't you? And who is this charming girl?'

Your daughter.

When I was eight, I spent a weekend with my grandmother in the large, dark house on Prince Arthur Avenue in Toronto. We ate breakfast together: tea on a silver service, Ryvita biscuits imported from England, with the London *Times* in a feathery edition two weeks late. I sat on the end of her bed and we had a conversation, tentative and serious across the gulf of time. I had never seen her hair down before, masses of it—grey, austere and luxuriant against the pillows. There is a kind of majesty in some old women, the deep red glow of a banked fire. I talked on and on, and she followed me with her eyes and a whisper of amusement on her lips.

Then there came a Sunday, not many months later, when I was ushered into the dark mahogany dining-room and knew at once from the slope of her shoulders, the terrible diminution of her presence, the slowness with which she turned to meet my eye, that she had no idea who I was. She stared out through the window at the blank wall of the new hotel rising to block her view. She said nothing. Her eyes were still and grey and vacant. I was speechless through lunch with her, and, when I left, I knew I would never see her again. She died several years later in a nursing home north of the city. Her will, that last relinquishing gesture of generosity in a generous life, enabled my father and mother to buy this house.

My mother is cool and lucid about her own prospects. I do not believe these things run in the family, and I tell her so. She nods and then says, 'I'm sure I would make a cheerful old nut. Don't you think so? In any case,' and here she picks up her drink and walks into the kitchen to look to her cooking, 'it's much worse for those you leave behind.'

IN THE next village, a theatre troupe is staging *Oedipus* on a tiny stage built into the sandstone cliffs at the foot of the village. There is a little boy in front of us in the stands, sitting between his mother and his father. He is about five. Oedipus and Jocasta circle each other slowly against the towering folds of sandstone: the eternal story unfolds in the night air. Oedipus turns his bleeding eyes upon us: 'Remember me, and you will never lose your happiness.'

The little boy rocks backwards and forwards on his seat. He says to himself in a small voice, 'Now I understand everything.'

Then he falls asleep on his mother's lap.

We stay behind afterwards while they dismantle the set. From the top row of the stands, the valley stretches out below us in the amber afterglow of nightfall. The vines and cane windbreaks are drained of colour. The first lights in the village appear. It was this landscape which made me into a European; man's hand is upon it, the millennia of labour, the patient arts of settlement. The stillness is human: the rim of light at the edge of a shutter, the snake of a headlight, the swish of the irrigation sprinklers drenching the earth in the dark. In Canada the silence among the great trees was menacing. No light for miles. The cold. I had no quarrel with the place. I just wanted to get out.

She is standing beside me looking out into the dark valley. She leans her weight against my shoulder. I met her in a street dance in London eight years ago. Within two weeks I had brought her here, knowing that this was the place which would reveal us to each other.

My favourite photograph of her was taken in the first week we spent in this country. She is on the terrace walking towards me, wearing a white dress and a red Cretan sash. Her right hand is pushing the hair back off her forehead. She is smiling, her gaze directly into mine, shy and fearless. It is the last photograph in which she is still a stranger, approaching but still out of reach, still on the other side of the divide, before we fell in love.

The valley below us is black now. A breeze lifts up from the earth and the olive groves. She points to the sparkling village perched ten miles away on a promontory of ochre: 'It's like an ocean liner.'

MICHAEL IGNATIEFF / 97

I am thinking of the *Andrea Doria*. She went down off Nantucket when I was nine. They sent divers down, and they took photographs. She was lying in shallow water, and the lights of her bridge, by some impossible chance, were still on. Like the livid eyes of some great beast staring at the hunter who has brought her down, the ship's lights streamed through the ocean darkness. As a child I used to dream about those pictures of the great ship glowing on the bottom of the sea. It seems to me now that those dreams were an image of what it would be like to die sinking in the folds of the ocean, your own eyes blazing in the salty dark.

On the way down the hill from the village, through the vaulted tunnel of the plane trees, white and phosphorescent in the headlights, she sings to me. Verdi as always. Flat as always, her head leaning back, her eyes staring up at the trees rushing by through the sun-roof.

'I am *not* flat.'

I am laughing.

She ignores me and sings on in a husky voice, '*Libera me . . . de morta aeterna.*'

From the village road, the house looks low and small, its back hunched against the mistral. By Christmas, when the *notaire* has filed the deed, it will belong to my brother and me. But whatever the deeds say, it will always be my father's house. I cannot sell it any more than I can disavow the man I became within its walls, any more than I can break the silences at the heart of family life.

The lights are out. My parents are both asleep, and our son is in his cot.

She says, 'Let's not go in yet.'

We climb up into the field behind the house where the beekeeper has his hives, and where you can see the whole of the Luberon mountains stretched out against the night sky. The shale is cool and the dew is coming down. We watch for satellites and for the night flights to Djibouti, Casablanca and Rome. There are many bright, cold stars. A dog barks. In the house, our child floats in his fathomless sleep.

'Cassiopeia, Ursa Major, Orion's Belt . . . I must learn the names, I want to teach him the names.'

Out of the dark, as if from far away, she says, 'What do you need to name them for?'

SEAMUS HEANEY

In discussing Dylan Thomas's "Do Not Go Gentle into That Good Night,"
Heaney identifies the villanelle as a form "so much a matter of crossings and
substitutions, of back-tracks and double-takes, turns and returns, that it is a
vivid figure for the union of opposites, for the father in the son, the son in the
father, for life in death and death in life." Heaney could just as easily have
been talking about "Follower" or "Digging," the seminal, "coarse-grained
navvy" of a father poem in which, for the first time, he "let down a shaft into
real life." Certainly in "Follower" father follows child, as child once followed
father. The father, Atlas Cyclops all in one, laboured for the child, as the
Heaney narrator now labours for and belabours the father. If as children we
can be a burden and nuisance to our father, so too the memory of our father,
his internalized presence, can be burden and nuisance for us. As children we
sail in the father's shadow, unconsciously absorbing his gait and his craft.
Whether farmer, sailor, or poet, as adults he shadows us still as we work his
field or our own. Although not a villanelle, "Follower" is a poem wrought in
"crossings and substitutions," in "back-tracks and double-takes," in "turns
and returns," in which follower becomes leader and leader follower.
"Wrought," by way of back-track and double-take, was a word common in
the mid-Ulster vernacular of Heaney's farmer father, a word for which
Heaney wisely and self-consciously substituted "worked" in the opening line
of the poem.

FOLLOWER

My father worked with a horse plough,
His shoulders globed like a full sail strung
Between the shafts and the furrow.
The horses strained at his clicking tongue.

An expert. He would set the wing
And fit the bright-pointed sock.
The sod rolled over without breaking.
At the headrig, with a single pluck

Of reins, the sweating team turned round
And back into the land. His eye
Narrowed and angled at the ground,
Mapping the furrow exactly.

I stumbled in his hobnailed wake,
Fell sometimes on the polished sod;
Sometimes he rode me on his back
Dipping and rising to his plod.

I wanted to grow up and plough,
To close one eye, stiffen my arm.
All I ever did was follow
In his broad shadow around the farm.

I was a nuisance, tripping, falling,
Yapping always. But today
It is my father who keeps stumbling
Behind me, and will not go away.

KEN SARO-WIWA, JR.

An anthology of father writings would not be complete without a Hamlet story, and Ken Saro-Wiwa, Jr.'s essay is a perfect example of such a story. His Nigeria, corrupt and murderous, is a second Denmark, and his response to his father's murder is every bit as tormented and reluctant as Hamlet's. Many sons and daughter take on the burden of trying to defend or uphold the public memory of deceased fathers. In this anthology alone, Miriam Toews, Winston Churchill, and even Edmund Gosse undertake that quixotic challenge. Ken Saro-Wiwa, Jr.'s task, however, is even more difficult. Haunted by the need to vindicate a murdered father, he is forced to subsume his life to his father's righteous cause, even to the extent of accepting his father's "old furniture and tastes." We come away from "In the Name of My Father" with deep sympathy for Ken Saro-Wiwa, Jr. and his country, and a greatly deepened understanding of Hamlet's dilemma.

IN THE NAME OF MY FATHER

'Your dad's dead.' For most of my adult life I'd lived in dread of hearing those words. Even before he became a global icon of social justice I was keenly aware that my father's death, whenever it came, would have a profound impact on my life. Years before they killed him I would imagine what it would be like to receive the news. I would rehearse scenarios in my head; how would I feel, how would I react? I never imagined, not even in my wildest calculations, that my father's death would have such an impact well beyond my personal universe.

On the day they killed him I remember walking up a hilly street in Auckland. I was 25 years old and had flown to New Zealand to try to lobby the Commonwealth Heads of State to intervene on behalf of my father, who had been sentenced to death at the end of October. At the top of the street I turned to view the sunset. Looking out over the city centre below me and out into the harbour in the distance, I watched the sun sink into the sea, casting a pale orange glow against the sky. I remember the exact moment he died. I was sitting in a restaurant chatting and laughing with friends when I felt a brief palpitation in my chest—it felt like a vital connection had been ruptured inside me and I just knew. It was midnight in Auckland and midday in Nigeria and my father had just been hanged; his broken body lay in a shallow sand pit in a hut at the condemned prisoners block at Port Harcourt Prison.

His death on 10 November 1995 shook the world. John Major described the trial that sent him to the gallows as a 'fraudulent trial, a bad verdict, an unjust sentence'. Nelson Mandela thundered that 'this heinous act by the Nigerian authorities flies in the face of appeals by the world community for a stay of execution'. Bill Clinton and the Queen added their voices to the worldwide condemnation, Nigeria was suspended from the Commonwealth, countries recalled their diplomats and there were calls for economic sanctions and a boycott of Shell oil.

Sitting here in my father's old office in the busy commercial quarter of the old town of Port Harcourt on the southern coast of Nigeria is a poignant place for me as I look back on his death. I've been travelling in and out of Nigeria since the end of military rule in 1999 dividing my time between my family in Canada and my father's business interests here, and earlier this year I took a decision to relocate my centre of gravity, moving my family back to England while I concentrated on running the business here.

People are always quick to remind me that I have replicated my father's arrangements. I usually smile sheepishly and protest that there are some subtle differences. Like his office, which I was happy to dust down and renovate to suit my own tastes only to be told by his friends and supporters that they preferred the place as it was with my father's old furniture and tastes that were fashionable in about 1982! I eventually gave in to their need to remember my father but the episode was a reminder that while I might feel I have moved on, my father's legacy remains the foundation stone on which we must build the future.

Outside here the streets vibrate to the rhythms of a town that mocks its nickname as the garden city. Where this part of Port Harcourt was once the genteel colonial quarters with elegant mansions and their spacious verandahs, postmodern Africa is busy decolonising the city with a familiar pattern of snarling traffic jams, uncollected refuse and brash expressions of architectural confusion; the whole noise and colour of a city floating on a wave of oil money that creates islands of startling wealth in a sea of dehumanising poverty.

I remember how I would often find my father staring out of these windows. 'Look out there,' he would say gesturing with his chin. 'Out there are all the stories a writer needs.' He would stare in silence with a frown on his face as if he was contemplating some regret. Looking back, I think of him sitting there trying to come to terms with what must have seemed like the impossible burden of bringing those untold stories to the attention of the world.

Writing was my father's great love—I'm never sure how many books he actually produced but he once claimed 25, including poetry anthologies, plays, memoirs, collections of essays, short stories and at least two novels. No doubt he would have loved to have been remembered as a man of letters and he had already arrogated to himself the literary ambition of forging the uncreated conscience of his people in his soul. In the end he never quite managed to publish that book but then the greatest story he ever told was to die for his people and it took his death to realise his ambition of placing his people on the world map.

If you head north east out of Port Harcourt and into the flat, gently sloping floodplains of the Niger River Delta you will likely arrive in my community. To foreign eyes Ogoni must look like any other rural community in sub-Saharan Africa. Off the main road that runs east-west right across the 404 square miles of Ogoni territory, the tarred roads eventually give way to dirt tracks of mud red earth that take you into the villages. You could travel around the 120 or so Ogoni villages and you might not see much evidence of the oil industry that has been at the core of this story but somewhere among the dense mangroves, the palm trees and the giant irokos are the flowstations and pipelines that have pumped 900 million barrels of oil out of the area since the natural resource was discovered there in 1958.

All told, there were once over a hundred oil wells, a petrochemical complex, two oil refineries and a fertiliser plant in the region. An area which, as my father once wrote, should have been as rich as a small Gulf state, stood as an example of how Africa's rich natural resources have impoverished its people and the land they live off.

Associated natural gas has been flared into the atmosphere for over 40 years in Nigeria—pumping noxious fumes into the environment. Nigeria alone accounts for 28 per cent of total gas flared in the world and the flared gas volume in Nigeria translates into the crude oil equivalent of 259,000 barrels per day.

Apart from the gas flares there are the oil spills, the matrix of pipelines that criss-cross Ogoni, sometimes over farmlands and often in close proximity to human habitation. The pipelines had been laid without impact assessment studies, without community consultation and were often laid over appropriated farmland with little or minimal compensation. Few locals dared to question the oil industry because to do so was to be seen to challenge the national security of the country since the governments of Nigeria are dependent on oil revenues for foreign exchange. It takes a brave man to block the flow of oil.

Few dared to question the cosy relationship between the oil companies and Nigeria's ruling elites until my father spoke out. Born on 10 October 1941, he grew up in a traditional home in Ogoni. He saw the coming of the oil industry and as a 17-year-old began writing letters to newspapers questioning the benefits when oil was first discovered in Ogoni. For the next 30 years his commentaries on the oil nexus escalated until he became best known in Nigeria for his trenchant criticisms of the industry.

By exposing the double standards of oil companies who preached sound ecological virtues in the north while singing from an entirely different song sheet in Nigeria, my father earned powerful enemies and became a marked man. Censored by editorial boards and denied a pulpit in a country where poverty made books a luxury, my father decided to abandon his writing and took his words to the streets. In 1990 he was instrumental in forming Mosop (Movement for the Survival of the Ogoni People), a grassroots organisation to mobilise our community to speak out for their rights. So successful was Mosop in raising awareness among the community that, within three years of forming the organisation, an estimated 300,000 of our people spilled out onto the streets of Ogoni during a protest march.

My father later insisted that if he had died that day he would have died a happy man. Instead, from that day, he was a marked man. He was arrested or detained on four separate occasions until his final arrest on 21 May 1994 following a riot in Ogoni at which four prominent chiefs were murdered. My father and hundreds of Ogoni were held for nine months without charge and when he was finally charged to court he was accused of procuring his supporters to murder the four chiefs.

When my father was finally brought before a civil disturbances tribunal the case had dubious merit even within the provisions of the Nigerian law under which he was prosecuted. International and independent observers of the trial criticised the proceedings as unfair and premeditated to deliver a miscarriage of justice and the trial became an international cause célèbre. The sentencing and execution of my father and eight Ogoni was the day my destiny was locked into a path that I had spent my entire adult life trying to resist.

Long before Ken Saro-Wiwa became a symbol of resistance for the Ogoni, Nigerians and social justice activists around the world, he was my father. As a child I had idolised Jeje, as I called him, but when he chose to send me to private schools in England, the cultural dislocation opened up a distance between us. Although my father always wanted the best education for his seven children, he had expected that we would return home to apply our expensively trained minds to the problems at home. It was a trajectory that many Nigerians had followed, returning home to good jobs and a society that could offer a good life and a basic standard of living to repatriated exiles loaded with degrees and doctorates. By the time I had sleepwalked through Tonbridge school and the University of London I had no real idea who I was, what I wanted to do with my life and where I wanted to apply that expensive education. My father was apoplectic and exasperated that his eldest son and namesake showed little or no ambition of following in his footsteps.

Whatever my misgivings about this country because of my father's murder, I knew deep down that I had no choice but to return; my father's multiple legacies, literary, business, personal and political are centred here. His life and death have anchored me to Nigeria and over the past five years of coming and going I have developed the same love-hate relationship with this country that my father had.

Life goes on but the pain never goes, especially as he remains a convicted murderer in Nigeria's statute books, despite UN resolutions to revisit the trial and the intense lobbying of the Nigerian government. The current administration is slowly coming to terms with Ken Saro-Wiwa. President Olusegun Obasanjo and the governor of my state Dr Peter Odili have been true to their word in allowing my family to retrieve my father's bones for a proper burial.

The process of rehabilitating, compensating and reconciling my family to Nigeria is proceeding but it has been too slow and too long in coming. My family remains committed and open to reconciliation and cordial relations between my family and members of the families of the four Ogoni chiefs murdered in May 1994 have been restored and our wounds are starting to heal from inside.

To my mind the 10th anniversary of his death is a symbolic occasion to begin the process in earnest but while I am happy to forgive I don't want to forget—I am mindful that there are still many who are afraid of my father in this country. There is an oil company which, though it has publicly admitted making 'mistakes' in Nigeria, refuses to account or atone for its role in the execution of my father.

That is why, in 1996, we filed a suit against Shell in the US under the Alien Torts Claims Act—which human rights lawyers have used to help non-US citizens file complaints against US companies in the US for torts in foreign jurisdictions. Bringing the case helped to fulfil my father's prophecy that Shell must one day have its day in court. But it is not and has never been about vengeance. On the day my father was executed I was interviewed by David Frost and when he asked me about Shell I very deliberately answered that Shell were part of the problem and must be part of the solution. I knew what I was saying and I knew the risks I was taking then. I still believe in those words that Shell remains part of the problem in the Niger Delta but my feeling is that the company mistakenly believes it can ride out the crisis and return to Ogoni one day. There have been many stillborn attempts to arrive at a resolution of many of the problems in Ogoni and in the Niger Delta as a whole. My family remains open to any process that is transparent, that insists as a gesture of good faith that my father's dignity is restored and the stain on his reputation as a murderer is erased from the statute books.

Returning home has been a bitter sweet experience because while it has undoubtedly been good for the soul, I remain guarded about it if only because the official stance on my father is still muted and divided and I am keenly aware that while Ken Saro-Wiwa has been widely honoured abroad he has not been afforded the same status by his own country.

Plans to commemorate the 10th anniversary of his execution around the world are reminders of what a tremendous legacy I have inherited and the good name that my father left his children. His story has touched ordinary people, is immortalised in songs, and in art. My father would have been so gratified that his death inspired John Le Carré's *The Constant Gardener* and that poets from around the world have contributed to an anthology in his name. Thirty PEN centres will mark the anniversary with a performance or readings of his last play, "On the Death of Ken Saro-Wiwa," written a few days before his execution. In the US a resolution is being deliberated in the Senate, private parties are being held around the US, in Canada there will be a celebration of music and readings by writers and musicians. In London the winner of the Living Memorial, an art competition launched to remember Ken Saro-Wiwa on the streets of London, will be announced. My father will be the second African, after Nelson Mandela to be given that honour.

Part of the inspiration for the Living Memorial came from Milan Kundera's observation that 'the struggle of man against power is the struggle of memory against forgetting'. It has become the motto for all the Ken Saro-Wiwa commemoration events but another way of looking at Kundera's observation is the old maxim that the shortest way to the future is via the past.

I often wonder what my own children will make of their grandfather and the name and history they carry. How will they interpret his story, my own, for their own future? Up until now I have tried to avoid speaking to them about my father for fear of traumatising them. There are hardly any mementos or memorials to my father's struggle in my house but this year my children will, for the first time, take part in some of those celebrations. My two boys, aged eight and five, are if nothing else, cut from the same cloth as their grandfather because they have inherited their grandfather's strong sense of right and wrong. I guess most children their age have a strong moral centre but I am conscious that they are already aware of their history. Inevitably they didn't need me to fill in the gaps in the family tree.

I am conscious that my relationship with my father, with their history and community, will have an impact on the direction of their lives. I am loathe to steer or direct them in any way for fear of repeating my father but my sense or at least my hope is that they will, like me, eventually find their own way and make an accommodation through his story. I feel that my job is to ensure that they learn the truth about my father, guide them and leave them with enough clues to give them a secure sense of the past so that they can shape their future.

RAYMOND CARVER

*In "Where He Was: Memories of My Father," an essay first published in
Esquire magazine and later republished in* The Granta Book of the
Family, *Raymond Carver rightly singled out "Photograph of My Father
in His Twenty-Second Year" for special attention. The poem is easily the
most accomplished of his numerous father poems. In comparison, poems
like "Prosser" or "Bobber" feel contrived and forced. Other poems, like
"My Dad's Wallet," "The Trestle," or even the darkly humorous, richly
allusive "Suspenders," are loose, sprawling affairs, more prose than poem.
Part of the strength of "Photograph of My Father in His Twenty-Second
Year" is that it contains as much self-criticism as it does criticism. As he
points out in the essay, Carver was inflicted with the same first name as
his father and afflicted with the same self-destructive need for alcohol. In
the poem's movement from the framing now of October and the "dank
kitchen" to the posed moment of the photograph and then on to the direct
address of the father, Carver uses poetic precision and structural skill to
reveal traces of self loathing and to hint at passive-aggressive bitterness.
The poem betrays as much of the narrator as it does of the father, yet it is
also a reminder and affirmation of the complexity and power of love.
Despite the narrator's denial, Carver does know "the places to fish," and
this is a trophy poem.*

PHOTOGRAPH OF MY FATHER
IN HIS TWENTY-SECOND YEAR

October. Here in this dank, unfamiliar kitchen
I study my father's embarrassed young man's face.
Sheepish grin, he holds in one hand a string
of spiny yellow perch, in the other
a bottle of Carlsbad beer.

In jeans and denim shirt, he leans
against the front fender of a 1934 Ford.
He would like to pose bluff and hearty for his posterity,
wear his old hat cocked over his ear.
All his life my father wanted to be bold.

But the eyes give him away, and the hands
that limply offer the string of dead perch
and the bottle of beer. Father, I love you,
yet how can I say thank you, I who can't hold my liquor either,
and don't even know the places to fish?

ANNIE DILLARD

"Do you know that in the head of the caterpillar of the ordinary goat moth there are two hundred twenty-eight separate muscles?"' Write this one yourselves. Read and reread An American Childhood. *Read and reread; think and rethink. Do the same with* The Writing Life. *Read and reread all of Dillard, all about Dillard, even interviews and biographical scraps. Let the words and the meanings enter your consciousness. Let them change your brain cells the way practicing music changes the brain cells of a pianist. Read and reread* Life on the Mississippi River. *Again, read, and reread Dillard. Read and reread* Walden. *Now write . . . and rewrite. Do the same for all the pieces in this anthology which have meaning for you. Read and reread. Think and rethink. Write and rewrite. Perhaps, even, look at your own father: look at yourself. See. Read and reread. Think and rethink. Write and rewrite. Envision and re-vision. "The mind fits the world and shapes it as a river fits and shapes its own banks."*

excerpt from *AN AMERICAN CHILDHOOD*

In 1955, when I was ten, my father's reading went to his head.

My father's reading during that time, and for many years before and after, consisted for the most part of *Life on the Mississippi*. He was a young executive in the old family firm, American Standard; sometimes he traveled alone on business. Traveling, he checked into a hotel, found a bookstore, and chose for the night's reading, after what I fancy to have been long deliberation, yet another copy of *Life on the Mississippi*. He brought all these books home. There were dozens of copies of *Life on the Mississippi* on the living-room shelves. From time to time, I read one.

Down the Mississippi hazarded the cub riverboat pilot, down the Mississippi from St. Louis to New Orleans. His chief, the pilot Mr. Bixby, taught him how to lay the boat in her marks and dart between points; he learned to pick a way fastidiously inside a certain snag and outside a shifting shoal in the black dark; he learned to clamber down a memorized channel in his head. On tricky crossings the leadsmen sang out the soundings, so familiar I seemed to have heard them the length of my life: "Mark four! . . . Quarter-less-four! . . . Half three! . . . Mark three! . . . Quarter-less . . ." It was an old story.

WHEN ALL this reading went to my father's head, he took action. From Pittsburgh he went down the river. Although no one else that our family knew kept a boat on the Allegheny River, our father did, and now he was going all the way with it. He quit the firm his great-grandfather had founded a hundred years earlier down the river at his family's seat in Louisville, Kentucky; he sold his own holdings in the firm. He was taking off for New Orleans.

NEW ORLEANS was the source of the music he loved: Dixieland jazz, O Dixieland. In New Orleans men would blow it in the air and beat it underfoot, the music that hustled and snapped, the music whose zip matched his when he was a man-about-town at home in Pittsburgh, working for the family firm; the music he tapped his foot to when he was a man-about-town in New York for a few years after college working for the family firm by day and by night hanging out at Jimmy Ryan's on Fifty-second Street with Zutty Singleton, the black drummer who befriended him, and the rest of the house band. A certain kind of Dixieland suited him best. They played it at Jimmy Ryan's, and Pee Wee Russell and Eddie Condon played it too—New Orleans Dixieland chilled a bit by its journey up the river, and smoothed by its sojourns in Chicago and New York.

Back in New Orleans where he was headed they would play the

old stuff, the hot, rough stuff—bastardized for tourists maybe, but still the big and muddy source of it all. Back in New Orleans where he was headed the music would smell like the river itself, maybe, like a thicker, older version of the Allegheny River at Pittsburgh, where he heard the music beat in the roar of his boat's inboard motor; like a thicker, older version of the wide Ohio River at Louisville, Kentucky, where at his family's summer house he'd spent his boyhood summers mucking about in boats.

GETTING READY for the trip one Saturday, he roamed around our big brick house snapping his fingers. He had put a record on: Sharkey Bonano, "Li'l Liza Jane." I was reading Robert Louis Stevenson on the sunporch: *Kidnapped*. I looked up from my book and saw him outside; he had wandered out to the lawn and was standing in the wind between the buckeye trees and looking up at what must have been a small patch of wild sky. Old Low-Pockets. He was six feet four, all lanky and leggy; he had thick brown hair and shaggy brows, and a mild and dreamy expression in his blue eyes.

WHEN OUR mother met Frank Doak, he was twenty-seven: witty, boyish, bookish, unsnobbish, a good dancer. He had grown up an only child in Pittsburgh, attended Shady Side Academy, and Washington and Jefferson College in Pennsylvania, where he studied history. He was a lapsed Presbyterian and a believing Republican. "Books make the man," read the blue bookplate in all his books. "Frank Doak." The bookplate's woodcut showed a square-rigged ship under way in a steep following sea. Father had hung around jazz in New York, and halfheartedly played the drums; he had smoked marijuana, written poems, begun a novel, painted in oils, imagined a career as a riverboat pilot, and acted for more than ten seasons in amateur and small-time professional theater. At American Standard, Amstan Division, he was the personnel manager.

But not for long, and never again; Mother told us he was quitting to go down the river. I was sorry he'd be leaving the Manufacturers' Building downtown. From his office on the fourteenth floor, he often saw suicides, which he reported at dinner. The suicides grieved him, but they thrilled us kids. My sister Amy was seven.

People jumped from the Sixth Street bridge into the Allegheny River. Because the bridge was low, they shinnied all the way up the steel suspension cables to the bridge towers before they jumped. Father saw them from his desk in silhouette, far away. A man vigorously climbed a slanting cable. He slowed near the top, where the cables hung almost vertically; he paused on the stone tower, seeming to sway against the sky, high over the bridge and the river below. Priests, firemen, and others—presumably family members or passersby—gathered on the bridge. In about half the cases, Father said, these people talked the suicide down. The ones who jumped kicked off from the tower so they'd miss the bridge, and fell tumbling a long way down.

Pittsburgh was a cheerful town, and had far fewer suicides than most other cities its size. Yet people jumped so often that Father and his colleagues on the fourteenth floor had a betting pool going. They guessed the date and time of day the next jumper would appear. If a man got talked down before he jumped, he still counted for the betting pool, thank God; no manager of American Standard ever wanted to hope, even in the smallest part of himself, that the fellow would go ahead and jump. Father said he and the other men used to gather at the biggest window and holler, "No! Don't do it, buddy, don't!" Now he was leaving American Standard to go down the river, and he was a couple of bucks in the hole.

WHILE I was reading *Kidnapped* on this Saturday morning, I heard him come inside and roam from the kitchen to the pantry to the bar, to the dining room, the living room, and the sun porch, snapping his fingers. He was snapping the fingers of both hands, and shaking his head, to the record—"Li'l Liza Jane"—the sound that was beating, big and jivey, all over the house. He walked lightly, long-legged, like a soft-shoe hoofer barely in touch with the floor. When he played the drums, he played lightly, coming down soft with the steel brushes that sounded like a Slinky falling, not making the beat but just sizzling along with it. He wandered into the sunporch, unseeing; he was snapping his fingers lightly, too, as if he were feeling between them a fine layer of Mississippi silt. The big buckeyes outside the glass sunporch walls were waving.

A week later, he bade a cheerful farewell to us—to Mother, who had encouraged him, to us oblivious daughters, ten and seven, and to the new baby girl, six months old. He loaded his twenty-four-foot cabin cruiser with canned food, pushed off from the dock of the wretched boat club that Mother hated, and pointed his bow downstream, down the Allegheny River. From there it was only a few miles to the Ohio River at Pittsburgh's point, where the Monongahela came in. He wore on westward down the Ohio; he watched West Virginia float past his port bow and Ohio past his starboard. It was 138 river miles to New Martinsville, West Virginia, where he lingered for some races. Back on the move, he tied up nights at club docks he'd seen on the charts; he poured himself water for drinks from dockside hoses. By day he rode through locks, twenty of them in all. He conversed with the lock-masters, those lone men who paced silhouetted in overalls on the concrete lock-chamber walls and threw the big switches that flooded or drained the locks: "Hello, up there!" "So long, down there!"

He continued down the river along the Kentucky border with Ohio, bumping down the locks. He passed through Cincinnati. He moved along down the Kentucky border with Indiana. After 640 miles of river travel, he reached Louisville, Kentucky. There he visited relatives at their summer house on the river.

It was a long way to New Orleans, at this rate another couple of months. He was finding the river lonesome. It got dark too early. It was September; people had abandoned their pleasure boats for the season; their children were back in school. There were no old salts on the docks talking river talk. People weren't so friendly as they were in Pittsburgh. There was no music except the dreary yacht-club juke-boxes playing "How Much Is That Doggie in the Window?" Jazz had come up the river once and for all; it wasn't still coming, he couldn't hear it across the water at night rambling and blowing and banging along high and tuneful, sneaking upstream to Chicago to get educated. He wasn't free so much as loose. He was living alone on beans in a boat and having witless conversations with lockmasters. He mailed out sad postcards.

From phone booths all down the Ohio River he talked to Mother. She told him that she was lonesome, too, and that three children—maid and nanny or no—were a handful. She said, further, that people were starting to talk. She knew Father couldn't bear people's talking. For all his dreaminess, he prized respectability above all; it was our young mother, whose circumstances bespoke such dignity, who loved to shock the world. After only six weeks, then—on the Ohio River at Louisville—he sold the boat and flew home.

I WAS JUST waking up then, just barely. Other things were changing. The highly entertaining new baby, Molly, had taken up residence in a former guest room. The great outer world hove into view and began to fill with things that had apparently been there all along: mineralogy, detective work, lepidopterology, ponds and streams, flying, society. My younger sister Amy and I were to start at private school that year: the Ellis School, on Fifth Avenue. I would start dancing school.

CHILDREN ten years old wake up and find themselves here, discover themselves to have been here all along; is this sad? They wake like sleepwalkers, in full stride; they wake like people brought back from cardiac arrest or from drowning: *in medias res,* surrounded by familiar people and objects, equipped with a hundred skills. They know the neighborhood, they can read and write English, they are old hands at the commonplace mysteries, and yet they feel themselves to have just stepped off the boat, just converged with their bodies, just flown down from a trance, to lodge in an eerily familiar life already well under way.

I woke in bits, like all children, piecemeal over the years. I discovered myself and the world, and forgot them, and discovered them again. I woke at intervals until, by that September when Father went down the river, the intervals of waking tipped the scales, and I was more often awake than not. I noticed this process of waking, and predicted with terrifying logic that one of these years not far away I would be awake continuously and never slip back, and never be free of myself again.

CONSCIOUSNESS converges with the child as a landing tern touches the outspread feet of its shadow on the sand: precisely, toe hits toe. The tern folds its wings to sit; its shadow dips and spreads over the sand to meet and cup its breast.

Like any child, I slid into myself perfectly fined, as a diver meets her reflection in a pool. Her fingertips enter the fingertips on the water, her wrists slide up her arms. The diver wraps herself in her reflection wholly, sealing it at the toes, and wears it as she climbs rising from the pool, and ever after.

I never woke, at first, without recalling, chilled, all those other waking times, those similar stark views from similarly lighted precipices: dizzying precipices from which the distant, glittering world revealed itself as a brooding and separated scene—and so let slip a queer implication, that I myself was both observer and observable, and so a possible object of my own humming awareness. Whenever I stepped into the porcelain bathtub, the bath's hot water sent a shock traveling up my bones. The skin on my arms pricked up, and the hair rose on the back of my skull. I saw my own firm foot press the tub, and the pale shadows waver over it, as if I were looking down from the sky and remembering this scene forever. The skin on my face tightened, as it had always done whenever I stepped into the tub, and remembering it all drew a swinging line, loops connecting the dots, all the way back. You again.

DYLAN THOMAS

If "Do Not Go Gentle" has become a chestnut of high school and English university courses, a poem to be served up hot in ritual fervour, it is still a chestnut capable of exploding, a living chestnut with a green and prickly husk. Dylan Thomas was deeply marked, not to say scarred, by his father, a touchy, bitter man, angry at himself for not having realized his dream of becoming a great poet. Dylan, of course, realized his father's dream for himself, though Freudians looking at his troubled life might argue that he did so at a grievous personal cost. The playwright Arthur Miller even suggested that Thomas precipitated his own death to make "amends by murdering the gift he had stolen from the man he loved." The power of "Do Not Go Gentle," though, as so often in Thomas' poetry, lies not in the personal but in the mythic. This is a poem which Ulysses might speak to the defeated, demoralized Laertes, or Edgar to Gloucester in King Lear. *William Tindall, Marc Cyr, and other critics have suggested that there are also strong echoes of Yeats in the poem. Be that as it may, the poem sublimates a son's griefs and grievances into a transcendent poetic tribute. The rolling refrains of the villanelle, traditionally a pastoral form, provide a rigid structure to contain a son's commingled pain and exultation at a father's decline. The father is dying, long live the father.*

DO NOT GO GENTLE INTO THAT GOOD NIGHT

Do not go gentle into that good night,
Old age should burn and rave at close of day;
Rage, rage against the dying of the light.

Though wise men at their end know dark is right,
Because their words had forked no lightning they
Do not go gentle into that good night.

Good men, the last wave by, crying how bright
Their frail deeds might have danced in a green bay,
Rage, rage against the dying of the light.

Wild men who caught and sang the sun in flight,
And learn, too late, they grieved it on its way,
Do not go gentle into that good night.

Grave men, near death, who see with blinding sight
Blind eyes could blaze like meteors and be gay,
Rage, rage against the dying of the light.

And you, my father, there on the sad height,
Curse, bless, me now with your fierce tears, I pray.
Do not go gentle into that good night.
Rage, rage against the dying of the light.

SAUL BELLOW

The terms "fictionalized recall" and "speculative biography" have both been applied to Saul Bellow's work. Certainly, "Memoirs of a Bootlegger's Son" straddles an uncertain line between fiction and autobiography. Written just after the publication of Bellow's breakthrough classic, The Adventures of Augie March, *and first published in the* Granta 41: Biography *issue of 1992, "Memoirs" shimmers with typical Bellovian exuberance, exaggeration, and distortion. Among hard, verifiable facts—the family's Russian Jewish background, the father's various career disasters, the Montreal childhood, and sister Zelda's piano playing—are numerous fictionalizations and distortions. Most notable of these is Bellow's presentation of the narrator as the eldest son. Bellow was the youngest of the four children. The sentimentalized portrait of the father as a self-pitying, self-dramatizing failure, no matter how true when Bellow was a child, also contains a fiction of sorts. In 1954, when Bellow wrote the lengthy manuscript from which the* Granta *piece was later excerpted, Abram Bellow was a successful businessman, while Saul Bellow was a struggling writer still accepting financial handouts from his father. Bellow, indeed, was in much the same position as the father-centered, father-tormented hero of his next, and possibly greatest, novel,* Seize the Day.

MEMOIRS OF A BOOTLEGGER'S SON)

'**G**ott *meiner*,' said my father to my mother. 'Again no money? But I gave you twelve dollars at the beginning of the week. What have you done with it?'

'I don't know. It went away.'

'So quickly . . . by Thursday? Impossible.'

'It couldn't be helped. Some of it I used to pay old bills. We've owed money to Herskovitz for I don't know how long.'

'But did you have to pay him this week?'

'He's right in the block. For two months now I've been coming home the long way around. I gave him three dollars.'

'How could you! Haven't you any sense? And what did you do with the rest? Joshua,' he said, turning to me furiously. 'Take a pencil and write these things down. I have to know where it all went. I bought eggs and butter on Tuesday.'

'Seventy-five cents to the milkman,' said Ma, earnest and frightened. She must have believed she had done something wrong.

'Write it,' he said.

I had taken a piece of Ma's checkered stationery and placed the figures carefully within the tiny boxes. I was shaken, too, and eager to escape condemnation.

'Willie had a tooth out. It cost fifty cents.'

'Fifty?' he said.

'Yes, it's usually a dollar an extraction. I sent him up alone and told him to say it was all he had. And after he was done, I waited for him downstairs. I was ashamed to show my face to Dr Zadkin.'

'Did it have to come out?'

'There was nothing left of it but the walls. Do you want to look at it? The child was in pain ... Then there was fifty cents to have the boys' hair cut.'

'I'm going to buy a pair of clippers and do it myself,' Pa said. He was always resolving to do this.

'Fifty cents for the gas meter. Twenty cents for a coal shovel. Twenty-five cents to the insurance man. Twenty cents for a flat-iron handle. Forty cents to the tinsmith for relining my copper pot. Leather mittens for Bentchka cost me thirty cents. I haven't even started on the bigger things yet, such as meat.'

'We have meat far too often,' Pa said. 'We don't need it. I prefer milk soups anyway.'

'Don't expect me to stint on the stomach,' my mother said with determination. 'If I do nothing else, I'm going to feed the children.'

'They don't look starved,' said Pa. 'Especially this one. I never look at him but what he's chewing.'

My appetite was large and I seemed never to have had enough. I ate all the leftovers. I chewed down apple parings, gristle, cold vegetables, chicken bones.

'If I knew how to do things more cheaply,' said Ma, as though she now consented to take the blame.

'You don't bargain enough,' my father said to her harshly. His accusation always was that she did not accept her condition and was not what the wife of a poor man ought to be. And yet she was. She was whatever would please him. She made over our clothes. On the table there often appeared the thick Russian linens she had brought, but on our beds were sheets that she had made of flour sacks.

'Like your sister Julia?' said my mother.

'Yes, Julia. That's why they're rich. It was she that made him so.'

I had been with Aunt Julia to the farmer's market and knew how she worked. 'How much'a der han?' she would say when she seized a rooster. 'Oh, *trop cher,*' she'd cry at the Canadian farmer, and she'd say to me in Yiddish, 'Thieves, every last man of them. But I will beat them down.' And in her Russian shawl, with her sharp nose jutting, she would shuffle to another wagon, and she always did as she promised.

'A wife *can* make the difference,' said Pa. 'I am as able as Jomin, and stronger.'

'They have grown children.'

'Yes, that's so,' said Pa. 'Whereas I have no one to turn to.'

He would often repeat this, and particularly to me. 'You can turn to me,' he'd say. 'But to whom can I turn? Everything comes from me and nothing to me. How long can I bear it? Is this what the life of a man is supposed to be? Are you supposed to be loaded until your back is broken? Oh my God, I think I begin to see. Those are lucky who die when their childhood is over and never live to know the misery of fighting in the world.'

When he flew into a rage, he forgot himself altogether and lost his sense of shame.

'Aren't you taking money for your brother?' he once shouted at Ma. 'Aren't you saving to send him . . . ?'

He meant her brother Mordecai in St Petersburg. Her brother Aaron had recently died. The Bolsheviks had come to his house and slashed open the beds and the furniture in their search for jewels and gold. They had taken everything from him and he was dead.

'No, no,' Ma cried, and it was obvious to me that she was not telling the truth. 'How can you say it?'

She greatly loved these two brothers. On the day she received the news of Aaron's death, when she had been doing a Monday wash, she sat sobbing by the tub. Except to mourn, Jews were forbidden to sit on the floor. She hung over the tub, and her arms, in grey sleeves, trailed in the water. I came up behind her to draw her from the water. My arms felt the beating of her heart through her bosom. It was racing, furious, sick and swift.

'Let me be, Joshua. Leave me alone, my son,' she said.

'Aha! You do save money for him, and for your mother,' said my father.

'And if I do?' said Ma. 'Think, Jacob. Did they do nothing for you?'

'And did they do nothing *to* me?' Pa was beside himself.

'If I do put aside a little money now and then, it's less than you spend on your tobacco.'

'And do you know how much money I'd have now if it weren't for you and the children?' he roared at her. 'I'd be worth ten thousand dollars. Ten thousand, do you hear? And be a free man. Do you hear what I say?' he glared with a strained throat. In his rage his face wore an expression that resembled hunger. His eyes grew huge, like those of a famished man. 'I say I might have had ten thousand dollars.'

'Why don't you leave then?' My mother wept.

'That's what I will do!'

He hurried out. It was night. He was gone for about an hour, and then I saw his cigarette glow on the front step, and he said to me, meekly, that he had only gone to buy a package of Honeysuckles.

'Will you please save the package for me, Papa?' said Willie, and Pa said to him, 'Of course, my boy. I'll remember this time and not throw it away.'

PA WAS a mercurial man, and very unlucky. He had the energy to be a millionaire but nothing came of it except poverty. From Aunt Julia, I knew the story of the dowry. In less than a year, Pa had lost the ten thousand roubles and went to Ma's brothers to ask for more. One of them, Uncle Mordecai, was very rich. He had run away to South Africa as a boy and made a fortune among the Kaffirs and later he sold cattle to the Russians during the Japanese war. When they lost they didn't settle their debt, but he made a fortune nevertheless. He came back to Russia after this, and until the War led the life of a rich man. According to Ma, he was princely, dashing, brave and open-handed. By Pa's account, he drank too much and spent his money on women and neglected his respectable wife. Pa would sometimes frown at me and say that I reminded him of Mordecai. He saw the faults of my mother's family embodied in me. In my own mind I came to accept this, and was not ashamed of it even when Pa would say, 'There's insanity in your mother's line. Her Uncle Poppe was a firebug, and he was very dangerous. He used to set the curtains afire. These things are inherited. There's no taint like that on my family.'

'Not if you don't count hard hearts and bad tempers,' Ma would occasionally, but too rarely, answer. Only occasionally, because she loved him. When he was away she'd say to the children, 'If you told Mordecai that you needed something, he put his hand in his pocket and gave you what was in it, without looking.'

In Petersburg, Pa had made a handsome living. He dealt in produce and travelled widely. He was the largest importer of Egyptian onions and Spanish fruit. And it was evident that he and Ma had been people of fashion. She still owned black taffeta petticoats and ostrich feathers, now out of fashion, and some jewellery, while Pa had a Prince Albert in the trunk, and a stovepipe hat, a brocaded vest and a fox-lined overcoat. Ma's fur coat was made over for Zelda and she wore it for four years at the Baron Byng school, complainingly. 'Over there, we had everything we needed,' Ma said. There were photos of Zelda in silk dresses, and of me in velvet pants, with long hair, like Rasputin. But every minute of this prosperity was stolen. Bribes made it possible. Then Pa was seized by the police for illegal residence. My uncles got him out of prison, and we escaped to Canada.

Within a year, the money he had brought from Russia was almost gone. The last of it he put into a partnership with three other men who owned a bakery. He had to drive a wagon, and he wasn't used to rough labour then. He had never before harnessed a horse. Over there, only coachmen and teamsters knew how to harness. Pa had to learn to do it by lantern light in the cold Canadian nights, with freezing hands which he would try to warm by the lantern-glass or against the horse's belly. His route lay in Lachine and Wilson's Pier, along the St Lawrence, by the Lachine Canal, around Monkey Park and the Dominion Bridge Company. Across the river, in Caughnawaga, the Indians lived in their old cottages. At this time Pa smelled of bread and his hair was somewhat floury. His partners were quarrelsome and rough, they swore obscenely and held Pa for a dude, and as the misery of his sudden fall was too much to hide they gave him a hard time. Why should it be so terrible to have become one of them? Ma said they gave him all the worst things to do.

THE BAKERY was a shanty. The rats took refuge from the winter there, and were drowned in the oil and fished out suffocated from the jelly. The dogs and cats could not police them, they were so numerous. The thick ice did not float leisurely, it ran in the swift current. In March and even April the snow still lay heavy. When it melted, the drains couldn't carry off the water. There were grey lagoons in the hollows of old ice; they were sullen or flashing according to the colour of the sky.

The partners had fist fights. Pa was no judge of the strength of others, and as he was very proud and reckless he usually got the worst of it. He came home with horrible bruises on his face and his voice broke as he told how it happened. Eliahu Giskin was the one with whom he had most trouble. Huge and stout, Eliahu had a shaved head and a tartar moustache. He drove one of the skinny, rusty wagons of the firm. The very rust was fading deeper, into mauve, and on it was spelled in a circle of blind letters *Pâtisserie de Choix Giskin*. He was a bawling and clutching kind of man. He bullied the horse so that it put forth the best speed for him. Scared of him, it turned its head sidewards from the whip and galloped with heavy, hairy ankles through the streets. On the ground, Giskin himself was awkward and moved with hampered steps because of the size of his belly and his enormous boots. Pa also walked in a certain peculiar smart way; he put more weight on the left heel than on the right and marched as he went. He almost limped. It was an old Jewish way of walking, with his hands held at his back.

He and Giskin had their worst fight one day in the yard of the bakery when my mother and I were there. Exactly why they were fighting I couldn't tell you. They grappled and Pa's shirt was torn from him. It was a Russian style of fighting. Each tried to carry the other down and there was no idea of self-defence, but just one desperate body squeezing the other. Pa was burned up with violence, and he was a strong muscular man in his young days. Giskin clawed and scratched his white back as they clinched while Pa struck him with his elbow and fists. They fell on the rutted ground. A baker and one of the helpers ran out from the shack and pulled them apart.

'How can this go on?' said Ma at home where she helped him to undress and washed the dirt from him.

Pa admitted that it couldn't. He might kill Giskin or Giskin him, he said. And Ma insisted that he should withdraw from the partnership, and he did so although he did not know what to turn to next.

HE TRIED the junk business, at which my Uncle Jomin had grown rich, and with the string of jingling junk bells stretched across the wagon he drove along the St Lawrence shore and up and down the shanty streets, the little brick streets, and put in at farms and monasteries to try to buy rags, paper and metal. He spoke ten words of French and not many more of English, then.

'*Might you could sell me iron, gentlemann?*' was what he said. I was often on the wagon-seat, and watched—the eldest son, though ten years old, the *b'chor* as I was called, I was supposed to go into the world with him. He was not submissive, though he appeared to be so. At least he was not submissive to men. It was to necessities that he hung down his head and not to the farmer or the Brother or housewife. He had hard matter in him. He smoked as he drove, with keen eyes. We wrapped burlap about our knees when fall weather blew. The cold little bells clinked. '*Gentlemann?*' Pa would begin, and something both anxious and bold played through him. To weigh paper, he had a scale in the wagon; his purse was in his hand to pay, a steel-billed leather purse. The term for it was also the slang word for the scrotum. The money in it was poor, seedy money, dark copper, bleak silver and a wrinkled green paper or two.

HE LEFT this business soon, never having earned more than a few dollars a week at it. In the winter it was too much for him. With Uncle Asher, Aunt Taube's husband, he went into the bag business. They rented a loft and some machines, and hired two women to operate them. It looked as if they might make good as manufacturers. Somehow Asher got an order for munitions-bags during the War. However, the contract was cancelled because the first batch was not up to specifications. When this happened, there was a big family quarrel. Everyone got into it. Aunt Taube was very haughty. Uncle Asher had great respect for Ma and was always civil to her. In fact, he was meek and good-tempered, not very clever. He boasted about his teeth and never ate candy. He was apt to repeat this too often, about candy. It was she, his sister, who said the worst things against Pa.

Ma told her, 'Don't be ungrateful, Taube.'

She meant that Taube and Asher owed their being in America to Pa. He had given them the money to marry, in his prosperous days.

'A great favour you did me,' said Taube, although her love affair with Asher was famous. The son of a mere stationmaster, he was not considered a match for her. She had seen him from a train-window while he stood idle on the platform. He was placid, and handsome because of it. My cousins, three small girls, were like him. Aunt Taube always wore a smile, but it was a shrewd smile. At the left corner of her mouth a few of the nerves were ailing and she could not govern her expressions well. She was the brainy one and wore the pants.

'It was Asher's fault,' Pa declared. 'He tried to save money on the material. That was why we lost the contract.'

'Jacob,' said my aunt, 'you must always blame someone else.'

'Well, what good does it do to fight about it now,' said Ma. 'That's what I'd like to know.'

Neither quarrelling nor peace made a difference. Pa had no trade, he would have found no work if he had had one, for there wasn't any to be found after the War. He was ready for any humiliation, even that of serving a master, and to him that was one of the deepest. He had come into the world to do business, and there was no limit to the strength and effort he would expend in this. His pride was beaten, or almost beaten, when he was ready to labour for another man.

'A beggar!' said Pa, describing himself. 'A *bettler*!'

The ragged old country *bettler*, hairy, dirty and often crazy, were to be seen then in the yellowish streets of Jewish Montreal. They carried burlap sacks in which were old rags and scraps of food. What they couldn't finish when you fed them they clutched with their beggar's fingers from the plate and stuffed into the sack: stew, bread, crumbs of sugar. Then they blessed, they mumbled insane things, and shouldered their sacks and went away. They were supposed to be like this.

Ma therefore smiled when Pa said that. 'Not yet, by any means,' was what she answered.

'Not far from it. How far do you think?'

He had gone into innumerable enterprises: jobbing, peddling, storekeeping, the produce business, the bottle business, the furniture business, the dairy business, the insurance business, matchmaking. There was no corner into which he didn't try to squeeze himself.

AT ONE time we thought of becoming farmers. I say 'we' because my parents discussed their projects over the kitchen table. Matters of business were always brought into the open. The children had to understand. If Herskovitz the grocer or Duval the landlord came to ask for their money, the children couldn't say that Pa or Ma were at home. We grasped these necessities very quickly.

Pa had heard of a farm, out beyond Huntington that was for sale or rent, and we went to see it. It was an excursion. We put on our best. Ma was very happy; she was not a city-woman by upbringing. We went down to the Grand Trunk Station on the trolley, buying some

half-spoiled Bartlett pears on the way. Pa said they had their best fla-
vour when they were like that and peeled them for us with his pen-
knife in his neat way. Some of his habits were very trim. Tobacco made
two fingers of his left hand dark brown.

There was a soft gloom in the station. The city air was heavy that
day. But as we were crossing the ponderous black bridge the sun
opened up on us. Beneath the funnel hole in the toilet the St Lawrence
winked. Quick death should we fall in, Then the stones of the roadbed,
scratched by much speed. It was bright and hot at the station when the
short trip ended. We were picked up in a buggy by the farmer, an old
man. Ma mounted the step with her pointed, black, button shoes, and
Zelda next, with her straw hat on which cloth roses were perishing.
The kids wore pongee suits with short pants, and I a pair of heavy
serge knickers that made me sweat. They were picked out for me
from a job lot Pa had once acquired. Blue flowers grew in the long, sta-
tion-side weeds. A mill-wheel was splashing in the town.

'Ah,' said Pa. "It's good to stand under that. It knocks your bones
into place. Best thing in the world for you.'

Bentchka had a habit of dropping his head and dreaming at things
with one eye. His hair was still long then. Ma would not let it be cut
though he was nearly five. On her other side sat Willie with his
bated-breath look; he stared at the hay, then lying over the stubble to
dry. The old farmer, Archie, described the country with flaps of his
whip. Ma's face softened with all the country pleasure, the warm sun
and the graceful hay, and fragrance, the giant trees and hoops of birds
that went about them, the perfect leaves and happy sun. She began to
have smooth creases of enjoyment about her mouth and chin instead
of her often sober and dark expression.

We arrived at the house, It was like silver with age, the wind had pol-
ished it so long. The old wife with her seamed skin came to the door and
called, in a clear voice, 'Arrrchie—the hens are in the garrrden.' Willie
ran to shoo them. Pa and Ma inspected the long door, went through the

house and then down toward the yard. Ma said, 'It just revives you to smell this air.' From the tone she took, Zelda and I knew that this was just a holiday in the country. And I had been imagining great things and let my mind build hopes that I could be a farmer's son and walk on those gold stubble fields from one horizon to another and not as a timid, fleshy city boy with these meek shoes, but in boots. But look! It was obvious. We couldn't live here. Glancing at me as if I would be the most prone to it, Ma said, 'We can't have the children growing up ignorant and boors. I couldn't hide my disappointment. It filled my face.

'I don't see why they should,' said Pa,

But Ma said it was plain enough. No synagogue, no rabbis, no kosher food, no music teachers, no neighbours, no young men for Zelda. It would be good for the health of the younger children, that was true, but she wasn't going to have us grow into cowherds, no finer feelings, no learning.

'Ach, too bad,' said Pa with gloom, but he nodded. He was sizing up the beast-world of the barnyard, and I don't doubt but that he was thinking what hardship it had been for him to learn to harness a horse. And our mother had strange ideas about association with animals. If I stroked a cat she'd occasionally warn me against it. She'd say, 'You'll be cat-witted.' Or a dog, the same. 'You'll be dog-souled.'

'No, no,' she said to my pleading. Zelda was on her side; Pa was not wholeheartedly on mine.

And when we were ready to leave, we had to search for Willie. He had wandered off to the river to watch the blackbirds plunge through the bulrushes and to try to catch toads in his handkerchief. This was enough for Ma. She was in a panic. A river! Small children wandering away. There was no more discussion of farms. The farmer drove us back to the station toward night, when a star like a chopped root flared in the sky.

Pa would often say afterwards that he still wished he owned a piece of land. Losing his temper he'd exclaim against my mother, 'There could have been bread. All we needed. But you had to have your city. Well, now we've got it. We've got bricks and stones'

THE NEXT business he tried was a dry goods store in Point St Charles, not a prosperous district. The streets ran into nothing after blocks of half-empty slum and goat-tracked snows. The store was in a wooden building. Stairs led down to it from the sidewalk. When you got down to the bottom, where the wood underfoot was shredded with age, you found a door in which there was a little pane, and when you opened it you encountered Pa and Cousin Henoch. They were setting up shop. Railroad overalls and ladies' drawers hung on exhibit, stockings, gloves, wool headwear, layettes, silk shirts and Hudson Bay blankets, and a lot of army goods. There was an odour of smoke from some of these articles; Pa had bought them at salvage sales. The business had no credit as yet and could not lay in an entirely new line. Pa got job lots wherever he could. Cousin Henoch had brought a little money into the partnership, and Pa had borrowed some from his sister Julia and her husband, who had plenty of it.

I participated in this, too. Pa, you see, thought that I was stupid and backward. He had a biased and low opinion of me and he was anxious for me to take shape, and quickly. He couldn't stand for me to remain boyish. He would say to me, 'You'll be a man soon and your head still lies in childish things. I don't know what will become of you. At twelve, thirteen, fourteen, I was already a man.' Oh, he was very impatient of childhood. One must not remain a child but be mature of understanding and carry his share of difficulty. He wouldn't have me studying magic or going to the baths with Daitch, or hiding in the free library.

Catching me there, he'd drive me into the street. When his temper was up, he thought nothing of gripping me by the ear and leading me away. Back from unseriousness. Back from heathen delusions. Back from vain and childish things. We'd march together while he gripped my ear.

'Do you know what you are?' he'd say full of rage. 'A chunk of fat with two eyes staring from it. But I'll make something of you. A man. A Jew. Not while I live will you become an idler, an outcast, an Epicurus.'

I was frightened and begged at him to let me go. I wasn't entirely a submissive son. But I didn't dare try to free my ear, though my voice went deep and hoarse when I said, 'Don't do that, Pa. Don't do that!' I yelled, 'Let me go!' while he gripped me and led me home. He made me look like a fool in the eyes of the old lady at the library. To him such things didn't matter. He kept his eye on the main business of life: to provide for us and teach us our duty.

After a family conference he often said, when it had been decided what to do, 'And you'll come with me.'

So I was with him when he went to make a loan of Aunt Julia and Uncle Jomin.

AUNT JULIA was his eldest sister, a very shrewd and sharp-minded woman, and rich, and her attitude toward many things was condemnatory. She had a thin face and a pinched nose, very unfeminine to my way of thinking; her colour was flushed and it made her look threatening sometimes. Yet she was witty, also, and often kept you laughing; and when you were laughing and out of breath, then came something that took the ground from under your feet. When she said something about you, you were criticized to the heart. It was merciless, for she was a harsh judge of character. Her face, I said, was thin, but her hair was heavy and glossy. She wore it in a single stout braid down her back. Her body was also heavy, in contrast with her face, and at home she wore a few unusual and choice garments—a man's undershirt, a pair of voluminous green bloomers and over them a scarlet crêpe de Chine wrapper, wool stockings and fleece slippers. She sat heavily or, cooking, cleaning, she stood and moved with heaviness, and at all times, in that unvarying nasal tone, she uttered the most damaging and shrewd remarks conceivable: a sort of poetry of criticism, faultfinding and abuse. She was always ingenious and there were very few offences that she forgave.

Though she oppressed me, I was crazy about her. She was a great show-woman and she said whatever she pleased with utter frankness, and she and Uncle Jomin, that mild person, were extremely salty. Because, you understand, they were outstanding people; they had a right and nobody would contest it. My Uncle Jomin was a brown man and slender. His beard was tight, short and black; it surrounded the broad teeth of his smiling mouth, of which one was gold. The bridge of his nose had an intense twist, and then the cartilages broadened—it became a saddle nose. He had the brown eyes of an intelligent, feeling, and yet satirical animal. He had a grim humour about him. The odour of his breath was tart and warm. I always found it agreeable to be near him. He enjoyed playing the hand-slapping game with me, a homely game that went like this: you laid your hands on his palms and were supposed to snatch them away before he could slap them. If he missed, it was your turn to try to slap his. Despite his slight trembling—he was not well, he had an enlarged heart—he was swifter than I. With a bent head that shook slightly he would hide a deep smile and gaze at my reddened hands. His crisp beard itself made a slight sound. My hands smarted. I would laugh, like the rest of them, but be angry at heart.

My cousins, grown men and all in business, stood watching.

'Faster, you duffer,' said Cousin Abba. He was nearest to me in age and already had an enterprise of his own; in summer he operated a fruit stand. Abba subscribed to *Chums* and *Magnet*, British schoolboy magazines. He talked continually of Bob Cherry and Tom Merry and Billy

Bunter and hamptuckers, and mixed 'jollies' and 'eh what's' with the fantastic Yiddish they all spoke, a French-Russian-Hebrew-British-Yiddish.

'Faster there, Houdini, you *golem*. Stay with it, now. Stiff upper lip does it. That's the spirit my man. Ay, what a *frask-o*. Bums, eh? Good for the circulation, I'll be bound.'

He whinnied when I cried out. He was all right, Abba. Not more open-handed than the rest of them. They didn't exactly have that reputation. But we were fond of each other and he often gave me good advice.

JOMIN'S business was junk. He was one of the biggest junk dealers in Montreal. In his yard there were piles, mountains of old metal shapes, the skeletons of machines and beds, plumbing fixtures. A deep, scaly red-brown beautiful rust shone like powdered chicory and dry blood to the sun. Cobwebs floated from it. I went around in the loft and tried to read funnies on the faces of paper bales or looked for locks that I could study, as Houdini had done. In the office swung chandeliers and princely metals. Long-armed and stooped in his cocoa-coloured sweater, Uncle Jomin stood in the middle of the yard and sorted scrap. He examined a piece of metal, classified it and threw it to the top of the appropriate pile. Iron here, zinc there, lead left, brass right and babbitt by the shed. Boys, Indians, old women, halfwits and greenhorns who did not know a word of English, arrived with junk in little carts and coasters. Junk men with wagons and plumed horses came. During the War Uncle Jomin did a vast business. The junk was needed at the shipyards and on the Western Front.

My aunt bought real estate, and my cousins went into business. Moneywise, they were among the first families. They lived simply, and they were known as hard dealers. In the synagogue, they rated very highly and had seats against the eastern wall, the best because the nearest to Jerusalem. The dark man and his sons, with other leading Jews, faced the rest of the congregation. Of these, most were meek immigrants, pedlars, factory workers, old grandfathers and boys. From the women's gallery Aunt Julia, thin-nosed, looked down. Her Hebrew was good and she prayed as well as any man. She wore glasses and read steadily from her book.

She'd say to me, 'What do you think of Tante Julia? Your old *Trante* is no fool.'

She could not let a word go by without giving a twist. She had a great genius with words.

One winter afternoon we came to make a touch for the store in Point St Charles. Naturally enough, Pa was a little scared of such a woman. Ma said, 'It will be hard but you have to do it. They can give you the money, and Jomin doesn't have a bad heart. Not even she can refuse her brother.'

Pa shrugged and turned his hands outward. He had been tramping the town, making his stops: he covered miles daily in his hunt for business opportunities, and did it in his outward-pointed stride, favouring the left heel, always, and his hands behind his back and his head dropped to one side. 'We'll see,' he said. He had stopped at home to get me to come with him, and so didn't take off his fox-lined overcoat—the orange fur was bald in places—and his scarf, the colour of creamed coffee, was wound thickly under his chin; it sparkled with melted frost, and so did the moustache that covered his handsome mouth. He diffused an odour of cigarettes; his fingers were dyed with the brown colour. Ma helped me into my sheepskin. She wasn't well that day, she suffered with her teeth and was heating buckwheat on the stove to apply to her cheek. Bentchka was ailing, too. He sat and looked through the bars of his bed at the sparrows as they ruffled on the wires and on the glass clusters of the telephone poles and dropped down to peck in the horse-churned, sleigh-tracked snow. You could leave him alone; he'd amuse himself for hours.

We changed cars at Place d'Armes; the snow stung like rock salt, and then we travelled another half an hour on the Notre Dame car and arrived at Aunt Julia's at sunset. Ribbons of red colour were buried in the dry snow. The sun seemed snarling, the moon pearly cold and peaceful. We went in. The stoves were hot and there was a bearskin on the sofa. The curl-tailed bitch barked. Her teeth were sharp, curved and small. My face smarted with heat and cold, and my mouth watered at the smell of gravy. Meat was roasting.

TANTE JULIA was thinking, as I took off my coat, how chunky I was. I knew. In her eyes this was not a bad thing, but meant I had a lot of good hard work in me.

Her floors were highly polished and gleamed with darkness, with stove lights and the final red of the roaring cold Canadian day. While she watched us take our outdoor clothes off her face judged us in a very masculine way. She knew what Pa was here for. Trust her for that.

'Come in the kitchen and have something,' she said nasally. She was not stingy when it came to food; she always fed you well. 'The lad must be hungry.'

'Give him something, yes,' said Pa.

'And you?'

'I'm not hungry.'

'Too worried to eat, ah?'

Nevertheless, Pa also ate several slices of delicious dry roast meat with carrots and grape jelly. We drank tea. Uncle Jomin was a slow eater. For every piece of bread he recited a blessing. Then he sliced away the crust and bent to the plate with a slow shake of his broad head.

'Tuck in, old top,' said Cousin Abba. 'Joshua is a *gefährlicher* trencherman.' All my cousins laughed. Everyone was present this evening. I laughed, too.

I WAS IN an odd way a favourite with them all, although they were also sardonic with me and gave me hell. I caught it from Cousin Moses because I tracked tar one summer day into his new Ford. He had bought it to court a girl—a rich girl related to Libutsky the bottle man.

I crept into Moses's car with tar on my feet, and he lost his temper and whacked me on the head—a favourite place; perhaps everyone felt that it was a thick place and I would take no harm there. I cried and said I would get him for that, and for a while we were enemies. At Huntington, where Aunt Julia had a summer house, Cousin Moses slapped my face once and I picked up a piece of wood and tried to kill him. I would have brained him; I was in a rage. It swept me away and I no longer knew or cared what I was doing. He was sitting on the swing with his fiancée; he was swarthy and she pale. He was grinning. A vine wove fiercely around the lattices; it grew a kind of cucumber, full of prickles and inedible. Moses teased me out of the side of his mouth. I gave him an angry answer because I couldn't stand to be ridiculed before the girl, and I suddenly felt a spirit of murder in my blood and ran at him with the piece of firewood. He knocked me over and picked me up by the collar, choked me with the neckband and beat some sense into me. He slapped me till I tasted blood in my saliva and then booted me in the tail. He told Aunt Julia he wouldn't have me around. He said I was a goy, an Ishmael, and that I'd have to go back to St Dominique Street. It was a holiday, you see. They would rescue each of us a few days at a time and give us some country air at their cottage. So back I went and Willie was sent down.

I made it up afterwards with Moses. Maybe it weighed on his conscience that he had beaten me so hard; I felt ashamed, too, that I had tried to murder him. Anyway, I got along better with him than with my cousin Philip. He was a law student at McGill and behaved very slyly toward me. They were all my seniors and dealt with me more as uncles than as cousins. Cousin Thelma, two years older than I, was fat and huge and had a bold savage temper. Her hair was frizzy and her teeth were obstinate and white.

'TELL, MY brother,' said Aunt Julia when everybody was present. 'I gather that things are going badly again.'

'They never went well,' said Pa. 'But I may be doing better soon, God willing.'

'Why, do you have something new in mind?'

'Yes,' said Pa.

'And why don't you stick to one thing,' his sister said. 'You jump from this to that, and here and there. You have no patience.'

'I have little children,' said Pa, in a lowered but not patient voice. 'I have to put bread on the table. I am no coward and I'm not idle, and I'm learning the language and the ways. I'm all over the city every day and digging in the cinders for a bone. I thank you for your advice. When a dog is drowning, everyone offers him a drink.'

'Yes, yes,' said my Aunt Julia. 'You don't have to tell us what it is to be poor immigrants. We know the taste of it. When Jomin came over he dug ditches. He worked with pick and shovel for the CPR and he has a hernia to this day. But I, you understand me, knew how to manage and I never thought I was a grand lady from St Petersburg with rich brothers and a carriage and summer house and servants.'

'She doesn't have them any more,' Pa said.

'You didn't know anything of such things either, before you met her,' said Aunt Julia, 'and don't pretend to *me* that you were born with a golden spoon in your mouth. I know better.'

'Yes, but what of it?'

'You cry because you've fallen so. And how humiliating it is. Common people couldn't see you, your windows were so high.'

'I never snubbed you, or anyone,' said Pa. 'My door always was open and my hand was too. I tasted prosperity once but I know something else now. Eliahu Giskin beat my bones, and *I haven't a piece of tin/To stop up a hole, or cover my skin*, as they say. I often feel as if I was buried alive.'

'My children had no pianos and violins. They knew they were poor. You have to know, and be, what you are. Be what you are. The rest is only pride. I sent them out to earn a penny. They collected bottles and bones and ran errands. They had no time to become musicians. Now, thank God, things have gone better. They will hire musicians when they marry. *Then,*' she said, 'we'll dance. And I hope you'll be there to share our joy.'

The Jomins owned the house we were sitting in, and other properties around town.

'A wife has a duty to her husband not to make him a slave to the children,' said Aunt Julia. 'If you saved the dollars that you spend to make Kreislers of your boys and a princess of your daughter you wouldn't have to dig in the cinders like a dog, as you say.'

THE BLOOD had risen to her face, which never was pale, her eyes were angry and her voice high and hard. As Pa had come to confess failure and ask for aid he was obliged to listen. Also, he may not have disagreed entirely; perhaps he wanted to hear Ma blamed. He was an influenceable man and sometimes said these very things himself. Pa didn't have a constant spirit. Depending on how he felt, he changed opinion. One night he'd sit and shed tears when Zelda played Beethoven, his heart touched; another time, he'd stamp his feet and say we were ruining him: 'Food! That's my duty. Shoes!—Shoes I'm obliged as a father to put on your feet. Whatever a father should do, I will do!' he'd shout at us all. 'But I will not lay down my health and strength for luxuries and nonsense.'

Aunt Julia said, sternly, with fierce eyes turned to me, 'Children have their part to do, too.'

'Oh,' said my father, 'he's a pretty good lad.' He put his hand on my head gently. I almost burst into tears at this. A moment before I was indignant with him because he said nothing in defence of Ma. I, you see, knew what she was up against. Fear of Aunt Julia and my other hard elders kept me from speaking. It was no time to have a burst of temper and hurt Pa's chances of a loan. But now when he touched me and said I was pretty good, I wanted to take his hand and kiss it, and say how well I understood what was happening, and how much I loved him. The roof of my mouth ached, and my throat closed. I didn't dare to move or to open my mouth.

'He should be that,' said Aunt Julia. 'He's got a good father—a father who watches over his children. He's old enough to understand the difference.'

I was old enough, certainly, to understand.

'What's this new business you have gone into, Uncle?' said Cousin Moses respectfully. It came hard, because Pa was an immigrant, all but a pauper. Also, like everyone else, Pa was subject to mockery, probably, as soon as his back was turned. I had seen all the Jomins take turns at mimicking some character. I had seen them put an entire Sunday afternoon on the porch into this wicked vaudeville—how so-and-so walked, stammered, wiped his nose on his sleeve or picked bones out of fish. My sister Zelda also had a great gift for this game. She didn't spare anyone. And I am positive that Pa was often taken off in Aunt Julia's house. And perhaps he had just done something typical, and they were barely able to hold back their laughter. However, respect for elders was drummed into all of us. Pa was Moses's uncle and Moses had to speak to him with considerable civility. It was quite a thing to watch, for a man like Moses had a strong spirit of satire. He smiled at the side of his mouth. He had a powerful, swarthy face, and passed air loudly through his nose to punctuate what he said.

His engagement to the Libutsky girl, now broken off, was the result of Pa's matchmaking. My parents had tried that, too, as a sideline, and had brought Moses and the girl together. Uncle Jomin read matrimonial notices aloud to his sons from the Yiddish paper. Widows with fortunes were the chief interest, and young women with large marriage portions from the Far West who needed Jewish husbands. My Aunt Julia told her children, 'Don't hold yourselves cheap. Marry rich.' The Libutsky girl had money, but it didn't work out. Ma thought well of Moses. However, she said, the girl was too gentle for him. He would need a bolder one.

'What is this business?' Moses said.

'A little dry goods store in Point St Charles.'

'Not a bad idea,' said Moses, 'Is it a good location?'

'Yes, we can make a living there. If the Lord will send a little luck. You know I've never been a lazy man. I've had money, and I'll have it again as surely as we're alive this day in the world . . .'

'With God's help, it happens,' said Uncle Jomin.

'It was hard for Sarah to get used to the life here, but . . .'

'You have a good wife,' said Uncle Jomin. 'I feel for her. And it is a strange country. But you have to keep your head. That's the main thing about strangeness.'

Aunt Julia interrupted, saying, 'I don't see what's so strange. You had to make your way over there, too. Would you want to be in Russia now? A fire!' she said. 'A destruction! Millions of corpses. Ploughing with cannon. Typhus. Famine and death. Didn't you have a taste of it? Don't you thank God that you escaped from those madmen?'

She told Pa this sternly, and glared at him that he could be so weak-minded, so forgetful, so ignorant as to talk loosely about the strangeness here. She showed you how the old country was sealed up in doom and death. She spoke strongly, and as though it was a credit to her to have come here. Escape? No, it was more like a triumph.

MELBA THE fox terrier sat in Uncle Jomin's lap and cunningly reached for scraps on his plate. She extended her head sidewise under his arm. Melba was privileged and the reason was that one night she woke Uncle Jomin when the house was afire. She pulled the blanket from him and saved the family. Therefore she had the run of things. She escorted Jornin to the junkyard in the morning and then she came home to accompany Aunt Julia to the market. They seemed to me exceptionally lucky in their dog. We could not have one. I brought a terrier in and he gave us fleas. We had to be treated with Paris Green. Pa went out and brought it home in a paper sack, mixed a paste and smeared it on our bodies. Another time an English bulldog followed me home. I fed him peppermint hard-balls, the red and white kind. However, he ran away. I ran after him all the way to Peel Street but couldn't get him back. We had cats, instead, many of them. They belonged to Bentchka.

Then, too, Aunt Julia had pictures on the wall that seemed to me of a high degree. Of these, the best was Queen Victoria with a veil and diadem, her flesh very fair and pure. She had her elbow on the table and her chin rested on her wrist. In addition, there was a painting of a basket of fruit. A peach sliced in half with a very rich red stone was in front. Another picture was of a faithful collie who had found a lamb in the snow and wouldn't abandon it. These were powerful and influential pictures. It wasn't any old thing that turned up in the junkyard that Aunt Julia would allow to hang on her walls. At home we had only one picture, of Moses holding up the tablets.

'I have a partner for the Point St Charles business,' said Pa.

'A partner! Why a partner?' said Aunt Julia. 'Why are you afraid to do anything by yourself? And who is this partner?'

'Henoch,' he told her.

'*Gottenyu!*' Aunt Julia raised her sarcastic eyes to heaven. She clasped her hands and wrung her fingers. Her long upraised nostrils were tense with laughter and horror at Pa's idiocies.

'That one?' said Cousin Moses.

Aunt Julia cried out, 'You poor beggar. You everlasting fool.'

'Is this,' said Philip, 'the Henoch who left his wife?'

Henoch was my mother's cousin, and he had brought his wife and family over, but then there had been a divorce. No one approved of that.

'I didn't want a partner,' Pa explained. 'But I had to take in someone. I couldn't do everything myself.'

'Not if you took Joshua out of school?'

'No, not even.'

Jomin said, 'What happened to Henoch's fish store?'

'Gone,' said Pa.

'Well, that's a fine omen,' said Aunt Julia. 'He ruined his own business, and now you want to give him a second opportunity in your store.'

'They say he's living with another woman,' said Moses.

Moses had a passion for gossip. He'd come and tell his mother things. That very evening, I heard him say to her in an undertone, 'Max Feldman, you remember . . .'

'Yes.'

'Was caught.'

'With another woman?'

'His own mother-in-law.'

'No!' she said, turning her fine sharp head to him, with alarm. 'Woe-to-us-not! Those wasters! Where?'

'Where do you think,' said Moses. 'In bed, of course.'

She gave a little scream of horror and satisfaction. 'What a beast of a woman, to do this to her daughter.'

'Well,' Pa said in reply to Moses's question about Henoch. 'I don't know where he's living.' His answer was uneasy, for it wasn't truthful.

'And such a sport yet,' said Aunt Julia, 'with his little moustache, and his crooked eyes and fat lips, and his belly, and that coat he wears with a split in the back, like a Prussian.'

She was a deadly observer. Cousin Henoch's coat did bear a resemblance to the Prussian military overcoat.

'And he stinks of fish,' she added. 'And he's rotten to the bone, and lazy, and he probably has syphilis. And if you think I am going to throw away money on a business like . . .'

'I'll give you my own note,' said Pa. 'Not his, mine.'

'. . . If you think we are going to throw away hard-earned money,' she said, 'you can go out in the woods, and find a bear, and pick up the bear's apron, and kiss the bear,' she said, fiercely nasal and high, 'right under the apron.'

The mirth of the Jomin family was a curious thing—it had a devil of a twist to it. They were dark, and they were all clever and subtle, and laughed like wolves, pointing their faces.

THE KITCHEN walls were hot. The stoves were bursting with heat. Where old pipe-holes entered the chimney there were circular asbestos plugs with flowers painted on them.

The Jomins laughed at Aunt Julia's wit, but Pa said angrily, 'You are heartless people! Hard people! One schleps himself out to earn a living for his wife and children, and another mocks him. You have it good in America. While my face is being ground.'

The hot kitchen filled with high, wrathful voices. The cries mounted.

'America is all yours, my dear brother,' cried Aunt Julia. 'Go and do as Jomin did. Work with a pick and shovel, as he did. Dig ditches and lay tracks. To this day he wears a truss.'

That was a fact. An elaborate truss with a cushion for the groin hung in the bathroom. I found it behind the bathroom door and tried it on. The pad pushed uncomfortably into the groin.

'He'll never be the same man. Don't expect me to waste his money on your wife's relatives.'

'A coarse, cruel character you have,' Pa shouted. 'Your brother's misery does you good, you devil, you.'

'You grudge me my good luck,' she cried. 'You're envious. You have the evil eye.'

'And you would murder people in the street, with your arrogant heart. And you are brazen. And you don't know what it is to pity. You're not a woman at all. I don't know what you are.'

They raged and yelled at each other. It was a quarrel of nearly forty years' duration, which now and then flared. Pa blamed her for his ruin in Canada. He called her a witch. He said she could have saved him any time she chose but preferred to see him struggle and go under.

Her face was red as Chinese paint. I am sure she knew of more sins and judgements than he could imagine if his anger lasted a month. She cried out, 'Why do you throw yourself on people? You fool! And don't you think I know better than to try to soak up the sea by flinging loaves of bread into it?'

It was Pa's outrage that she found intolerable.

'You may kiss my—!' she told him.

'You may lie in your grave before then,' he shouted, 'and not a penny will you have there.'

Melba barked at him so shrilly that Abba finally took her away, and it appeared as if her barking had incited Pa and Aunt Julia, for when her dog-shrieks ended, they both grew calmer. I too was susceptible to dogs' barking.

And Uncle Jomin on his own lent Pa 150 dollars to go into business in Point St Charles, and took Pa's note for the amount. He sternly warned him against his partner. Uncle Jomin had a pair of eyes of gloomy strength; they had great power to warn and threaten. But what good does it do to threaten a desperate man?

FOR ONE brief year we had the feeling of a family that owned a business. It was a store. People went everywhere else to buy their dry goods—if the French and Irish families in this sparse slum bought anything at all. But there was a little store, nevertheless. The partner, as predicted, was no good. He put his entire trust in Pa, and so did nothing. Every afternoon he took a nap on an old bench at the back of the store, which must have come out of the waiting-room of a station. He flirted with the Ukrainian and French women who came, and Pa said we had to keep an eye on him, he might give things away. All the men in Ma's family had this weakness for women, he told me. Henoch snoozed, during vacant summer afternoons when the air was warm and grey. Pa went out to hunt bargains, job lots, and to check on prices in other stores. I read books and practised tricks, and tried to discipline my body. I was ambitious to learn to tie knots with my toes. Houdini could both tie and untie them. I studied the books of spiritualists, too: Oliver Lodge, A. Conan Doyle, and a book called *The Law of Psychic Phenomena*, by Hudson.

The dry goods store soon went on the rocks.

THEODORE ROETHKE

Pathos is often an element in our relationship with our fathers, and it is hard not to read "My Papa's Waltz" without feeling the pathos of the son's situation. Loving a drunk is never easy, even when the drunk is your long-dead father. Poems, of course, need not be autobiographical, and strict critics may think an identification of the narrator with the poet and of Papa with the poet's father presumptuous. Presumptuous or not, it is hard not to make such an identification. Roethke's gardener father, hands caked with dirt, loomed large in his imagination, and Roethke's feelings toward his father were as deeply ambivalent as the feelings evoked in this poem. The search for the father is always more difficult when the father disappears in the writer's childhood or youth, and Roethke's father died when Roethke was only 15. "My Papa's Waltz" is a declaration both of love and of reproach, all the more powerful for its restraint. Roethke, incidentally, never became a father, though he did become an alcoholic.

MY PAPA'S WALTZ

The whiskey on your breath
Could make a small boy dizzy;
But I hung on like death:
Such waltzing was not easy.

We romped until the pans
Slid from the kitchen shelf;
My mother's countenance
Could not unfrown itself.

The hand that held my wrist
Was battered on one knuckle;
At every step you missed
My right ear scraped a buckle.

You beat time on my head
With a palm caked hard by dirt,
Then waltzed me off to bed
Still clinging to your shirt.

MORDECAI RICHLER

The number of Jews writing about their fathers is worth pointing out, and Mordecai Richler provides a good pretext for doing so ... if only because at least three of his children—Emma, Jacob, and Noah—have also written about him. In addition to Richler's essay, this anthology includes 'patremoirs' by Saul Bellow, Leonard Cohen, Mary Gordon, Franz Kafka, and Philip Roth, and it could easily have included pieces by other Jewish writers such as Paul Auster, A. M. Klein, Maxine Kumin, Stanley Kunitz, Phillip Lopate, and Art Spiegelman. This abundance of powerful father pieces by Jewish writers may arise from the patriarchal nature of Jewish culture, the Jewish emphasis on origins and identity, or the strong exegetical and critical training which Jewish culture provides. Further, such pieces may also find their roots in concerns about assimilation and loss of Jewish identity. For many writers with a Jewish heritage, writing about the father is an act of ethnic autobiography. As Adrienne Rich says, "I have to claim my father, for I have my Jewishness from him ... and ... in order to claim him I have in a sense to expose him." If Richler exposes his father, if he presents his father as a weak man—possibly a coward, certainly a cuckold—his essay also looks beyond the father's failings. His essay is a secular Kaddish. It is an act of filial contrition which proves that when it comes to difficult fathers, emotions matter more than facts. Whatever the facts, there is no emotional falsity in the poignant, climactic exchange between father and son:"What do you know?' 'Nothing,' I replied, hugging him." Indeed, Richler's love, so evident in this exchange, eventually led him to transform his father into a benevolent minor deity, into the loveable, streetwise, tough guy father of Joshua Then and Now.

MY FATHER'S LIFE

After the funeral, I was given my father's *talis,* his prayer shawl, and (oh my God) a file containing all the letters I had written to him while I was living abroad, as well as carbon copies he had kept of the letters he had sent to me.

December 28, 1959: "Dear Son, Last week I won a big Kosher Turkey, by bowling, when I made the high triple for the week. How I did it I do not know, I guess I was lucky for once, or was it that the others were too sure of themselves, being much better at the game than I am."

February 28, 1963: "This month has been a cold one, making it difficult, almost impossible to work outside. Yes! it's been tough. Have you found a title for your last novel? What can you do with a title like this? 'UNTIL DEBT DO US PART'?"

His letter of February 28, 1963, like so many others written that year, begins, "Thanks for the cheque." For by that time we had come full circle. In the beginning it was my father who had sent checks to me. Included in the file I inherited were canceled checks, circa 1945, for $28 monthly child support, following the annulment of my parents' marriage. A bill dated January 15, 1948, for a Royal portable, my first typewriter, a birthday gift. Another bill, from Bond Clothes, dated August 21, 1950, on the eve of my departure for Europe, for "1 Sta. Wag. Coat, $46.49."

My own early letters to my father, horrendously embarrassing for me to read now, usually begin with appeals for money. No, *demands.* There is also a telegram I'd rather forget. March 11, 1951. IMPERATIVE CHECK SENT PRONTO MADRID C O COOKS WAGON LITS ALCALA NR 23 MADRID. BROKE. MORDECAI.

Imperative, indeed.

I WAS also left a foot-long chisel, his chisel, which I now keep on a shelf of honor in my workroom. Written with a certain flourish in orange chalk on the oak shaft is my father's inscription:

Used by M.I. Richler
Richler Artificial Stone Works
1922
De La Roche Street
NO SUCCESS.

My father was twenty years old then, younger than my eldest son is now. He was the firstborn of fourteen children. Surely that year, as every year of his life, on Passover, he sat in his finery at a dining-room table and recited, "We were once the slaves of Pharaoh in Egypt, but the Lord our God brought us forth from there with a mighty hand and an outstretched arm." But, come 1922, out there in the muck of his father's freezing backyard on De La Roche Street in Montreal—yet to absorb the news of his liberation—my father was still trying to make bricks with insufficient straw.

Moses Isaac Richler.

Insufficient straw, *NO* SUCCESS, was the story of his life. Neither of his marriages really worked. There were searing quarrels with my older brother. As a boy, I made life difficult for him. I had no respect. Later, officious strangers would rebuke him in the synagogue for the novels I had written. Heaping calumny on the Jews, they said. If there was such a thing as a reverse Midas touch, he had it. Not one of my father's penny mining stocks ever went into orbit. He lost regularly at gin rummy. As younger, more intrepid brothers and cousins began to prosper, he assured my mother, "The bigger they come, the harder they fall."

My mother, her eyes charged with scorn, laughed in his face. "You're the eldest and what are you?"

Nothing.

After his marriage to my mother blew apart, he moved into a rented room. Stunned, humiliated. St. Urbain's cuckold. He bought a natty straw hat. A sports jacket. He began to use aftershave lotion. It was then I discovered that he had a bottle of rye whiskey stashed in the glove compartment of his Chevy. My father. Rye whiskey. "What's that for?" I asked, astonished.

"For the femmes," he replied, wiggling his eyebrows at me. "It makes them want it."

I remember him as a short man, squat, with a shiny bald head and big floppy ears. Richler ears. My ears. Seated at the kitchen table at night in his Penman's long winter underwear, wetting his finger before turning a page of the *New York Daily Mirror*, reading Walter Winchell first. Winchell, who knew what's what. He also devoured *Popular Mechanics, Doc Savage,* and *Black Mask.* And, for educational purposes, *Reader's Digest.* My mother, on the other hand, read Keats and Shelley. *King's Row. The Good Earth.* My father's pranks did not enchant her. A metal ink spot on her new chenille bedspread. A felt mouse to surprise her in the larder. A knish secretly filled with absorbent cotton. Neither did his jokes appeal to her. "Hey, do you know why we eat hard-boiled eggs dipped in salt water just before the Passover meal?"

"No, Daddy. Why?"

"To remind us that when the Jews crossed the Red Sea they certainly got their balls soaked."

Saturday mornings my brother and I accompanied him to the Young Israel synagogue on Park Avenue near St. Viateur. As I was the youngest, under bar-mitzvah age, and therefore still allowed to carry on the Sabbath, I was the one who held the prayer shawls in a little purple velvet bag. My father, who couldn't stomach the rabbi's windy speeches, would slip into the back room to gossip with the other men before the rabbi set sail. "In Japan," my father once said, "there is a custom, time-honored, that before he begins, a speaker's hands are filled with ice cubes. He can shoot his mouth off for as long as he can hold the ice cubes in his hands. I wouldn't mind it if the rabbi had to do that."

He was stout, he was fleshy. But in the wedding photographs that I never saw until after his death the young man who was to become my father is as skinny as I once was, his startled brown eyes unsmiling behind horn-rimmed glasses. Harold Lloyd. Allowed a quick no-promises peek at the world and what it had to offer, but clearly not entitled to a place at the table.

My father never saw Paris. Never read Yeats. Never stayed out with the boys drinking too much. Never flew to New York on a whim. Nor turned over in bed and slept in, rather than report to work. Never knew a reckless love. What did he hope for? What did he want? Beyond peace and quiet, which he seldom achieved, I have no idea. So far as I know he never took a risk or was disobedient. At his angriest, I once heard him silence one of his cousins, a cousin bragging about his burgeoning real estate investments, saying, "You know how much land a man needs? Six feet. And one day that's all you'll have. Ha, ha!"

Anticipating Bunker Hunt, my father began to hoard American silver in his rented room. A blue steamer trunk filling with neatly stacked piles of silver dollars, quarters, dimes. But decades before their worth began to soar, he had to redeem them at face value. "I'm getting hitched again," he told me, blushing. He began to speculate in postage stamps. When he died at the age of sixty-five I also found out that he had bought a city backlot somewhere for $1200 during the Forties. In 1967, however—riding a bloated market, every fool raking it in—the estimated value of my father's property had shrunk to $900. All things considered, that called for a real touch of class.

I was charged with appetite, my father had none. I dreamed of winning prizes, he never competed. But, like me, my father was a writer. A keeper of records. His diary, wherein he catalogued injuries and insults, betrayals, family quarrels, bad debts, was written in a code of his own invention. His brothers and sisters used to tease him about it. "Boy, are we ever afraid! Look, I'm shaking!" But as cancer began to consume him, they took notice, fluttering about, concerned. "What about Moishe's diary?"

I wanted it. Oh, how I wanted it. I felt the diary was my proper inheritance. I hoped it would tell me things about him that he had always been too reticent to reveal. But his widow, an obdurate lady, refused to let me into the locked room in their apartment where he kept his personal papers. All she would allow was, "I'm returning your mother's love letters to her. The ones he found that time. You know, from the refugee."

That would have been during the early Forties, when my mother began to rent to refugees, putting them up in our spare bedroom. The refugees, German and Austrian Jews, had been interned as enemy aliens in England shortly after war was declared in 1939. A year later they were transported to Canada on a ship along with the first German and Italian prisoners of war. On arrival at the dock in Quebec City, the army major who turned them over to their Canadian guards said, "You have some German officers here, very good fellows, and some Italians, they'll be no trouble. And over there," he added, indicating the refugees, "the scum of Europe."

The refugees were interned in camps, but in 1941 they began to be released one by one. My father, who had never had anybody to condescend to in his life, was expecting real *greeners* with sidecurls. Timorous innocents out of the *shtetl,* who would look to him as a master of magic. Canadian magic. Instead, they patronized him. A mere junk dealer, a dolt. The refugees turned out to speak better English than any of us did, as well as German and French. After all they had been through over there, they were still fond of quoting a German son of a bitch called Goethe. "Imagine that," my father said. They also sang opera arias in the bathtub. They didn't guffaw over the antics of Fibber McGee 'n' Molly on the radio; neither were they interested in the strippers who shook their nookies right at you from the stage of the Gayety Theatre, nor in learning how to play gin rummy for a quarter of a cent a point. My mother was enthralled.

MY FATHER was afraid of his father. He was afraid of my unhappy mother, who arranged to have their marriage annulled when I was thirteen and my brother eighteen. He was also afraid of his second wife. Alas, he was even afraid of me when I was a boy. I rode street-cars on the Sabbath. I ate bacon. But nobody was ever afraid of Moses Isaac Richler. He was far too gentle.

The Richler family was, and remains, resolutely Orthodox, follow-ers of the Lubavitcher rabbi. So when my mother threatened divorce, an all but unheard-of scandal in those days, a flock of grim rabbis in flapping black gabardine coats descended on our cold-water flat on St. Urbain Street to plead with her. But my mother, dissatisfied for years with her arranged marriage, in love at last, was adamant. She had had enough. The rabbis sighed when my father, snapping his suspenders, rocking on his heels—speaking out—stated his most deeply felt marital grievance. When he awakened from his Saturday afternoon nap there was no tea. "Me, I like a cup of hot tea with lemon when I wake up."

In the end, there was no divorce. Instead, there was an annul-ment. I should explain that in the Province of Quebec at that time each divorce called for parliamentary approval. A long, costly pro-cess. A lawyer, a family friend, found a loophole. He pleaded for an annulment. My mother, he told the court, had married without her father's consent when she had still been a minor. He won. Techni-cally speaking, as I used to brag at college, I'm a bastard.

WEEKDAYS my father awakened every morning at six, put on his phylacteries, said his morning prayers, and drove his truck through the wintry dark to the family scrapyard near the waterfront. He worked there for my fierce, hot-tempered grandfather and a pompous younger brother. Uncle Solly, who had been to high school, had been made a partner in the yard, but not my father, his firstborn. He was a mere employee, working for a salary, which fed my mother's wrath. Younger brothers, determined to escape an overbearing father, had slipped free to form their own business, but my father was too timid to join them. "When times are bad they'll be back. I remember the Depression. Oh, boy!"

"Tell me about it," I pleaded.

But my father never talked to me about anything. Not his own boyhood. His feelings. Or his dreams. He never even mentioned sex to me until I was nineteen years old, bound for Paris to try to become a writer. Clutching my Royal portable, wearing my Sta. Wag. coat. "You know what safes are. If you have to do it—*and I know you*—use 'em. Don't get married over there. They'd do anything for a pair of nylon stockings or a Canadian passport."

Hot damn, I hoped he was right. But my father thought I was crazy to sail for Europe. A graveyard for the Jews. A continent where everything was broken or old. Even so, he lent me his blue steamer trunk and sent me $50 a month support. When I went broke two years later, he mailed me my boat fare without reproach. I told him that the novel I had written over there was called *The Acrobats* and he immediately suggested that I begin the title of my second novel with a B, the third with a C, and so on, which would make a nifty trademark for me. Writing, he felt, might not be such a nutty idea after all. He had read in *Life* that this guy Mickey Spillane, a mere *goy*, was making a fortune. Insulted, I explained hotly that I wasn't that kind of writer. I was a serious man.

"So?"

"I only write out of my obsessions."

"Ah, ha," he said, sighing, warming to me for once, recognizing another generation of family failure.

EVEN when I was a boy his admonitions were few. "Don't embarrass me. Don't get into trouble."

I embarrassed him. I got into trouble.

In the early Forties, my father's father rented a house directly across the street from us on St. Urbain, ten of his fourteen children still single and rooted at home. The youngest, my Uncle Yankel, was only three years older than I was and at the time we were close friends. But no matter what after-school mischief we were up to, we were obliged to join my grandfather at sunset in the poky little Gallicianer *shul* around the comer for the evening prayers, a ritual I didn't care for. One evening, absorbed in a chemistry experiment in our "lab" in my grandfather's basement, we failed to appear. On his return from *shul,* my grandfather descended on us, seething, his face bleeding red. One by one he smashed our test tubes and our retorts and even our cherished water distiller against the stone wall. Yankel begged forgiveness, but not me. A few days later I contrived to get into a scrap with Yankel, leaping at him, blackening his eye. Oh boy, did that ever feel good. But Yankel squealed on me. My grandfather summoned me into his study, pulled his belt free of his trousers, and thrashed me.

Vengeance was mine.

I caught my grandfather giving short weight on his scrapyard scales to a drunken Irish peddler. My grandfather, Jehovah's enforcer. Scornful, triumphant, I ran to my father and told him his father was no better than a cheat and a hypocrite.

"What do you know?" my father demanded.

"Nothing."

"They're anti-Semites, every one of them."

My grandfather moved to Jeanne Mance Street, only a few blocks away, and on Sunday afternoons he welcomed all the family there. Children, grandchildren. Come Hanukkah, the most intimidating of my aunts was posted in the hall, seated behind a bridge table piled high with Parcheesi games one year, Snakes and Ladders another. As each grandchild filed past the table he was issued a game. "Happy Hanukkah."

My grandfather was best with babies, rubbing his spade beard into their cheeks until they squealed. Bouncing them on his lap. But I was twelve years old now and I had taken to strutting down St. Urbain without a hat, and riding streetcars on the Sabbath. The next time my father and I started out for the house on Jeanne Mance on a Sunday afternoon, he pleaded with me not to disgrace him yet again, to behave myself for once, and then he thrust a *yarmulke* at me. "You can't go in there bareheaded. Put it on."

"It's against my principles. I'm an atheist."

"What are you talking about?"

"Charles Darwin," I said, having just read a feature article on him in *Coronet*, "or haven't you ever heard of him?"

"You put on that *yarmulke*," he said, "or I cut your allowance right now."

"O.K., O.K."

"And Jewish children are not descended from monkeys, in case you think you know everything."

"When I have children of my own I'll be better to them."

I had said that, testing. Sneaking a sidelong glance at my father. The thing is I had been born with an undescended testicle and my brother, catching me naked in the bathroom, had burst out laughing and assured me that I would never be able to have children or even screw. "With only one ball," he said, "you'll never be able to shoot jism."

My father didn't rise to the bait. He had worries of his own. My mother. The refugee in the spare bedroom. His father. "When you step in the door," he said, "the *zeyda* will ask you which portion of the Torah they read in *shul* yesterday." He told me the name of the chapter. "Got it?"

"I'm not afraid of him."

My grandfather, his eyes hot, was lying in wait for me in the living room. Before a court composed of just about the entire family, he denounced me as a violator of the Sabbath. A *shabus goy*. Yankel smirked. My grandfather grabbed me by the ear, beat me about the face, and literally threw me out of the house. I lingered across the street, waiting for my father to seek me out, but when he finally appeared, having endured a bruising lecture of his own, all he said was, "You deserved what you got."

"Some father you are."

Which was when I earned another belt on the cheek.

"I want you to go back in there like a man and apologize to the *zeyda*."

"Like hell."

I never spoke to my grandfather again.

But when he died, less than a year after the annulment of my parents' marriage, my mother insisted it was only proper that I attend his funeral. I arrived at the house on Jeanne Mance to find the coffin set out in the living room, uncles and aunts gathered round. My Uncle Solly drove me into a comer. "So here you are," he said.

"So?"

"You hastened his death; you never even spoke to him even though he was sick all those months"

"I didn't bring on his death."

"Well, smart guy, you're the one who is mentioned first in his will."

"Oh."

"You are not a good Jew and you are not to touch his coffin. It says that in his will. Don't you dare touch his coffin."

I turned to my father. Help me, help me. But he retreated, wiggling his eyebrows.

SO MANY things about my father's nature still exasperate or mystify me. All those years he was being crushed by his own father, nagged by my mother, teased (albeit affectionately) by his increasingly affluent brothers and cousins, was he seething inside, plotting a vengeance in his diary? Or was he really so sweet-natured as not to give a damn? Finally, there is a possibility I'd rather not ponder. Was he not sweet-natured at all, but a coward? Like me. Who would travel miles to avoid a quarrel. Who tends to remember slights—recording them in my mind's eye—transmogrifying them—finally publishing them in a code more accessible than my father's. Making them the stuff of fiction.

Riddles within riddles.

My father came to Montreal as an infant, his father fleeing Galicia. Pogroms. Rampaging Cossacks. But, striptease shows aside, the only theatre my father relished, an annual outing for the two of us, was the appearance of the Don Cossack Choir at the St. Denis Theatre. My father would stamp his feet to their lusty marching and drinking songs; his eyes would light up to see those behemoths, his own father's tormentors, prance and tumble on stage. Moses Isaac Richler, who never marched, nor drank, nor pranced.

Obviously, he didn't enjoy his family. My mother, my brother, me. Sundays he would usually escape our cold-water flat early and alone and start out for the first-run downtown cinemas, beginning with the Princess, which opened earliest, continuing from there to the Capitol or the Palace, and maybe moving on to the Loew's, returning to us bleary-eyed, but satiated, after dark. Astonishingly, he kept a sharp eye out for little production errors. Discovering them filled him with joy. Once, for instance, he told us, "Listen to this, Clark Gable is sitting there in this newspaper office and he tells Claudette Colbert he will be finished typing his story in an hour. But when she comes back and we are supposed to believe an hour has passed, *the hands on the clock on the wall haven't moved. Not an inch*." Another time it was, "Franchot Tone is in this tank in the desert, you're not going to believe this, and he says 'O.K., men, let's go. Attack!' And they attack. But if you look closely inside the tank just before they push off, the fuel gauge is indicating EMPTY. No gas. Get it?"

The Best Years of Our Lives overwhelmed him.

"There's a scene in there where Fredric March burps. He's hung over, he drinks an Alka-Seltzer or something, and he lets out a good one. Right there on screen. Imagine."

My mother was fond of reminding me that the night I was born, my father had not waited at the hospital to find out how she was, or whether it was a boy or a girl, but had gone to the movies instead. What was playing, I wondered.

My father didn't dream of Italy, where the lemon trees bloomed. He never went for a walk in the country or read a novel, unless he had to, because it was one of mine and he might be blamed for it. Bliss for him was the Gayety Theatre on a Saturday night. My father and a couple of younger brothers, still bachelors, seated front row center. On stage, Peaches, Anne Curie, or the legendary Lili St. Cyr. My father rapt, his throat dry, watching the unattainable Lili simulating intercourse with a swan as the stage lights throbbed, then trudging home through the snow to sit alone at the kitchen table, drinking hot milk with matzohs before going to sleep.

We endured some rough passages together. Shortly after the marriage annulment, I fought with my father. Fists flew. We didn't speak for two years. Then, when we came together again, meeting once a week, it wasn't to talk, but to play gin rummy for a quarter of a cent a point. My father, I began to suspect, wasn't reticent. He didn't understand life. He had nothing to say to anybody.

IN 1954, some time after my return to Europe, where I was to remain rooted for almost two decades, I married a *shiksa* in London. My father wrote me an indignant letter. Once more, we were estranged. But no sooner did the marriage end in divorce than he pounced: "You see, mixed marriages never work."

"But, Daddy, your first marriage didn't work either and Maw was a rabbi's daughter."

"What do you know?"

"Nothing," I replied, hugging him.

When I married again, this time for good, but to another *shiksa,* he was not overcome with delight, yet neither did he complain. For after all the wasting years, we had finally become friends. My father became my son. Once, he had sent money to me in Paris. Now, as the scrapyard foundered, I mailed monthly checks to him in Montreal. On visits home, I took him to restaurants. I bought him treats. If he took me to a gathering of the Richler clan on a Sunday afternoon, he would bring along a corked bottle of 7-Up for me, filled with scotch whisky. "There'll be nothing for you to drink there, and I know you."

"Hey, Daddy, that's really very thoughtful."

During the Sixties, on a flying trip to Montreal, my publishers put me up at the Ritz-Carlton Hotel, and I asked my father to meet me for a drink there.

"You know," he said, joining me at the table, "I'm sixty-two years old and I've never been here before. Inside, I mean. So this is the Ritz."

"It's just a bar," I said, embarrassed.

"What should I order?"

"Whatever you want, Daddy."

"A rye and ginger ale. Would that be all right here?"

"Certainly."

WHAT I'M left with are unresolved mysteries. A sense of regret. Anecdotes for burnishing.

My wife, a proud lady, showing him our firstborn son, his week-old howling grandchild, saying, "Don't you think he looks like Mordecai?"

"Babies are babies," he responded, seemingly indifferent.

Some years later my father coming to our house, pressing chocolate bars on the kids. "Who do you like better," he asked them, "your father or your mother?"

In the mid-Sixties, I flew my father to London. He came with his wife. Instead of slipping away with him to the Windmill Theatre or Raymond's Revue Bar, another strip joint, like a fool I acquired theatre tickets. We took the two of them to *Beyond the Fringe*. "What did you think?" I asked as we left the theatre.

"There was no chorus line," he said.

Following his last operation for cancer, I flew to Montreal, promising to take him on a trip as soon as he was out of bed. The Catskills. Grossinger's. With a stopover in New York to take in some shows. Back in London, each time I phoned, his doctor advised me to wait a bit longer. I waited. He died. The next time I flew to Montreal it was to bury him.

LEONARD COHEN

While Cohen has written far more personal pieces about his father, this song is included here because of the uses it makes of the story of Abraham and Isaac. In interviews and concerts, Cohen has commented frequently, if cryptically, on this song. For instance, at a 1974 Paris concert he said, "There is a place where the generations often meet. A very curious place. It's generally an altar or a chopping block. This is a song for my father." Ever the mythmaker and the iconoclast, Cohen inverts the myth of Abraham and Isaac by offering his father up on the altar of his song. From medieval times on, the story of Abraham and Isaac was seen to prefigure the relationship between God and Christ. In Cohen's iconography there is also the strong possibility that both Abraham and Isaac are versions of himself. After all, in The Favourite Game *he writes that to have no father "made you more grown up. You carved the chicken, you sat where he sat." If the son becomes his own father, when the father sacrifices the son, it is really the son sacrificing an earlier version of himself so as to be transfigured. In this scriptural parody, Cohen plays (as many children do) both Abraham and Isaac.*

STORY OF ISAAC

The door it opened slowly,
    my father he came in;
    I was nine years old.
And he stood so tall above me,
    his blue eyes they were shining
    and his voice was very cold.
He said, "I've had a vision
    and you know I'm strong and holy,
    I must do what I've been told."
So we started up the mountain;
    I was running, he was walking,
    and his axe was made of gold.

The trees they got much smaller,
    the lake a lady's mirror,
    when we stopped to drink some wine.
Then he threw the bottle over,
    I heard it break a minute later,
    and he put his hand on mine.
I thought I saw an eagle
    but it might have been a vulture,
    I never could decide.
Then my father built an altar,
    he looked once behind his shoulder,
    but he knew I would not hide.

You who build these altars now
      to sacrifice the children,
      you must not do it any more.
A scheme is not a vision
      and you never have been tempted
      by a demon or a god.
You who stand above them now,
      your hatchets blunt and bloody,
      you were not there before:
when I lay upon a mountain
      and my father's hand was trembling
      with the beauty of the word.

And if you call me Brother now,
      forgive me if I inquire,
      Just according to whose plan?
When it all comes down to dust,
   I will kill you if I must,
   I will help you if I can.
When it all comes down to dust,
   I will help you if I must,
   I'll kill you if I can.
And mercy on our uniform,
      man of peace, man of war—
      the peacock spreads his fan!

PHILIP ROTH

This passage is from the second chapter of Philip Roth's Patrimony: A True Story. *Although the book's title hints at a postmodern game, there is nothing playful about the clear-eyed, plain-spoken integrity with which Roth observes his father's dying and remembers his father's life. The father lives on in the "modest no-frills style," and the book is remarkable as a strong tribute paid by a strong son to a strong father. Despite simplicity of style,* Patrimony *is an epic, with Roth as a Hercules labouring on his father's behalf. In fierce, moving, often comic vignettes he takes on a ghoulish, hate-filled neighbour, a psychotic cab driver, denial of anti-Semitism by Metropolitan Life, a pornographic Holocaust survivor, a quintuple bypass, his father's excrement, and, repeatedly, his father himself. In a previous book,* The Facts: A Novelist's Autobiography, *Roth had said of his father that "narrative is the form his knowledge takes." In* Patrimony: A True Story, *he links his father's narrative gifts to memory: "You mustn't forget anything—that's the inscription on his coat of arms. To be alive, to him, is to be made of memory—to him if a man's not made of memory, he's made of nothing." Memory and narrative, along with the "shit" of "nothing less or more than lived reality" are Roth's patrimony—a patrimony which he transmutes into this profound and heartfelt testament. Book, son, and father merge into "the vernacular, unpoetic and expressive and pointblank, with all the vernacular's glaring limitations, and all its durable force."*

excerpt from *PATRIMONY*

My father's retirement pension from Metropolitan Life provided him with more than enough to live on in the modest no-frills style that seemed to him natural and sufficient for someone who grew up in near-poverty, worked slavishly for some forty years to give his family a secure, if simple, home life, and lacked the slightest interest in conspicuous consumption, ostentation, or luxury. In addition to the pension he'd been receiving now for twenty-three years, he drew Social Security income and the interest on his accumulated wealth—some eighty thousand dollars' worth of savings accounts, CDs, and municipal bonds. Despite his solid financial situation, however, in advanced old age he had become annoyingly tight about spending anything on himself. Though he did not hesitate to give generous gifts to his two grandsons whenever they needed money, he was continually saving inconsequential sums that deprived him of things he himself liked or needed.

Among the more distressing economies was his refusal to buy his own *New York Times*. He worshiped that paper and loved to spend the morning reading it through, but now, instead of buying his own, he waited all day long to have a copy passed on to him by somebody in his building who had been feckless enough to fork over the thirty-five cents for it. He'd also given up buying the *Star-Ledger,* a fifteen-cent daily that, along with the defunct *Newark News*, he had read ever since I was a child and it was called the *Newark Star-Eagle*. He also refused to re-tain, on a weekly basis, the cleaning woman who used to help my mother with the apartment and the laundry. The woman now came one day a month, and he cleaned the apartment himself the rest of the time. "What else do I have to do?" he asked. But as he was nearly blind in one eye and had a cataract thickening in the other and was no longer as agile as he liked to imagine, no matter how hard he worked the job he did do was awful. The bathroom smelled, the carpets were dirty, and few of the appliances in the kitchen could have passed muster with a health inspector who hadn't been bribed.

It was a comfortably furnished, rather ordinary three-room apartment, decorated with neither flair nor bad taste. The living room carpet was a pleasant avocado green and the furniture there mostly antique reproductions, and on the walls were two large reproductions (chosen for my parents nearly forty years back by my brother, who had been to art school) of Gauguin landscapes framed in wormwood as well as an expressionistic portrait that my brother had painted of my father in his early seventies. There were thriving plants by the row of windows that faced a quiet, tree-lined, residential street to the south; there were photos in every room—of children, grandchildren, daughters-in-law, nephews, nieces—and the few books on the shelves in the dining area were either by me or on Jewish subjects. Aside from the lamps, which were a little glitzily ornate and surprisingly uncharacteristic of my mother's prim, everything-in-its-place aesthetic, it was a warm, welcoming apartment whose gleaming appearance—at least when my mother was still alive—was somewhat in contrast to the depressing lobby and hallways of the thirty-year-old building, which were uninvitingly bare and growing slightly dilapidated.

Ever since my father had been alone, when I was visiting, I'd sometimes wind up, after having used the toilet, scouring the sink, cleaning the soap dish, and rinsing out the toothbrush glass before I returned to sit with him in the living room. He insisted on washing his underclothes and his socks in the bathroom rather than parting with the few quarters that it cost to use the washer/dryer in the basement laundry room; every time I came to see him, there were his grayish, misshapen things draped over wire hangers on the shower rod and the towel racks. Though he prided himself on being nattily dressed and always enjoyed putting on a nicely tailored new sports jacket or a three-piece Hickey-Freeman suit (enjoyed it particularly when he'd bought it at an end-of-season sale), he had taken to cutting corners on whatever wasn't visible to anyone else. His pajamas and handkerchiefs, like his underwear and socks, looked as though they hadn't been replaced since my mother's death.

When I got to his apartment that morning—after the inadvertent visit to my mother's grave—I quickly excused myself and went off to the toilet. First I'd missed a turnoff, and now in the bathroom I was taking another few minutes to rehearse for a final time the best way to tell him about the tumor. While I stood over the bowl, his undergarments hung all around me like remnants strung out by a farmer to scare the birds away. On the open shelves above the toilet, where there was an assortment of prescription drugs, as well as his Polident, Vaseline, and Ascriptin, his boxes of tissues, Q-tips, and absorbent cotton, I spotted the shaving mug that had once been my grandfather's; in it my father kept his razor and a tube of shaving cream. The mug was pale blue porcelain; a delicate floral design enclosed a wide white panel at the front, and inside the panel the name "S. Roth" and the date "1912" were inscribed in faded gold Gothic lettering. The mug was our one family heirloom as far as I knew, aside from a handful of antique snapshots the only thing tangible that anyone had cared to save from the immigrant years in Newark. I had been intrigued by it ever since my grandfather had died a month short of my seventh birthday and it made its way into our Newark bathroom, back when my father was still shaving with a bristle brush and shaving soap.

Sender Roth had been a remote, mysterious presence to me as a small boy, an elongated man with an undersized head—the forebear whom my own skeleton most resembles—and about whom all I knew was that he smoked all day long, spoke only Yiddish, and wasn't much given to fondling the American grandchildren when we all showed up with our parents on Sundays. After his death, the shaving mug in our bathroom brought him much more fully to life for me, not as a grandfather but, even more interestingly then, as an ordinary man among men, a customer of a barbershop where his mug was kept on a shelf with the mugs of the other neighborhood immigrants. It reassured me as a child to think that in that household where, according to all reports, there was never a penny to spare, a dime was set aside every week for him to go to the barbershop and get his Sabbath shave.

My grandfather Roth had studied to be a rabbi in Polish Galicia, in a small town not far from Lemberg, but when he arrived in America alone in 1897, without his wife and his three sons (my uncles Charlie, Morris, and Ed), he took a job in a hat factory to earn the money to bring his family over and worked there more or less most of his life. There were seven children born between 1890 and 1914, six sons and a daughter, and all but the last two of the boys and the one girl left school after the eighth grade to find jobs to help support the family. The shaving mug inscribed "S. Roth" had seemed to free my grandfather—if only momentarily, if only for those few minutes he quietly sat being shaved in the barber's chair late on a Friday afternoon—from the dour exigencies that had trapped him and that, I imagined, accounted for his austere, uncommunicative nature. His mug emitted the aura of an archaeological find, an artifact signaling an unexpected level of cultural refinement, an astonishing superfluity in an otherwise cramped and obstructed existence—in our ordinary little Newark bathroom, it had the impact on me of a Greek vase depicting the mythic origins of the race.

By 1988 what amazed me about it was that my father hadn't thrown it out or given it away. Over the years, when it was within his power, he had gotten rid of just about everything "useless" to which any of us might have been thought to have a sentimental attachment. Though these seizures of largess were, on the whole, admirably motivated, they sometimes lacked sensitivity to innate property rights. So eager was he to answer the need (real or imagined) of the recipient that he did not always think about the effect of his impulsiveness on the unwitting donor.

My two-volume stamp collection, for instance, studiously acquired by me throughout my late grade school years—a collection partially inspired by the example of the country's most famous philatelist, Franklin Delano Roosevelt, and underwritten with virtually all my riches—he gave away to a great-nephew of his the year I went off to college. I didn't know this until ten years later, when I was thinking of drawing on my scholarly discoveries as a boy stamp collector for an episode in a piece of fiction and went down to my parents' house in Moorestown to get the albums out of the attic. It was only after I had searched thoroughly, but in vain, through the cartons I'd stored there that my mother reluctantly—and not until we were off alone together—explained how they had come to disappear. She assured me that she had tried to stop him, that she had told him that my stamps weren't his to dispose of, but he wouldn't listen. He told her that I was grown up, away at college, didn't "use" the stamps anymore, whereas Chickie, his great-nephew, could bring them with him to school, et cetera, et cetera, et cetera. I suppose I could have found out if any part of my collection even existed any longer by contacting Chickie—a relative who was virtually a stranger to me and by then a young married man—but I decided to let the whole thing drop. I was terrifically irritated to hear what he had done—and, when I remembered how much of my childhood had gone into that collection, genuinely pained—but as it was so long ago that he had done it and as I had rather more difficult problems to deal with (I was in the midst of an acrimonious marital separation) I said nothing to him. And even if I had been inclined to, it would have been no easier for me to criticize him to his face at twenty-eight than it had been at eighteen or eight, since his most blatantly thoughtless acts were invariably ignited by this spontaneous impulse to support, to assist, to rescue, to save, prompted by the conviction that what he was doing—giving away my stamps, for example—was generous, helpful, and morally or educationally efficacious.

I believe another motive was operating in him—one harder to fathom and name—when we came back from burying my mother in May of 1981, and even as the apartment began filling up with family and friends, he disappeared into the bedroom and started emptying her bureau drawers and sorting through the clothes in her closet. I was still at the door with my brother, welcoming the mourners who'd followed us back from the cemetery, and so I wouldn't right off have known what he was up to had not my mother's sister Millie rushed out of the bedroom and down the hallway calling for help. "You better go in there and do something, darling," she whispered into my ear; "your father's throwing everything out. "

Not even my opening the bedroom door and coming into the room and firmly saying, "Dad, what are you doing?" did anything to slow him down. The bed was already strewn with dresses, coats, skirts, and blouses pulled from the closet, and he was now busily chucking things from a corner of her lowest bureau drawer into a plastic garbage bag. I put my hand on his shoulder and gripped it forcefully. "People are here for you," I said; "they want to see you, to talk to you—" "What good is this stuff anymore? It's no good to me hanging here. This stuff can go to Jewish relief—it's in mint condition—" "Stop, please—just stop. There's time for all this later. We'll do it together later. Stop throwing things out," I said. "Pull yourself together. Go into the living room where you're needed."

But he *was* pulled together. He didn't appear to be either in a daze or in the throes of a hysterical fit—he was simply doing what he had done all his life: the next difficult job. Thirty minutes before, we had buried her body; now to dispose of her things.

I ushered him out of the bedroom, and once among the guests who had come to offer condolences, he immediately began talking away, assuring everyone that he was fine. I returned to the bedroom to remove from the garbage bag the pile of mementos that he'd already discarded and that my mother had neatly and carefully saved over the years—among them, in a tiny brown envelope, my Phi Beta Kappa key, which she had coveted, a collection of programs to family graduation exercises, birthday cards from my brother and me, a handful of telegrams announcing good news, clippings friends had sent her about me and my books, specially prized snapshots of her two grandsons as small boys. They were all items for which my father could imagine no function now that she who had treasured them was gone, the sentimental keepsakes of someone whose sentiments had been snuffed out forever two nights earlier at a seafood restaurant where, as was their custom, they had gone with friends for Sunday night dinner. My mother had just been served clam chowder, a favorite dish of hers; to everyone's surprise she had announced, "I don't want this soup"; and those were her last words—a moment later she was dead of a massive coronary.

It was my father's primitivism that stunned me. Standing all alone emptying her drawers and her closets, he seemed driven by some instinct that might be natural to a wild beast or an aboriginal tribesman but ran counter to just about every mourning rite that had evolved in civilized societies to mitigate the sense of loss among those who survive the death of a loved one. Yet there was also something almost admirable in this pitilessly realistic determination to acknowledge, instantaneously, that he was now an old man living alone and that symbolic relics were no substitute for the real companion of fifty-five years. It seemed to me that it was not out of fear of her things and their ghostlike power that he wanted to rid the apartment of them without delay—to bury *them* now, too—but because he refused to sidestep the most brutal of all facts.

Never in his life, as far as I knew, had he been one to try to elude the force of a dreadful blow, and yet, as I later learned, on the evening of her death he had fled from her corpse. This occurred not at the restaurant, where she had in fact died, but at the hospital, where she was declared dead after the paramedics had worked in vain to revive her on the ambulance ride from the restaurant to the emergency room. At the hospital, they pushed her stretcher into a cubicle of its own, and when my father, who had followed the ambulance in his car, went in by himself to look at her, he could not stand to see what he saw and so he ran. It was months before he could speak about this to anyone; and when he did, it wasn't to me or to my brother but to Claire, who, as a woman, could grant him the womanly absolution he required to begin to shed his shame.

Though he wasn't himself equipped to account for why he'd run away like that, I wondered if it hadn't something to do with his realizing that he might have contributed to the heart attack by pushing my mother that afternoon to walk beyond her endurance. She had been suffering for some time from severe shortness of breath and, unknown to me, from angina; during the previous winter there had also been a long siege of arthritic pain that had demoralized her terribly. That winter she'd had all she could do just to sit up comfortably in a chair, but on the day she died, because the May weather was so beautiful and she was finally out of doors getting some exercise, they'd walked as far as the drugstore, three very long city blocks away, and then, because he insisted it would be good for her, they'd also walked all the way home. According to Aunt Millie—whom my mother had phoned before they went out for the evening—by the time they'd reached the drugstore, she was already hopelessly exhausted. "I didn't think I could get back," she'd reported to my aunt, but instead of calling a taxi or waiting for a bus, they had rested a little on a nearby bench, and then he'd got her up on her feet for the return trek. "You know your father," my aunt had said to me. "He told her she could do it." She had spent the rest of the afternoon on the bed, trying to recover enough strength to go out to dinner.

As it happened, only an hour or so before they'd left for their walk, I'd made my customary Sunday call from England and told her playfully that I expected her to go a mile with me down the country road outside my house when she and my father came to visit that summer. She replied, "I don't know if it'll be a mile, dear, but I'll try." She was sounding bright and confident for the first time in months and could well have gone off that afternoon hoping to begin to prepare herself for our summer stroll.

In fact, when I arrived back in America the next day and took a taxi from Kennedy directly over to Elizabeth, my father's first words to me were "Well, she won't be taking that walk, Phil." He was in her reclining chair, his body decrepit, his face battered-looking and drained of all life. I thought (not incorrectly, as it turned out), "This is what he will look like when *he* is dead." My brother, Sandy, and his wife, Helen, had arrived earlier in the day from Chicago and were at the apartment when I got there. Sandy had already been to the funeral home to arrange for the burial the next day. Before he'd gone, my father had spoken on the phone to the elderly funeral director, a man with whom my mother had attended Elizabeth's Battin High around the end of the First World War. My father, in tears, had told him, "Take care of her body, take good care of it, Higgins," then for the rest of the day he went on weeping, there in that chair in which she would stretch out after supper and try to get some relief from her arthritis while they watched the news together. "She ordered New England clam chowder," he told me as I kneeled beside him, still in my coat and holding his hand, "and I ordered Manhattan. When it came she said, 'I don't want this soup.' I said, 'Take mine—we'll switch,' but she was gone. Just slumped forward. Didn't even fall. Made no trouble for anyone. The way she always did everything."

Over and over again he recounted for me the pure prosaicness of the seconds preceding her extinction, while all the while I was thinking, "What are we going to do with this old guy?" To have ministered to my mother's needs, had she been the elderly survivor of their marriage, would have seemed manageable and natural enough; it was she who was the repository of our family past, the historian of our childhood and growing up, and, as I now realized, it was she around whose quietly efficient presence the family had continued to cohere in the decades since my brother and I had left home. My father was a more difficult personality, far less seductive and less malleable, too; bluntly resisting points of view that diverged only slightly from his own reigning biases was, in fact, one of his most rigorously unthinking activities. Still kneeling before him with his hand in mine, I understood just how much we were going to have to help him—what I couldn't understand was how we were going to get through to him.

His obsessive stubbornness—his stubborn obsessiveness—had very nearly driven my mother to a breakdown in her final years: since his retirement at the age of sixty-three, her once spirited, housewifely independence had been all but extinguished by his anxious, overbearing bossiness. For years he had believed that he was married to perfection, and for years he wasn't far wrong—my mother was one of those devoted daughters of Jewish immigrants who raised housekeeping in America to a great art. (Don't talk to anyone in my family about cleaning—we saw cleaning in its heyday.) But then my father retired from one of the Metropolitan Life's big South Jersey offices, where he'd been managing a staff of fifty-two people, and the efficient, clear-cut division of labor that had done so much to define their marriage as a success gradually began to be obliterated—by him. He had nothing to do and she had everything to do—and that wouldn't do. "You know what I am now?" he told me sadly on his sixty-fifth birthday. "I'm Bessie's husband." And by neither temperament nor training was he suited to be that alone. So, after a couple of years of volunteer work—stints at the V.A. Hospital in East Orange, with Jewish relief groups and the Red Cross—and even of working as an underling for a friend who owned a hardware store, he settled down to become Bessie's boss—only my mother happened not to need a boss, having been her own since her single-handed establishment of a first-class domestic-management and mothering company back in 1927, when my brother was born.

Just the summer before her death, during a weekend visit to Connecticut, when we two were alone having a cup of tea in the kitchen, she had announced that she was thinking of getting a divorce. To hear the word "divorce" from my mother's lips astonished me almost as much as it would have if she had uttered an obscenity. But then the inmost intertwining of mother and father's life together, the difficulties and disappointments and enduring strains, remain mysterious, really, forever, perhaps particularly if you grew up as a good boy in a secure, well-ordered home—and simultaneously as a good girl. People don't always realize what good girls we grew up as, too, the little sons suckled and gurgled by mothers as adroit as my own in the skills of nurturing domesticity. For a very long and impressionable time the male who's not around all day remains much more remote and mythological than the palpable woman of wizardly proficiency anchored firmly, during the decades when I was young, in the odorous kitchen where her jurisdiction was absolute and her authority divine. "But, Ma," I said, "it's late for a divorce, no? You're seventy-six." But she was crying quite pitifully already. That astonished me too. "He doesn't listen to what I say," she said. "He interrupts all the time to talk about something else. When we're out, that's the worst. Then he won't let me speak at all. If I start to, he just shuts me up. In front of everyone. As though I don't exist." "Tell him not to do it," I said. "It wouldn't make any difference." "Then tell him a second time and if it still doesn't work, get up and say 'I'm going home.' And go." "Oh, darling, I couldn't. No, I couldn't embarrass him like that. Not with company." "But you tell me he embarrasses you when you're with company." "That's different. He's not like me. He couldn't take it, Philip. He would crumble up. It would kill him."

ROBERT HAYDEN

Quick as children are to set their fathers up on pedestals and, sometimes, to knock them down again, the dogged courage of fatherhood is rarely celebrated. Perhaps that is why "Those Winter Sundays" is so popular: it chooses praise instead of blame. The poem triumphs in wringing "a certain kind of affirmation and a certain kind of faith out of things that were really negative and troublesome." Although the father in this poem is a poetic subject equal to the complex, difficult figures of Harriet Tubman in "Runagate Runagate," and Nat Turner in "The Ballad of Nat Turner," craft and genius combine to make "Those Winter Sundays" a poem of transformation and resurrection. As the harsh plosive b's and k's of the opening lines dissolve into the open vowels and soft n's and l's of the conclusion, the father lives again in quiet heroism. Hayden made no bones about the autobiographical skeleton of "Those Winter Sundays," a poem "written for my foster father, who made it possible for me to go to college and all the rest of it." Where once the son would rise and dress in response to the father's love and call, now, in the plain, polished words of this poem, it is the father who is raised to life by the belated expression of the son's love and gratitude.

THOSE WINTER SUNDAYS

Sundays too my father got up early
and put his clothes on in the blueblack cold,
then with cracked hands that ached
from labor in the weekday weather made
banked fires blaze. No one ever thanked him.

I'd wake and hear the cold splintering, breaking.
When the rooms were warm, he'd call,
and slowly I would rise and dress,
fearing the chronic angers of that house,

speaking indifferently to him,
who had driven out the cold
and polished my good shoes as well.
What did I know, what did I know
of love's austere and lonely offices?

JAMES BALDWIN

More than just a father essay, "Notes of a Native Son" is a passionate yet restrained indictment of racism and its consequences. It is also American blues in essay form, blues in which Baldwin uses his father as an instrument to convey and, simultaneously, to transcend the bleak reality of the African American experience. Whether we recognize it or not, fathers are always instruments of culture, instruments shaped and shaping. By understanding how his father was shaped, Baldwin was able to escape or alter some of his father's shaping influences. By titling his essay (and the collection of pieces in which it was first published) "Notes of a Native Son," Baldwin was also riffing off of Richard Wright's novel Native Son (1940). *Though Baldwin described* Native Son *as "the most powerful and celebrated statement we have yet had of what it means to be a Negro in America," two of the eleven essays in* Notes of a Native Son, *"Everybody's Protest Novel" and "Many Thousands Gone," are critical of Wright's novel. In fact, Baldwin shared a common quarrel with his father and with Wright—the man whom, in his 1961 essay "Alas, Poor Richard," he referred to as "my ally and my witness, and alas! my father." Both men, Baldwin felt, had been damaged by the "bleak boundaries" which racism fixed to their lives. Both men had succumbed to bitterness. "Notes of a Native Son" is Baldwin's attempt to reject that bitterness without rejecting his fathers.*

One final note: Baldwin's title also plays off of Notes of a Son and Brother, *the title of a 1914 autobiographical work by Henry James.*

NOTES OF A NATIVE SON

On the 29th of July, in 1943, my father died. On the same day, a few hours later, his last child was born. Over a month before this, while all our energies were concentrated waiting for these events, there had been, in Detroit, one of the bloodiest race riots of the century. A few hours after my father's funeral, while he lay in state in the undertaker's chapel, a race riot broke out in Harlem. On the morning of the 3rd of August, we drove my father to the graveyard through a wilderness of smashed plate glass.

The day of my father's funeral had also been my nineteenth birthday. As we drove him to the graveyard, the spoils of injustice, anarchy, discontent, and hatred were all around us. It seemed to me that God himself had devised, to mark my father's end, the most sustained and brutally dissonant of codas. And it seemed to me, too, that the violence which rose all about us as my father left the world had been devised as a corrective for the pride of his eldest son. I had declined to believe in that apocalypse which had been central to my father's vision; very well, life seemed to be saying, here is something that will certainly pass for an apocalypse until the real thing comes along. I had inclined to be contemptuous of my father for the conditions of his life, for the conditions of our lives. When his life had ended I began to wonder about that life and also, in a new way, to be apprehensive about my own.

I had not known my father very well. We had got on badly, partly because we shared, in our different fashions, the vice of stubborn pride. When he was dead I realized that I had hardly ever spoken to him. When he had been dead a long time I began to wish I had. It seems to be typical of life in America, where opportunities, real and fancied, are thicker than anywhere else on the globe, that the second generation has no time to talk to the first. No one, including my father, seems to have known exactly how old he was, but his mother had been born during slavery. He was of the first generation of free men. He, along with thousands of other Negroes, came North after 1919 and I was part of that generation which had never seen the landscape of what Negroes sometimes call the Old Country.

He had been born in New Orleans and had been a quite young man there during the time that Louis Armstrong, a boy, was running errands for the dives and honky-tonks of what was always presented to me as one of the most wicked of cities—to this day, whenever I think of New Orleans, I also helplessly think of Sodom and Gomorrah. My father never mentioned Louis Armstrong, except to forbid us to play his records; but there was a picture of him on our wall for a long time. One of my father's strong-willed female relatives had placed it there and forbade my father to take it down. He never did, but he eventually maneuvered her out of the house and when, some years later, she was in trouble and near death, he refused to do anything to help her.

He was, I think, very handsome. I gather this from photographs and from my own memories of him, dressed in his Sunday best and on his way to preach a sermon somewhere, when I was little. Handsome, proud, and ingrown, "like a toenail," somebody said. But he looked to me, as I grew older, like pictures I had seen of African tribal chieftains: he really should have been naked, with war-paint on and barbaric mementos, standing among spears. He could be chilling in the pulpit and indescribably cruel in his personal life and he was certainly the most bitter man I have ever met; yet it must be said that there was something else in him, buried in him, which lent him his tremendous power and, even, a rather crushing charm. It had something to do with his blackness, I think—he was very black—with his blackness and his beauty, and with the fact that he knew that he was black but did not know that he was beautiful. He claimed to be proud of his blackness but it had also been the cause of much humiliation and it had fixed bleak boundaries to his life. He was not a young man when we were growing up and he had already suffered many kinds of ruin; in his outrageously demanding and protective way he loved his children, who were black like him and menaced, like him; and all these things sometimes showed in his face when he tried, never to my knowledge with any success, to establish contact with any of us. When he took one of his children on his knee to play, the child always became fretful and began to cry; when he tried to help one of us with our homework the absolutely unabating tension which emanated from him caused our minds and our tongues to become paralyzed, so that he, scarcely knowing why, flew into a rage and the child, not knowing why, was punished. If it ever entered his head to bring a surprise home for his children, it was, almost unfailingly, the wrong surprise and even the big watermelons he often brought home on his back in the summertime led to the most appalling scenes. I do not remember, in all those years, that one of his children was ever glad to see him come home. From what I was able to gather of his early life, it seemed that this inability to establish contact with other people had always marked him and had been one of the things which had driven him out of New Orleans. There was something in him, therefore, groping and tentative, which was never expressed and which was buried with him. One saw it most clearly when he was facing new people and hoping to impress them. But he never did, not for long. We went from church to smaller and more improbable church, he found himself in less and less demand as a minister, and by the time he died none of his friends had come to see him for a long time. He had lived and died in an intolerable bitterness of spirit and it frightened me, as we drove him to the graveyard through those unquiet, ruined streets, to see how powerful and overflowing this bitterness could be and to realize that this bitterness now was mine.

When he died I had been away from home for a little over a year. In that year I had had time to become aware of the meaning of all my father's bitter warnings, had discovered the secret of his proudly pursed lips and rigid carriage: I had discovered the weight of white people in the world. I saw that this had been for my ancestors and now would be for me an awful thing to live with and that the bitterness which had helped to kill my father could also kill me.

He had been ill a long time—in the mind, as we now realized, reliving instances of his fantastic intransigence in the new light of his affliction and endeavoring to feel a sorrow for him which never, quite, came true. We had not known that he was being eaten up by paranoia, and the discovery that his cruelty, to our bodies and our minds, had been one of the symptoms of his illness was not, then, enough to enable us to forgive him. The younger children felt, quite simply, relief that he would not be coming home anymore. My mother's observation that it was he, after all, who had kept them alive all these years meant nothing because the problems of keeping children alive are not real for children. The older children felt, with my father gone, that they could invite their friends to the house without fear that their friends would be insulted or, as had sometimes happened with me, being told that their friends were in league with the devil and intended to rob our family of everything we owned. (I didn't fail to wonder, and it made me hate him, what on earth we owned that anybody else would want.)

His illness was beyond all hope of healing before anyone realized that he was ill. He had always been so strange and had lived, like a prophet, in such unimaginably close communion with the Lord that his long silences which were punctuated by moans and hallelujahs and snatches of old songs while he sat at the living-room window never seemed odd to us. It was not until he refused to eat because, he said, his family was trying to poison him that my mother was forced to accept as a fact what had, until then, been only an unwilling suspicion. When he was committed, it was discovered that he had tuberculosis and, as it turned out, the disease of his mind allowed the disease of his body to destroy him. For the doctors could not force him to eat, either, and, though he was fed intravenously, it was clear from the beginning that there was no hope for him.

In my mind's eye I could see him, sitting at the window, locked up in his terrors; hating and fearing every living soul including his children who had betrayed him, too, by reaching towards the world which had despised him. There were nine of us. I began to wonder what it could have felt like for such a man to have had nine children whom he could barely feed. He used to make little jokes about our poverty, which never, of course, seemed very funny to us; they could not have seemed very funny to him, either, or else our all too feeble response to them would never have caused such rages. He spent great energy and achieved, to our chagrin, no small amount of success in keeping us away from the people who surrounded us, people who had all-night rent parties to which we listened when we should have been sleeping, people who cursed and drank and flashed razor blades on Lenox Avenue. He could not understand why, if they had so much energy to spare, they could not use it to make their lives better. He treated almost everybody on our block with a most uncharitable asperity and neither they, nor, of course, their children were slow to reciprocate.

The only white people who came to our house were welfare workers and bill collectors. It was almost always my mother who dealt with them, for my father's temper, which was at the mercy of his pride, was never to be trusted. It was clear that he felt their very presence in his home to be a violation: this was conveyed by his carriage, almost ludicrously stiff, and by his voice, harsh and vindictively polite. When I was around nine or ten I wrote a play which was directed by a young, white schoolteacher, a woman, who then took an interest in me, and gave me books to read and, in order to corroborate my theatrical bent, decided to take me to see what she somewhat tactlessly referred to as "real" plays. Theater-going was forbidden in our house, but, with the really cruel intuitiveness of a child, I suspected that the color of this woman's skin would carry the day for me. When, at school, she suggested taking me to the theater, I did not, as I might have done if she had been a Negro, find a way of discouraging her, but agreed that she should pick me up at my house one evening. I then, very cleverly, left all the rest to my mother, who suggested to my father, as I knew she would, that it would not be very nice to let such a kind woman make the trip for nothing. Also, since it was a schoolteacher, I imagine that my mother countered the idea of sin with the idea of "education," which word, even with my father, carried a kind of bitter weight.

Before the teacher came my father took me aside to ask *why* she was coming, what *interest* she could possibly have in our house, in a boy like me. I said I didn't know but I, too, suggested that it had something to do with education. And I understood that my father was waiting for me to say something—I didn't quite know what; perhaps that I wanted his protection against this teacher and her "education." I said none of these things and the teacher came and we went out. It was clear, during the brief interview in our living room, that my father was agreeing very much against his will and that he would have refused permission if he had dared. The fact that he did not dare caused me to despise him: I had no way of knowing that he was facing in that living room a wholly unprecedented and frightening situation.

Later, when my father had been laid off from his job, this woman became very important to us. She was really a very sweet and generous woman and went to a great deal of trouble to be of help to us, particularly during one awful winter. My mother called her by the highest name she knew: she said she was a "christian." My father could scarcely disagree but during the four or five years of our relatively close association he never trusted her and was always trying to surprise in her open, Midwestern face the genuine, cunningly hidden, and hideous motivation. In later years, particularly when it began to be clear that this "education" of mine was going to lead me to perdition, he became more explicit and warned me that my white friends in high school were not really my friends and that I would see, when I was older, how white people would do anything to keep a Negro down. Some of them could be nice, he admitted, but none of them were to be trusted and most of them were not even nice. The best thing was to have as little to do with them as possible. I did not feel this way and I was certain, in my innocence, that I never would.

But the year which preceded my father's death had made a great change in my life. I had been living in New Jersey, working in defense plants, working and living among southerners, white and black. I knew about the south, of course, and about how southerners treated Negroes and how they expected them to behave, but it had never entered my mind that anyone would look at me and expect *me* to behave that way. I learned in New Jersey that to be a Negro meant, precisely, that one was never looked at but was simply at the mercy of the reflexes the color of one's skin caused in other people. I acted in New Jersey as I had always acted, that is as though I thought a great deal of myself—I had to *act* that way—with results that were, simply, unbelievable. I had scarcely arrived before I had earned the enmity, which was extraordinarily ingenious, of all my superiors and nearly all my co-workers. In the beginning, to make matters worse, I simply did not know what was happening. I did not know what I had done, and I shortly began to wonder what *anyone* could possibly do, to bring about such unanimous, active, and unbearably vocal hostility. I knew about jim-crow but I had never experienced it. I went to the same self-service restaurant three times and stood with all the Princeton boys before the counter, waiting for a hamburger and coffee; it was always an extraordinarily long time before anything was set before me; but it was not until the fourth visit that I learned that, in fact, nothing had ever been set before me: I had simply picked something up. Negroes were not served there, I was told, and they had been waiting for me to realize that I was always the only Negro present. Once I was told this, I determined to go there all the time. But now they were ready for me and, though some dreadful scenes were subsequently enacted in that restaurant, I never ate there again.

It was the same story all over New Jersey, in bars, bowling alleys, diners, places to live. I was always being forced to leave, silently, or with mutual imprecations. I very shortly became notorious and children giggled behind me when I passed and their elders whispered or shouted—they really believed that I was mad. And it did begin to work on my mind, of course; I began to be afraid to go anywhere and to compensate for this I went places to which I really should not have gone and where, God knows, I had no desire to be. My reputation in town naturally enhanced my reputation at work and my working day became one long series of acrobatics designed to keep me out of trouble. I cannot say that these acrobatics succeeded. It began to seem that the machinery of the organization I worked for was turning over, day and night, with but one aim: to eject me. I was fired once, and contrived, with the aid of a friend from New York, to get back on the payroll; was fired again, and bounced back again. It took a while to fire me for the third time, but the third time took. There were no loopholes anywhere. There was not even any way of getting back inside the gates.

That year in New Jersey lives in my mind as though it were the year during which, having an unsuspected predilection for it, I first contracted some dread, chronic disease, the unfailing symptom of which is a kind of blind fever, a pounding in the skull and fire in the bowels. Once this disease is contracted, one can never be really care-free again, for the fever, without an instant's warning, can recur at any moment. It can wreck more important things than race relations. There is not a Negro alive who does not have this rage in his blood—one has the choice, merely, of living with it consciously or surrendering to it. As for me, this fever has recurred in me, and does, and will until the day I die.

My last night in New Jersey, a white friend from New York took me to the nearest big town, Trenton, to go to the movies and have a few drinks. As it turned out, he also saved me from, at the very least, a violent whipping. Almost every detail of that night stands out very clearly in my memory. I even remember the name of the movie we saw because its title impressed me as being so patly ironical. It was a movie about the German occupation of France, starring Maureen O'Hara and Charles Laughton and called *This Land Is Mine.* I remember the name of the diner we walked into when the movie ended: it was the "American Diner." When we walked in the counterman asked what we wanted and I remember answering with the casual sharpness which had become my habit: "We want a hamburger and a cup of coffee, what do you think we want?" I do not know why, after a year of such rebuffs, I so completely failed to anticipate his answer, which was, of course, "We don't serve Negroes here." This reply failed to discompose me, at least for the moment. I made some sardonic comment about the name of the diner and we walked out into the streets.

This was the time of what was called the "brown-out," when the lights in all American cities were very dim. When we re-entered the streets something happened to me which had the force of an optical illusion, or a nightmare. The streets were very crowded and I was facing north. People were moving in every direction but it seemed to me, in that instant, that all of the people I could see, and many more than that, were moving toward me, against me, and that everyone was white. I remember how their faces gleamed. And I felt, like a physical sensation, a *click* at the nape of my neck as though some interior string connecting my head to my body had been cut. I began to walk. I heard my friend call after me, but I ignored him. Heaven only knows what was going on in his mind, but he had the good sense not to touch me—I don't know what would have happened if he had—and to keep me in sight. I don't know what was going on in my mind, either; I certainly had no conscious plan. I wanted to do something to crush these white faces, which were crushing me. I walked for perhaps a block or two until I came to an enormous, glittering, and fashionable restaurant in which I knew not even the intercession of the Virgin would cause me to be served. I pushed through the doors and took the first vacant seat I saw, at a table for two, and waited.

I do not know how long I waited and I rather wonder, until today, what I could possibly have looked like. Whatever I looked like, I frightened the waitress who shortly appeared, and the moment she appeared all of my fury flowed towards her. I hated her for her white face, and for her great, astounded, frightened eyes. I felt that if she found a black man so frightening I would make her fright worth-while.

She did not ask me what I wanted, but repeated, as though she had learned it somewhere, "We don't serve Negroes here." She did not say it with the blunt, derisive hostility to which I had grown so accustomed, but, rather, with a note of apology in her voice, and fear. This made me colder and more murderous than ever. I felt I had to do something with my hands. I wanted her to come close enough for me to get her neck between my hands.

So I pretended not to have understood her, hoping to draw her closer. And she did step a very short step closer, with her pencil poised incongruously over her pad, and repeated the formula: ". . . don't serve Negroes here."

Somehow, with the repetition of that phrase, which was already ringing in my head like a thousand bells of a nightmare, I realized that she would never come any closer and that I would have to strike from a distance. There was nothing on the table but an ordinary watermug half full of water, and I picked this up and hurled it with all my strength at her. She ducked and it missed her and shattered against the mirror behind the bar. And, with that sound, my frozen blood abruptly thawed, I returned from wherever I had been, I *saw*, for the first time, the restaurant, the people with their mouths open, already, as it seemed to me, rising as one man, and I realized what I had done, and where I was, and I was frightened. I rose and began running for the door. A round, potbellied man grabbed me by the nape of the neck just as I reached the doors and began to beat me about the face. I kicked him and got loose and ran into the streets. My friend whispered, "*Run!*" and I ran.

My friend stayed outside the restaurant long enough to misdirect my pursuers and the police, who arrived, he told me, at once. I do not know what I said to him when he came to my room that night. I could not have said much. I felt, in the oddest, most awful way, that I had somehow betrayed him. I lived it over and over and over again, the way one relives an automobile accident after it has happened and one finds oneself alone and safe. I could not get over two facts, both equally difficult for the imagination to grasp, and one was that I could have been murdered. But the other was that I had been ready to commit murder. I saw nothing very clearly but I did see this: that my life, my *real* life, was in danger, and not from anything other people might do but from the hatred I carried in my own heart.

II

I HAD returned home around the second week in June—in great haste because it seemed that my father's death and my mother's confinement were both but a matter of hours. In the case of my mother, it soon became clear that she had simply made a miscalculation. This had always been her tendency and I don't believe that a single one of us arrived in the world, or has since arrived anywhere else, on time. But none of us dawdled so intolerably about the business of being born as did my baby sister. We sometimes amused ourselves, during those endless, stifling weeks, by picturing the baby sitting within in the safe, warm dark, bitterly regretting the necessity of becoming a part of our chaos and stubbornly putting it off as long as possible. I understood her perfectly and congratulated her on showing such good sense so soon. Death, however, sat as purposefully at my father's bedside as life stirred within my mother's womb and it was harder to understand why he so lingered in that long shadow. It seemed that he had bent, and for a long time, too, all of his energies towards dying. Now death was ready for him but my father held back.

All of Harlem, indeed, seemed to be infected by waiting. I had never before known it to be so violently still. Racial tensions throughout this country were exacerbated during the early years of the war, partly because the labor market brought together hundreds of thousands of ill-prepared people and partly because Negro soldiers, regardless of where they were born, received their military training in the south. What happened in defense plants and army camps had repercussions, naturally, in every Negro ghetto. The situation in Harlem had grown bad enough for clergymen, policemen, educators, politicians, and social workers to assert in one breath that there was no "crime wave" and to offer, in the very next breath, suggestions as to how to combat it. These suggestions always seemed to involve playgrounds, despite the fact that racial skirmishes were occurring in the playgrounds, too. Playground or not, crime wave or not, the Harlem police force had been augmented in March, and the unrest grew—perhaps, in fact, partly as a result of the ghetto's instinctive hatred of policemen. Perhaps the most revealing news item, out of the steady parade of reports of muggings, stabbings, shootings, assaults, gang wars, and accusations of police brutality, is the item concerning six Negro girls who set upon a white girl in the subway because, as they all too accurately put it, she was stepping on their toes. Indeed she was, all over the nation.

I had never before been so aware of policemen, on foot, on horse-back, on corners, everywhere, always two by two. Nor had I ever been so aware of small knots of people. They were on stoops and on corners and in doorways, and what was striking about them, I think, was that they did not seem to be talking. Never, when I passed these groups, did the usual sound of a curse or a laugh ring out and neither did there seem to be any hum of gossip. There was certainly, on the other hand, occurring between them communication extraordinarily intense. An-other thing that was striking was the unexpected diversity of the peo-ple who made up these groups. Usually, for example, one would see a group of sharpies standing on the street corner, jiving the passing chicks; or a group of older men, usually, for some reason, in the vicinity of a barber shop, discussing baseball scores, or the numbers, or making rather chilling observations about women they had known. Women, in a general way, tended to be seen less often together—unless they were church women, or very young girls, or prostitutes met together for an unprofessional instant. But that summer I saw the strangest combina-tions: large, respectable, churchly matrons standing on the stoops or the corners with their hair tied up, together with a girl in sleazy satin whose face bore the marks of gin and the razor, or heavy-set, abrupt, no-non-sense older men, in company with the most disreputable and fanatical "race" men, or these same "race" men with the sharpies, or these sharpies with the churchly women. Seventh Day Adventists and Meth-odists and Spiritualists seemed to be hobnobbing with Holyrollers and they were all, alike, entangled with the most flagrant disbelievers; some-thing heavy in their stance seemed to indicate that they had all, incredi-bly, seen a common vision, and on each face there seemed to be the same strange, bitter shadow.

The churchly women and the matter-of-fact, no-nonsense men had children in the Army. The sleazy girls they talked to had lovers there, the sharpies and the "race" men had friends and brothers there. It would have demanded an unquestioning patriotism, happily as uncommon in this country as it is undesirable, for these people not to have been disturbed by the bitter letters they received, by the newspaper stories they read, not to have been enraged by the posters, then to be found all over New York, which described the Japanese as "yellow-bellied Japs." It was only the "race" men, to be sure, who spoke ceaselessly of being revenged—how this vengeance was to be exacted was not clear—for the indignities and dangers suffered by Negro boys in uniform; but everybody felt a directionless, hopeless bitterness, as well as that panic which can scarcely be suppressed when one knows that a human being one loves is beyond one's reach, and in danger. This helplessness and this gnawing uneasiness does something, at length, to even the toughest mind. Perhaps the best way to sum all this up is to say that the people I knew felt, mainly, a peculiar kind of relief when they knew that their boys were being shipped out of the south, to do battle overseas. It was, perhaps, like feeling that the most dangerous part of a dangerous journey had been passed and that now, even if death should come, it would come with honor and without the complicity of their countrymen. Such a death would be, in short, a fact with which one could hope to live.

It was on the 28th of July, which I believe was a Wednesday, that I visited my father for the first time during his illness and for the last time in his life. The moment I saw him I knew why I had put off this visit so long. I had told my mother that I did not want to see him because I hated him. But this was not true. It was only that I *had* hated him and I wanted to hold on to this hatred. I did not want to look on him as a ruin: it was not a ruin I had hated. I imagine that one of the reasons people cling to their hates so stubbornly is because they sense, once hate is gone, that they will be forced to deal with pain.

We traveled out to him, his older sister and myself, to what seemed to be the very end of a very Long Island. It was hot and dusty and we wrangled, my aunt and I, all the way out, over the fact that I had recently begun to smoke and, as she said, to give myself airs. But I knew that she wrangled with me because she could not bear to face the fact of her brother's dying. Neither could I endure the reality of her despair, her unstated bafflement as to what had happened to her brother's life, and her own. So we wrangled and I smoked and from time to time she fell into a heavy reverie. Covertly, I watched her face, which was the face of an old woman; it had fallen in, the eyes were sunken and lightless; soon she would be dying, too.

In my childhood—it had not been so long ago—I had thought her beautiful. She had been quick-witted and quick-moving and very generous with all the children and each of her visits had been an event. At one time one of my brothers and myself had thought of running away to live with her. Now she could no longer produce out of her handbag some unexpected and yet familiar delight. She made me feel pity and revulsion and fear. It was awful to realize that she no longer caused me to feel affection. The closer we came to the hospital the more querulous she became and at the same time, naturally, grew more dependent on me. Between pity and guilt and fear I began to feel that there was another me trapped in my skull like a jack-in-the-box who might escape my control at any moment and fill the air with screaming.

She began to cry the moment we entered the room and she saw him lying there, all shrivelled and still, like a little black monkey. The great, gleaming apparatus which fed him and would have compelled him to be still even if he had been able to move brought to mind, not beneficence, but torture; the tubes entering his arm made me think of pictures I had seen when a child, of Gulliver, tied down by the pygmies on that island. My aunt wept and wept, there was a whistling sound in my father's throat; nothing was said; he could not speak. I wanted to take his hand, to say something. But I do not know what I could have said, even if he could have heard me. He was not really in that room with us, he had at last really embarked on his journey; and though my aunt told me that he said he was going to meet Jesus, I did not hear anything except that whistling in his throat. The doctor came back and we left, into that unbearable train again, and home. In the morning came the telegram saying that he was dead. Then the house was suddenly full of relatives, friends, hysteria, and confusion and I quickly left my mother and the children to the care of those impressive women, who, in Negro communities at least, automatically appear at times of bereavement armed with lotions, proverbs, and patience, and an ability to cook. I went downtown. By the time I returned, later the same day, my mother had been carried to the hospital and the baby had been born.

III

FOR MY father's funeral I had nothing black to wear and this posed a nagging problem all day long. It was one of those problems, simple, or impossible of solution, to which the mind insanely clings in order to avoid the mind's real trouble. I spent most of that day at the downtown apartment of a girl I knew, celebrating my birthday with whiskey and wondering what to wear that night. When planning a birthday celebration one naturally does not expect that it will be up against competition from a funeral and this girl had anticipated taking me out that night, for a big dinner and a night club afterwards. Sometime during the course of that long day we decided that we would go out anyway, when my father's funeral service was over. I imagine *I* decided it, since, as the funeral hour approached, it became clearer and clearer to me that I would not know what to do with myself when it was over. The girl, stifling her very lively concern as to the possible effects of the whiskey on one of my father's chief mourners, concentrated on being conciliatory and practically helpful. She found a black shirt for me somewhere and ironed it and, dressed in the darkest pants and jacket I owned, and slightly drunk, I made my way to my father's funeral.

The chapel was full, but not packed, and very quiet. There were, mainly, my father's relatives, and his children, and here and there I saw faces I had not seen since childhood, the faces of my father's one-time friends. They were very dark and solemn now, seeming somehow to suggest that they had known all along that something like this would happen. Chief among the mourners was my aunt, who had quarrelled with my father all his life; by which I do not mean to suggest that her mourning was insincere or that she had not loved him. I suppose that she was one of the few people in the world who had, and their incessant quarrelling proved precisely the strength of the tie that bound them. The only other person in the world, as far as I knew, whose relationship to my father rivalled my aunt's in depth was my mother, who was not there.

It seemed to me, of course, that it was a very long funeral. But it was, if anything, a rather shorter funeral than most, nor, since there were no overwhelming, uncontrollable expressions of grief, could it be called—if I dare to use the word—successful. The minister who preached my father's funeral sermon was one of the few my father had still been seeing as he neared his end. He presented to us in his sermon a man whom none of us had ever seen—a man thoughtful, patient, and forbearing, a Christian inspiration to all who knew him, and a model for his children. And no doubt the children, in their disturbed and guilty state, were almost ready to believe this; he had been remote enough to be anything and, anyway, the shock of the incontrovertible, that it was really our father lying up there in that casket, prepared the mind for anything. His sister moaned and this grief-stricken moaning was taken as corroboration. The other faces held a dark, non-committal thoughtfulness. This was not the man they had known, but they had scarcely expected to be confronted with *him*; this was, in a sense deeper than questions of fact, the man they had not known, and the man they had not known may have been the real one. The real man, whoever he had been, had suffered and now he was dead: this was all that was sure and all that mattered now. Every man in the chapel hoped that when his hour came he, too, would be eulogized, which is to say forgiven, and that all of his lapses, greeds, errors, and strayings from the truth would be invested with coherence and looked upon with charity. This was perhaps the last thing human beings could give each other and it was what they demanded, after all, of the Lord. Only the Lord saw the midnight tears, only He was present when one of His children, moaning and wringing hands, paced up and down the room. When one slapped one's child in anger the recoil in the heart reverberated through heaven and became part of the pain of the universe. And when the children were hungry and sullen and distrustful and one watched them, daily, growing wilder, and further away, and running head-long into danger, it was the Lord who knew what the charged heart endured as the strap was laid to the backside; the Lord alone who knew what one *would* have said if one had had, like the Lord, the gift of the living word. It was the Lord who knew of the impossibility every parent in that room faced: how to prepare the child for the day when the child would be despised and how to *create* in the child—by what means?—a stronger antidote to this poison than one had found for oneself. The avenues, side streets, bars, billiard halls, hospitals, police stations, and even the playgrounds of Harlem—not to mention the houses of correction, the jails, and the morgue—testified to the potency of the poison while remaining silent as to the efficacy of whatever antidote, irresistibly raising the question of whether or not such an antidote existed; raising, which was worse, the question of whether or not an antidote was desirable; perhaps poison should be fought with poison. With these several schisms in the mind and with more terrors in the heart than could be named, it was better not to judge the man who had gone down under an impossible burden. It was better to remember: *Thou knowest this man's fall; but thou knowest not his wrassling.*

While the preacher talked and I watched the children—years of changing their diapers, scrubbing them, slapping them, taking them to school, and scolding them had had the perhaps inevitable result of making me love them, though I am not sure I knew this then—my mind was busily breaking out with a rash of disconnected impressions. Snatches of popular songs, indecent jokes, bits of books I had read, movie sequences, faces, voices, political issues—I thought I was going mad; all these impressions suspended, as it were, in the solution of the faint nausea produced in me by the heat and liquor. For a moment I had the impression that my alcoholic breath, inefficiently disguised with chewing gum, filled the entire chapel. Then someone began singing one of my father's favorite songs and, abruptly, I was with him, sitting on his knee, in the hot, enormous, crowded church which was the first church we attended. It was the Abyssinia Baptist Church on 138th Street. We had not gone there long. With this image, a host of others came. I had forgotten, in the rage of my growing up, how proud my father had been of me when I was little. Apparently, I had had a voice and my father had liked to show me off before the members of the church. I had forgotten what he had looked like when he was pleased but now I remembered that he had always been grinning with pleasure when my solos ended. I even remembered certain expressions on his face when he teased my mother—had he loved her? I would never know. And when had it all begun to change? For now it seemed that he had not always been cruel. I remembered being taken for a haircut and scraping my knee on the footrest of the barber's chair and I remembered my father's face as he soothed my crying and applied the stinging iodine. Then I remembered our fights, fights which had been of the worst possible kind because my technique had been silence.

I remembered the one time in all our life together when we had really spoken to each other.

It was on a Sunday and it must have been shortly before I left home. We were walking, just the two of us, in our usual silence, to or from church. I was in high school and had been doing a lot of writing and I was, at about this time, the editor of the high school magazine. But I had also been a Young Minister and had been preaching from the pulpit. Lately, I had been taking fewer engagements and preached as rarely as possible. It was said in the church, quite truthfully, that I was "cooling off."

My father asked me abruptly, "You'd rather write than preach, wouldn't you?"

I was astonished at his question—because it was a real question. I answered, "Yes."

That was all we said. It was awful to remember that that was all we had *ever* said.

The casket now was opened and the mourners were being led up the aisle to look for the last time on the deceased. The assumption was that the family was too overcome with grief to be allowed to make this journey alone and I watched while my aunt was led to the casket and, muffled in black, and shaking, led back to her seat. I disapproved of forcing the children to look on their dead father, considering that the shock of his death, or, more truthfully, the shock of death as a reality, was already a little more than a child could bear, but my judgment in this matter had been overruled and there they were, bewildered and frightened and very small, being led, one by one, to the casket. But there is also something very gallant about children at such moments. It has something to do with their silence and gravity and with the fact that one cannot help them. Their legs, somehow, seem *exposed*, so that it is at once incredible and terribly clear that their legs are all they have to hold them up.

I had not wanted to go to the casket myself and I certainly had not wished to be led there, but there was no way of avoiding either of these forms. One of the deacons led me up and I looked on my father's face. I cannot say that it looked like him at all. His blackness had been equivocated by powder and there was no suggestion in that casket of what his power had or could have been. He was simply an old man dead, and it was hard to believe that he had ever given anyone either joy or pain. Yet, his life filled that room. Further up the avenue his wife was holding his newborn child. Life and death so close together, and love and hatred, and right and wrong, said something to me which I did not want to hear concerning man, concerning the life of man.

After the funeral, while I was downtown desperately celebrating my birthday, a Negro soldier, in the lobby of the Hotel Braddock, got into a fight with a white policeman over a Negro girl. Negro girls, white policemen, in or out of uniform, and Negro males—in or out of uniform—were part of the furniture of the lobby of the Hotel Braddock and this was certainly not the first time such an incident had occurred. It was destined, however, to receive an unprecedented publicity, for the fight between the policeman and the soldier ended with the shooting of the soldier. Rumor, flowing immediately to the streets outside, stated that the soldier had been shot in the back, an instantaneous and revealing invention, and that the soldier had died protecting a Negro woman. The facts were somewhat different—for example, the soldier had not been shot in the back, and was not dead, and the girl seems to have been as dubious a symbol of womanhood as her white counterpart in Georgia usually is, but no one was interested in the facts. They preferred the invention because this invention expressed and corroborated their hates and fears so perfectly. It is just as well to remember that people are always doing this. Perhaps many of those legends, including Christianity, to which the world clings began their conquest of the world with just some such concerted surrender to distortion. The effect, in Harlem, of this particular legend was like the effect of a lit match in a tin of gasoline. The mob gathered before the doors of the Hotel Braddock simply began to swell and to spread in every direction, and Harlem exploded.

The mob did not cross the ghetto lines. It would have been easy, for example, to have gone over Morningside Park on the west side or to have crossed the Grand Central railroad tracks at 125th Street on the east side, to wreak havoc in white neighborhoods. The mob seems to have been mainly interested in something more potent and real than the white face, that is, in white power, and the principal damage done during the riot of the summer of 1943 was to white business establishments in Harlem. It might have been a far bloodier story, of course, if, at the hour the riot began, these establishments had still been open. From the Hotel Braddock the mob fanned out, east and west along 125th Street, and for the entire length of Lenox, Seventh, and Eighth avenues. Along each of these avenues, and along each major side street—116th, 125th, 135th, and so on—bars, stores, pawnshops, restaurants, even little luncheonettes had been smashed open and entered and looted—looted, it might be added, with more haste than efficiency. The shelves really looked as though a bomb had struck them. Cans of beans and soup and dog food, along with toilet paper, corn flakes, sardines, and milk tumbled every which way, and abandoned cash registers and cases of beer leaned crazily out of the splintered windows and were strewn along the avenues. Sheets, blankets, and clothing of every description formed a kind of path, as though people had dropped them while running. I truly had not realized that Harlem *had* so many stores until I saw them all smashed open; the first time the word *wealth* ever entered my mind in relation to Harlem was when I saw it scattered in the streets. But one's first, incongruous impression of plenty was countered immediately by an impression of waste. None of this was doing anybody any good. It would have been better to have left the plate glass as it had been and the goods lying in the stores.

It would have been better, but it would also have been intolerable, for Harlem had needed something to smash. To smash something is the ghetto's chronic need. Most of the time it is the members of the ghetto who smash each other, and themselves. But as long as the ghetto walls are standing there will always come a moment when these outlets do not work. That summer, for example, it was not enough to get into a fight on Lenox Avenue, or curse out one's cronies in the barber shops. If ever, indeed, the violence which fills Harlem's churches, pool halls, and bars erupts outward in a more direct fashion, Harlem and its citizens are likely to vanish in an apocalyptic flood. That this is not likely to happen is due to a great many reasons, most hidden and powerful among them the Negro's real relation to the white American. This relation prohibits, simply, anything as uncomplicated and satisfactory as pure hatred. In order really to hate white people, one has to blot so much out of the mind—and the heart—that this hatred itself becomes an exhausting and self-destructive pose. But this does not mean, on the other hand, that love comes easily: the white world is too powerful, too complacent, too ready with gratuitous humiliation, and, above all, too ignorant and too innocent for that. One is absolutely forced to make perpetual qualifications and one's own reactions are always canceling each other out. It is this, really, which has driven so many people mad, both white and black. One is always in the position of having to decide between amputation and gangrene. Amputation is swift but time may prove that the amputation was not necessary-or one may delay the amputation too long. Gangrene is slow, but it is impossible to be sure that one is reading one's symptoms right. The idea of going through life as a cripple is more than one can bear, and equally unbearable is the risk of swelling up slowly, in agony, with poison. And the trouble, finally, is that the risks are real even if the choices do not exist.

"But as for me and my house," my father had said, "we will serve the Lord." I wondered, as we drove him to his resting place, what this line had meant for him. I had heard him preach it many times. I had preached it once myself, proudly giving it an interpretation different from my father's. Now the whole thing came back to me, as though my father and I were on our way to Sunday school and I were memorizing the golden text: *And if it seem evil unto you to serve the Lord, choose you this day whom you will serve; whether the gods which your fathers served that were on the other side of the flood, or the gods of the Amorites, in whose land ye dwell: but as for me and my house, we will serve the Lord.* I suspected in these familiar lines a meaning which had never been there for me before. All of my father's texts and songs, which I had decided were meaningless, were arranged before me at his death like empty bottles, waiting to hold the meaning which life would give them for me. This was his legacy: nothing is ever escaped. That bleakly memorable morning I hated the unbelievable streets and the Negroes and whites who had, equally, made them that way. But I knew that it was folly, as my father would have said, this bitterness was folly. It was necessary to hold on to the things that mattered. The dead man mattered, the new life mattered; blackness and whiteness did not matter; to believe that they did was to acquiesce in one's own destruction. Hatred, which could destroy so much, never failed to destroy the man who hated and this was an immutable law.

It began to seem that one would have to hold in the mind forever two ideas which seemed to be in opposition. The first idea was acceptance, the acceptance, totally without rancor, of life as it is, and men as they are: in the light of this idea, it goes without saying that injustice is a commonplace. But this did not mean that one could be complacent, for the second idea was of equal power: that one must never, in one's own life, accept these injustices as commonplace but must fight them with all one's strength. This fight begins, however, in the heart and it now had been laid to my charge to keep my own heart free of hatred and despair. This intimation made my heart heavy and, now that my father was irrecoverable, I wished that he had been beside me so that I could have searched his face for the answers which only the future would give me now.

RITA DOVE

Through family and family stories, almost every father roots his children to the past, while at the same time growing different possible futures for them through present actions. Understanding of "Grape Sherbet" is deepened by the knowledge that Rita Dove's father was the first black man to work as a chemist for the Goodyear Tire and Rubber Company of Akron, Ohio. The sherbet is a miracle of chemistry, a reality-altering colour transformation with implications as deep as Memorial Day's origins in the end of the Civil War. Like the children who name "each stone / for a lost milk tooth," who make the dead a positive part of natural growth, the father of the poem may not understand all the implications of what he does. The grandmother's "pure refusal" almost certainly is fuelled more by racial anxiety than it is by diabetes. However, because of history, because of family, because of her father—a Dove who wears "his cap turned up / so the bib resembles a duck"—Rita Dove can accept what the grandmother of her poem cannot. She can see why her father bothered, how he overcame pressures from both sides of the colour line, pressures both from within and from without, and because of his miracle she can face the past without ducking, without refusal. As she invents or recreates her father's feat, using secret recipes of her own, her "Grape Sherbet" burns with a grateful, playful smile.

GRAPE SHERBET

The day? Memorial.
After the grill
Dad appears with his masterpiece—
swirled snow, gelled light.
We cheer. The recipe's
a secret and he fights
a smile, his cap turned up
so the bib resembles a duck.

That morning we galloped
through the grassed-over mounds
and named each stone
for a lost milk tooth. Each dollop
of sherbet, later,
is a miracle,
like salt on a melon that makes it sweeter.

Everyone agrees—it's wonderful!
It's just how we imagined lavender
would taste. The diabetic grandmother
stares from the porch,
a torch
of pure refusal.

We thought no one was lying
there under our feet,
we thought it
was a joke. I've been trying
to remember the taste,
but it doesn't exist.
Now I see why
you bothered,
father.

BLISS BROYARD

"My Father's Daughter" was first published in the edgy essay anthology, Personals: Dreams and Nightmares From the Lives of 20 Young Writers. *The skill and power of this essay lies both in what it says and in what it does not say. Anatole Broyard was a coloured man who passed as white, and without outside knowledge, there is an inexplicable, subtly disturbing obsessiveness to this essay and the way in which Broyard pursues and haunts her father's traces. By not revealing her father's secret, the secret which he kept from her while alive, Broyard truly makes herself her father's daughter: her secrecy towards the reader duplicates her father's secrecy towards her. The following passage, taken from her memoir* One Drop, *reveals part of her own method in creating the subtle, moving pleasures of "My Father's Daughter":*

To reveal the young colored boy that my father had been, I had to carefully strip away the father that I had known. It was like uncovering a pentimento, the part of a painting that is hidden beneath the surface of the paint, the artist's first try.

MY FATHER'S DAUGHTER

There is a particular type of older man I like. He must be at least twenty years my senior, preferably thirty years or more. Old enough to be my father, it's fair to say. This man is handsome, stylish, a connoisseur of women, intelligent, cultured and witty, old-fashioned and romantic. He has male friends whom he loves as brothers. He knows how to dance the old dances: the lindy, the cha-cha, the samba, even the tango. He's vain about his appearance and is unabashedly delighted any time I tell him he is looking trim or healthy or particularly handsome. When I compliment his fedora, he tilts it to an even more jaunty angle. He reads the romantic poets and can quote their lines in a way that doesn't sound corny. He has fought in wars, has traveled a good bit of the world and has a reputation of being a ladies' man in his day. He tells me stories about girls he knew overseas: geishas and lonely nurses. He notices what I am wearing; he notices if I have changed my hairstyle or done my makeup in a new way. Each time I see him, he tells me I've never looked better. Our conversation is playful, mischievous, saucy. He sometimes makes pronouncements about women that make me blush and often also make me angry—things I would object to from a man my own age. Many of the traits in my favorite type of older man I would find foolish, affected, or tiresome in a younger man, but with you, old sport, I am always charmed.

Our relationship is not intimate, though our conversations often are. I tell this older man about whom I am dating and make not-so-subtle innuendos about my sex life: this one didn't understand that conversation is a necessary part of seduction, that one had the eagerness of a boy and a boy's lack of self-control; another one clutched his machismo between the sheets like a security blanket. We both shake our heads and mourn the shortage of decent young men out there these days. We both secretly believe that my charms belong to another era, a better and more refined world, his world. In his day, no doubt, I would have been a smash. At least this is my fantasy of what he is thinking.

Where do I meet these men? Mostly they are my father's friends. And since he died six years ago at the age of seventy, I have been transfigured from being my father's daughter into a young woman friend of these men in my own right.

Vincent, the oldest of my father's friends, lives in Greenwich Village, still carrying on the same sort of life he and my father led when they were young there together. There is Davey, the youngest of my father's friends, who over the years was his summer playmate for touch football and volleyball and beach paddle and who is now a father himself. Mike was the closest to my dad, serving as his primary reader during his long career as a writer and book critic. When Mike and I talk on the phone, he seems to miss my dad as much as I do. Finally there is Ernest, my father's most contentious friend. My dad used say that he had to befriend Ernest, otherwise Ernest wouldn't have any friends at all, although I think he secretly took pride in being able to tolerate his pal's notorious crankiness.

Though the ages of these men span more than twenty-five years and they come from a variety of backgrounds, I think of them as natives of a singular world, a world belonging to the past and a particular place: Greenwich Village, where my father's friendships with these men—if not actually born there—were consummated. Like any world, it has its own language and culture. There is a hip, playful rhythm to the conversation and an angle of the observations that makes everything appear stylized, either heroically or calamitously. In this world, folks don't walk, they swagger; they don't talk, they declaim. Women are crazy, beautiful, impeccably bred, tragic. They are rarely boring. No one has much money, but happiness, as my father liked to say, could be bought cheaply. A man's status is determined by his wit and intelligence and, most of all, his successes with women. A woman's status is a product of her beauty and her novelty, not a fresh kind of novelty because that would imply innocence—and you couldn't have too much innocence if you were with this crowd—but the kind of novelty that places you on the cutting edge of things. To be described as modern is a high compliment.

Of course, nostalgia has smoothed out these memories to make them uniform and sweet, and the world that I know from my father's stories is pristinely preserved in my mind as though it were contained in one of those little glass spheres that fills with snow when you shake it. I imagine, though, that by stepping in I can unsettle this scene with my presence and make it come back to life; then I will find a world that is more cozy than the one I live in, a world that is as reassuring and familiar as those winter idylls captured under glass.

VINCENT has lived in the same apartment on Perry Street for over forty years, and as I walk up the five flights to visit him, the years slip away behind me. Everyone lived in four- and five-floor walk-ups in the old days, Vincent has told me. All cold-water flats.

"Your father and I once went to a party at Anaïs Nin's, and I rang the bell and flew up the five flights as fast as I could. Your dad had briefed me that Anaïs gauged her lovers' stamina and virility by how long it took them to reach her floor without puffing"

This is a story I heard from my father, though many of the stories Vincent tells me about the old days I have not. Those are the ones I have come to hear.

Vincent's apartment is decorated with things collected from his years traveling the world as a cruise director on ships. Geometric Moroccan tiles and bits of Persian carpet and copper-colored patches of stucco cover every inch of the walls. Through a beaded curtain is his bedroom, where tapestries form a canopy over a daybed heaped with Turkish pillows. The tub located in the entrance hall is concealed by day with a sort of shiny green lamina which, when you gaze upon it, is reminiscent of an ancient Roman bath. Also off the entrance hall is the toilet, concealed only with a thin strip of fabric. Once, after I'd used it, Vincent asked me if I noticed how the base was loose. I hadn't.

"Well, it's been like that for almost forty years" he explained. "Once I loaned the apartment to your dad so he could take a girl he'd met somewhere private. Afterward, the toilet was a little rocky. I asked him what the hell he was doing in there, and he told me they were taking in the view." Vincent took me back into the bathroom and pointed out the Empire State Building, barely visible between two other buildings. "I won't have the toilet fixed," he said, "because I love being reminded of that story." I headed down the stairs with Vincent's laughter trailing behind me.

Should a daughter know such things about her father? Should she have an image of him that she must rush past, one that is a little too vivid and too private to be promptly forgotten? It is easy to become embarrassed by such stories, to let my own paternal memories sweep them under some psychic rug, but my father's past is like a magnet I can't pull myself away from. This is my history too, I argue to myself. I've had my own sexual adventures, my own versions of making love on a shaky toilet, an aspect of my life that I have been sure to share with my father's friends. I have paraded a host of boyfriends past them, have brought along young men to their apartments, or out to dinner, or for an evening of dancing. When the fellow gets up to fetch another round of drinks, I might lean back in my chair and watch him walk off.

"So," I'll say offhandedly, "I'm not sure I'm going to keep this one. He's bright and successful too, but maybe not quite sexy enough."

"You are your father's daughter," the man answers, laughing, which is just what I'd hoped to hear.

Of course, with my own contemporaries I am never so cavalier. I have argued on behalf of honesty and respect in relationships. I have claimed to believe in true love. I will even admit that I am looking for my own version of a soulmate (although I can confess to this only in an ironic tone of voice, all too aware of its sentimental implications). Nevertheless, this desire runs in me alongside a desire for a successful writing career, children, and a house in the country with dogs and flower beds and weekend guests visiting from the city—a lot like the kind of life my father left New York to build with my mother, a move that shocked many of his friends.

All of my father's friends share a boyish quality, one that is often delightful with its playfulness and vitality but that contains an underside too: a sort of adolescent distrust of any threat to the gang. A silent pact was made never to grow up. And though I wouldn't be here if my father, at the age of forty, hadn't managed finally to break free of this hold to marry my mother, I carry on this pact with his friends in spite of myself.

Some of these men eventually did marry and have children now themselves, have daughters who one day, no doubt, they hope to see married. If I would let them, they would probably wish for me a similar simple and happy fate. But I don't want to be seen in the same light as their daughters. Just as they knew my father as a friend first, rather than a dad or husband, I want them to view me as their friend rather than my father's daughter. Otherwise, I would never learn anything about him at all. I search out these men to discover the man behind my father, that is who I've come to meet.

Besides all this, these men are exceptional, and to be accepted by them, my aspirations must be sophisticated, more rarefied and imaginative than my dreams of a husband and house in the country.

Once out for dinner with the contentious friend, Ernest, we argued about the value of monogamy in relationships. Over the years, Ernest has taken me to some of New York's finest restaurants. Everywhere the maitre d's know him by name, probably because he is the worst kind of customer: he demands special dishes which he then complains about, is rude to the waiters, and usually leaves a shabby tip. I put up with his behavior for the same reason a parent puts up with a misbehaving child in a restaurant—to challenge Ernest would only egg him on. What I had forgotten was that in conversation he is the same way.

His expression grew increasingly pitying and snide while he listened to my argument for monogamy, which—best as I can recall—went something like this: monogamy in a relationship engendered trust and trust was the only means to a profound intimacy, not the kind of combustible sexual intimacy that Ernest favored (I added pointedly), but the kind that requires a continual commitment of faith, not unlike the effort to believe in God. And the rewards of this type of intimacy—the compassion, the connection—were infinitely greater. Trust was the only route to a person's soul!

I was only about twenty-five at the time, and while my line of reasoning was hardly original and smacked somewhat of piteous posturing, I remember being pleased that I was able to unfold my rationale in a composed, yet passionate manner. Sometimes when I was talking with my father or his friends, I would grab panic-struck for a word only to find it out of my reach. By the end of my speech, Ernest looked amused. He dabbed at his mouth with his linen napkin and sat back in his chair. "I had no idea you were so bourgeois," he said. "How in the world did your father manage to raise such a bourgeois daughter?"

"Bourgeois" was one of those words that floated through the air of my childhood, occasionally landing on a dinner guest or neighbor or the parent of one of my friends. I wasn't sure when I was young what it meant, but I didn't miss how efficiently the term dismissed the person as though he or she had been made to vanish into thin air.

For weeks after that dinner with Ernest, I carried on an internal debate with myself about the value of monogamy and, more fundamentally, wondered from what source I had formed my opinions on it: Was this something that my father believed, if perhaps not in practice, then in theory? Was I falling into a conventional, clichéd way of thinking? Or did I actually believe the stance I'd taken with Ernest for the very reason that it was not my father's position. This was not the first time I had tried to locate myself behind his shadow.

Although my father was a critic of books by profession, he could be counted on to have an opinion on just about anything. At a gathering back at my house following his cremation, I sat around the dining room table, reminiscing with a group of family friends. We began listing all the things my father liked, and after one trip around the table, we ran out of things to say. Then someone offered up "thick arms on a woman," and someone else jumped in with "kung fu movies and cream sauces," starting us on a long and lively conversation about all the things my father disliked. What surprised me during this discussion (besides the welcome relief it provided to that bleak day) was how many of my own opinions were either my father's—or the exact opposite. I remember thinking that rather than having a unique personality, I was merely an assemblage of reactions, a mosaic of agreements and disagreements with my dad—a feeling that has reoccurred intermittently since. I keep hoping to find the line where he stops and I begin.

VINCENT keeps scrapbooks. He has scrapbooks from his travels, scrapbooks from his days in Cuba where he first encountered the Afro-Cuban music that became his and my father's passion, scrapbooks from his youth with my dad in New York City. Sometimes before heading out to dinner or to a club to hear some salsa band, Vincent and I will have a drink in his apartment—we always drink champagne or sherry—and flip through these books. One evening I pointed out the pictures of people I didn't recognize. Vincent became irritated when I didn't know their names. Machito. Milton. Willie. You must know who these people are! How can you have not heard these stories? You should have paid more attention to your father when he was alive, he scolded. Are you listening to what I am telling you? Your father was a beautiful man! He lived a beautiful life!

Nostalgia made us quiet when we were out on the street. Vincent was nostalgic for a past that seemed in danger of being forgotten, and me—I was nostalgic for a history that both was and wasn't mine.

Vincent has worked as a tour guide on and off for most of his life and he walks very fast. That evening, I let him lead me around by my elbow. He rushed me across the intersections, hurrying me along in a variety of foreign languages: *vite, rapido*, quick-quick-quick. He began to talk as we twisted and turned through the labyrinth of streets, pointing out various buildings and explaining their significance: *there was an illegal nightclub here where we went to hear Machito drum, you had to know the code word to be let inside; this was where your dad had his bookstore and Milton and Willie hung out talking, talking, talking about books.* We turned a corner to arrive on a quiet, tree-lined street. He pointed out the top floor of a brownstone. *Your dad lived there for a while. He had a girlfriend in the next house over, and rather than walk down the five flights to the street and then up another five flights to her apartment, he would climb across the roof to her window like a cat burglar.*

I pointed out the steep pitch of the roofs and said that my dad must have really liked the girl to put himself at such risk. "Oh, he wasn't afraid of risks," Vincent answered knowingly, and I had no idea at that moment whether this assessment was true or not, a realization that brought tears to my eyes. After a moment, I remarked quietly that men didn't do that anymore—climb over rooftops for a woman—at least none that I'd ever met.

ONLY when a parent dies does it seem that a child gains a right to know that parent's life. While my father was alive, his life, as it should have, belonged to him. Besides, we were too involved with each other for me to step back and gain some objective view. But now that his life contains both a beginning *and* an end, it seems possible to shape some complete picture. I can't help regretting, though, that so much of my information must come secondhand. Perhaps Vincent is right. I should have paid more attention to my father when he was alive. Perhaps if I had asked him more questions about his past, I could have learned these things from him myself. Perhaps if he had lived longer, if we had moved on from being father and daughter to being friends, we would have arrived at some understanding of each other, or rather I would have arrived at some understanding of him that would allow me incorporate such anecdotes like a splash of color into the portrait I held of him rather than their changing the portrait completely.

But when my father was alive, I was too busy trying to figure out what he thought of me—another question that I now lay at the feet of his friends, as though he had handed off his judgment like a baton in a relay race.

At another, earlier dinner with Ernest, I watched him as he studied my face. I hadn't seen him in a few years, and I knew that since our last encounter I had evolved from looking like a girl to looking like a woman.

"You've grown up to be attractive," he finally decided. "For a while there it seemed that you wouldn't. Your features were so sharp and you were always frowning. You should keep your hair long, though. It softens your face."

I wish I could say that if my father had been present he would have reprimanded Ernest for this cold comment, but I know that he wouldn't have. Over the years I came to learn that being my father didn't limit his ability to assess me critically. He had opinions about my hairstyle, he picked out the clothes that he thought best brought out what he referred to as my "subtle appeal"; he noticed anytime I gained a few pounds. And while I realize now that in his world a woman was as powerful as her beauty, that doesn't lessen the hurt caused by such impartial opinions.

At times with these friends I have felt like an impostor or a spy, trying to lure them into a conversation where they will unwittingly reveal some assessment of me my father had shared with them, or that, since they knew him and his tastes and were able to observe us with the clarity of a spectator's view, they will reveal some insight about our relationship that remained hidden from me. On occasion, I have just asked point-blank what it is I want to know.

Recently I had a wedding to go to in the Long Island town where my dad's youngest friend, Davey, now lives with his wife, Kate, and their three teenage children. Davey has been in my life for as long as I can remember. And my father was in Davey's life as long as Davey can remember. They first met in the summer of 1950 on Fire Island. Davey was a chubby, cheerful boy of four, and my father was a trim, athletic bachelor of thirty. It's hard for me to picture the start of this friendship; nevertheless, during the ensuing summers on Fire Island, the man and boy became friends. They would remain close friends until my father's death. Davey spoke at my father's memorial service, recalling how when he was sixteen he helped move my parents from one five-story walk-up in Greenwich Village to another a few blocks away. Theirs was a friendship sealed by carrying books, he said. Throughout my childhood, Davey visited us each summer on Martha's Vineyard, and he and my father would write in the mornings (Davey eventually became a successful playwright) and then the two men would head to the beach for an afternoon of touch football or beach paddle, or they would just stroll and talk.

DURING this recent visit, Davey and I strolled on the beach ourselves and talked about *our* writing. He had been feeling discouraged recently about the unsteady progress of his career. I had just finished a graduate school degree in creative writing and was nervous about reentering the world with this new label of *writer*. We had walked a short distance when Davey mentioned that his back was bothering him and asked if we could sit down. We lay on the sand, a bit damp from the previous night's rain, and looked out over the choppy ocean.

A few days before, TWA flight 800 had crashed not far from where we lay, and earlier that day bits of fuselage and an airline drinking cup were found on a neighboring beach. Groups of people searched along the shoreline—airline officials, family members, curiosity seekers. Davey talked about his own kids, how well they were all doing, how different they were from one another and from him and Kate. It was clear in listening to him how much he respected and loved them, but I was surprised at how objectively he was able to assess their talents and weaknesses. I asked him what my father thought of me.

"Well, of course he loved you," he said, and then looked away toward the beachcombers. I could see that my question had upset him. Perhaps he was wondering if his children would ever ask such a thing. I was searching too, there on that beach, but my debris was not the result of some tragic, sudden accident; rather, my father had died slowly from the common illness of cancer when I was twenty-three, an age when most children are letting go of their parents in order to establish their own independence. I was lost somewhere between missing my father and trying to move past him. Davey looked back at me and said again with a surprising urgency in his voice that I must believe my father loved me. And I do, but in an abstract way, believing in my father's love the same way that I believe that all parents must love their children. What I am searching for is the shape of that love. These men are bright men, observant and persuasive. They are my father's friends, after all. I want them to make elegant arguments, peppered with indisputable examples and specific instances of the how and why and where of that love.

When all this searching makes me too weary, I call Mike. He is a psychologist and a writer too. Besides his interest and insight into human nature, he has most of Western literature for reference at his fingertips, which makes him wonderful to talk with. Over the years, even when he and my father lived in separate states, my dad would read to him the first drafts of almost everything he wrote. I can remember my father stretched out on his bed for an hour at a time, laying in the dark room, telephone in hand, chatting with his pal. Their talk was filled with elegant phrasing, animated starts and stops, black humor, and the sort of conversational shorthand one develops with an old, close friend. When signing off, my father would say, "All right, man, work hard and I will too."

I called Mike up recently with some gossip about the size of an advance for a book written by one of his colleagues. Mike is working on a new book and with one kid about to enter college and another following closely behind, he's hoping for a sizable advance himself. Before long we have moved on to the subject of his new book: how difficult and necessary it is to console yourself to the disappointment of life and the world. Doesn't scream best-seller, I joked, since no one likes to admit to this truth. I talked about how this disappointment often feels like a large white elephant in the corner of the room that no one will acknowledge, and how that denial makes you feel like you're crazy. Given the choice between feeling crazy and feeling disappointed, I don't understand why more people don't opt for the latter.

"You're exactly right, Blissie," Mike agreed. "That's just what I am trying to get at."

I was stretched out on my own bed now, watching the afternoon shadows lengthen down my wall. Talking with Mike was like walking down a familiar path that leads toward home. Here is the oak tree; around the bend is the stone wall. Talking with Mike was almost like talking with my father.

Both men shared a predilection for cutting through hypocrisy and looking past denial. They viewed the world with a bittersweet affection, appreciating the shadows of life's events as much as the events themselves. I once asked my dad why all the great stories were sad ones. Most good stories are mysteries, he said. The author is like a detective trying to get to the bottom of some truth, and happiness is a mystery that can come apart in your hands when you try to unravel it. Sadness, on the other hand, is infinitely more resilient. Scrutiny only adds to its depth and weight.

I don't ask Mike what my father thought of me. Mike's a shrink, after all, and he knows that I'm the only one who could answer that question.

What I realize when I am with the older men in my life is that the older man I want most is my father, and no amount of colorful anecdotes, no amount of recreating the kind of outings he might have had with his pals, can conjure him up in a satisfying way. Grief, like sadness, is too resilient for such casual stand-ins.

After I finished talking with Mike, I remained lying on my bed. Outside my window it was dark, and I hadn't bothered to turn on the light. I was thinking about how it is an odd time to get to know your father, after he has died. And it is odd to get to know him through his friends. I wondered why I should assume that they knew him any better than I did. If some aspects of his life before I knew him were mysterious to me, certainly the reverse was true as well: there are parts that only I know about. Would his friends be surprised to learn that when I was a baby, after my bath, my father would carry me around the house seated naked in the palm of his hand, holding me high up over his head like a waiter with a tray? Or that he would spend afternoons tossing my brother and me, torpedo-like, from the corner of the bedroom onto my parents' bed, the far wall piled high with pillows? Before each toss, he would inspect our teeth to make sure they were clenched so we wouldn't bite our tongues. Would his friends be surprised to know that when I was in college he would sometimes call me up in the middle of the day because he was feeling lonely in the empty house? Or when standing over him in his hospital bed, my throat choked with all the questions I realized there wasn't time to ask and his mouth filled with a pain beyond articulation, he suddenly seized my hand and raised it to his lips? "You're my daughter," he assured me. "You're my daughter."

When my father and I went out dancing together, we didn't dance the old dances, as Vincent and I tried to do when we went to hear a salsa band. Vincent had great hopes for my talent as a dancer, since my father was such a good one, but as he attempted to lead me across the floor, I kept overanticipating his moves. The slightest pressure of his hand would send me off in a new direction.

My dad relied on me to introduce him to the new music, the new dances. Competitive as always, he wanted to be sure that he could keep up with the times. In our living room, the rug pulled back and the coffee table pushed aside, I blasted *Word Up* by Cameo. I led the way across the smooth wooden floor, shouting out the lyrics, my hands waving in the air, my hips bumping left and right. I can still hear his encouragement as he followed along behind me. With my eyes closed, in the quiet of my dark bedroom, his hoots rise out of the silence.

DEREK WALCOTT

By his early death, Walcott's civil servant father "became one of his shadows / wavering and faint," thus liberating Walcott to know and use his father in ways unimpeded by directives and direct demands. The moving irony is that while some living fathers try to bend their children to their ends, young Walcott made it a "sacred duty" to voluntarily fly the flag of the dead father. In his 1965 essay "Leaving School," reminiscing over relics of his father's avocation as a painter, Walcott wrote, "These objects had established my vocation, and made it as inevitable as that of any craftsman's son, for I felt that my father's work, however minor, was unfinished." "A Letter from Brooklyn" captures some of the sense of responsibility Walcott feels towards his father's memory. The sinewy yet tender evocation of Mable Rawlins, "[g]rey-haired, thin-voiced, perpetually bowed," with her "veined hand / Pellucid as paper," does more than affirm community, caring, and kindness: "A Letter From Brooklyn" triumphantly proclaims the wisdom of Walcott's decision to be about his father's business. Just as Mable's faith and letter keep the father alive, so too the poem transcends death in its celebration of old lady, father, and art. There is belief and consolation worthy of a Shakespearian sonnet, as artist father lives on in the work of poet son.

A LETTER FROM BROOKLYN

An old lady writes me in a spidery style,
Each character trembling, and I see a veined hand
Pellucid as paper, travelling on a skein
Of such frail thoughts its thread is often broken;
Or else the filament from which a phrase is hung
Dims to my sense, but caught, it shines like steel,
As touch a line and the whole web will feel.
She describes my father, yet I forget her face
More easily than my father's yearly dying;
Of her I remember small, buttoned boots and the place
She kept in our wooden church on those Sundays
Whenever her strength allowed;
Grey-haired, thin-voiced, perpetually bowed.

"I am Mable Rawlins," she writes, "and know both your parents";
He is dead, Miss Rawlins, but God bless your tense:
"Your father was a dutiful, honest,
Faithful, and useful person."
For such plain praise what fame is recompense?
"A horn-painter, he painted delicately on horn,
He used to sit around the table and paint pictures."
The peace of God needs nothing to adorn
It, nor glory nor ambition.
"He is twenty-eight years buried," she writes, "he was called home,
And is, I am sure, doing greater work."

The strength of one frail hand in a dim room
Somewhere in Brooklyn, patient and assured,
Restores my sacred duty to the Word.
"Home, home," she can write, with such short time to live,
Alone as she spins the blessings of her years;
Not withered of beauty if she can bring such tears,
Nor withdrawn from the world that breaks its lovers so;
Heaven is to her the place where painters go,
All who bring beauty on frail shell or horn,
There was all made, thence their *lux-mundi* drawn,
Drawn, drawn, till the thread is resilient steel,
Lost though it seems in darkening periods,
And there they return to do work that is God's.

So this old lady writes, and again I believe.
I believe it all, and for no man's death I grieve.

ADRIENNE RICH #1

"Split at the Root" was written for Nice Jewish Girls: A Lesbian Anthology, *and later reprinted in Ursula Owen's* Fathers: Reflections by Daughters. *At the time of this essay's first publication, Rich was also working on "Sources," a remarkable, if deeply conflicted, poem of self-exploration. Essay and poem are companion pieces in which Rich, with her typical courage and anger, tries to make sense of herself and her relationship with her father. In her poem "Sources," she describes herself as "the eldest daughter in a house with no son, she who must overthrow the father." She addresses her father directly, saying: "For years I struggled with you: your categories, your will, the cruelty which came inextricably from your love." In her writings, Rich has the clarity of vision and the courage to see herself as wounded, as split at the root. Even in attacking and rejecting her father, she has the courage to recognize her kinship with him. His wounds are her wounds, and her split is engendered by his. Questor and quested, she is the "token" daughter of a "token" man; and in order to heal her "split consciousness" she has to overcome her father's legacy of denial. Only by recognizing and giving voice to his wounds can she start to heal her own.*

SPLIT AT THE ROOT:
AN ESSAY ON JEWISH IDENTITY (1982)

Adrienne Rich has declined permission for "Split at the Root: An Essay on Jewish Identity (1982)" to be used in this anthology. Those interested in reading this essay can find it in *Blood, Bread, and Poetry: Selected Prose 1979-1985,* or in the two anthologies mentioned in the introduction preceding this page.

ADRIENNE RICH #2

"After Dark" is included in part to provide a pretext for editorial comment. The decision to place Adrienne Rich at or near the center of this anthology is a deliberate one. So, too, is the decision to include both an essay and a poem by her. Other writers could easily have had two pieces included—Raymond Carver, for instance, or May Sarton. If Rich is the only writer to be so honoured, it is because her writings and her life are central to the values of this anthology. For Rich, literature is an instrument of vision and re-vision. For Rich, writing is an instrument of change. While much of her writing may be uncomfortable to read—and sometimes difficult to like—Adrienne Rich constantly challenges us to examine our assumptions about ourselves and our society. Poet and political activist, "glass-blower" and "missile-thrower," she demands that we see clearly and that we change and act accordingly.

The father is always part of the child, and in their struggles to free themselves from the father some children do violence to themselves. "After Dark" is an expression of such violence. The narrative self, after all, is "self-maimed." Written four years before her father's death, and eighteen years before the essay "Split at the Root" and the poem "Sources," "After Dark" lacks the insight and understanding of those later works. Anger, not acceptance, drives this poem. This anger is perhaps best seen in the multiplicity of Shakespearean voices, as the speaker by turns echoes or paraphrases Regan, Cordelia, Lear, and Ariel. While the later Rich usually tries to do justice to her multiple identities, here there is no justice, no understanding, and the multiple voices ring forced and false. At best, they are evidence of "Underground Seizures." In other poems of this period, Rich had already distanced herself from Shakespeare and the literary models drilled into her by her father. Here, despite the protective tenderness and the apparent reconciliation of the final line, the narrative self remains "torn at the roots"—scarred by the past and unable to assimilate it successfully. In this early attempt to come to terms with her father, Rich had yet to see that fathers cannot be escaped by self-mutilation.

AFTER DARK

Adrienne Rich has declined permission for "After Dark" to be used in this anthology. Those interested in reading this essay can find it most easily in the Norton Critical Edition of *Adrienne Rich's Poetry and Prose* or in *The Longman Anthology of Contemporary American Poetry* (2nd Edition).

ALICE MUNRO

Unclean castings, "all disfigured with what looked like warts or barnacles," and green sand, used for molds, invite meaning. Like many of the authors in this anthology—like Phillip Roth and Saul Bellow, for instance—to get at truths Alice Munro knowingly blurs and blasts the boundaries between fact and fiction. As all traces of the enterprise are destroyed, her writing glows with shadowy, metafactual possibilities—even while remaining "as truthful as our notion of the past can ever be." The Foundry can be reached by back roads, without having to go through town. When the daughter delivers a message to the father, and discovers that the work father is different from the home father, father truths emerge. Fathers are a product of their environment, and there is a Heisenberg location effect, as well as a Heisenberg observer effect. Fathers behave differently depending on where they are and on who is watching. The Foundry father is different from the domestic father. The work father surrounded by fellows is freer in form than the home father surrounded by family. Yet fathers can grow through families. Responsibilities make them heroic, and they do for family what they might not do for themselves. For family, some fathers fight through drifts and survive. The lessons learned are not just lessons of character and the evolution and molding of self required to be a good father. They also include lessons of possibility: the father watching the child, and sometimes in small ways living through the child, discovers unknown possibilities within himself. The child does deliver a message. After fox, foundry, and turkey, Robert Laidlaw surprised himself by following his daughter's path, writing stories and completing a novel about pioneer life. "Many of the offspring will have their father's colour," writes Munro, and sometimes fathers can find self and future in their children's shadings.

excerpt from *THE VIEW FROM CASTLE ROCK*

On a spring evening in 1949—the last spring, in fact the last whole season, that I was to live at home—I was riding my bicycle to the Foundry, to deliver a message to my father. I seldom rode my bicycle anymore. For a while, maybe all through the fifties, it was considered eccentric for any girl to be riding a bicycle after she was old enough, say, to wear a brassiere. But to get to the Foundry I could travel on back roads, I didn't have to go through town.

My father had started working in the Foundry in 1947. It had become apparent the year before that not just our fox farm but the whole fur-farming industry was going downhill very fast. Perhaps the mink would have tided us over if we had gone more heavily into mink, or if we had not owed so much money still, to the feed company, to my grandmother, to the bank. As it was, mink could not save us. My father had made the mistake many fox farmers made just at that time. It was believed that a new paler kind of fox, called a platinum, was going to save the day, and with borrowed money my father had bought two male breeders, one an almost snowy-white Norwegian platinum and one called a pearl platinum, a lovely bluish-gray. People were sick of silver foxes, but surely with these beauties the market would revive.

Of course there is always the chance, with a new male, of how well he will perform, and how many of the offspring will have their father's color. I think there was trouble on both fronts, though my mother would not allow questions or household talk about these matters. I think one of the males had a standoffish nature and another sired mostly dark litters. It did not matter much, because the fashion went against longhaired furs altogether.

When my father went looking for a job it was necessary to find a night job, because he had to spend all day going out of business. He had to pelt all the animals and sell the pelts for whatever he could get and he had to tear down the guard fence, the Old Sheds and the New

Sheds, and all the pens. I suppose he did not have to do that immediately, but he must have wanted all traces of the enterprise destroyed.

He got a job as night watchman at the Foundry, covering the hours from five in the afternoon till ten o'clock in the evening. There was not so much money in being a night watchman, but the good fortune in it was that he was able to do another job at that time as well. This extra job was called shaking down floors. He was never finished with it when his watchman's shift was over, and sometimes he got home after midnight.

The message I was taking to my father was not an important message, but it was important in our family life. It was simply a reminder that he must not forget to call in at my grandmother's house on his way home from work, no matter how late he was. My grandmother had moved to our town, with her sister, so that she could be useful to us. She baked pies and muffins and mended our clothes and darned my father's and my brother's socks. My father was supposed to go around by her house in town after work, to pick up these things, and have a cup of tea with her, but often he forgot. She would sit up knitting, dozing under the light, listening to the radio, until the Canadian radio stations went off at midnight and she would find herself picking up distant news reports, American jazz. She would wait and wait and my father wouldn't come. This had happened last night, so tonight at suppertime she had phoned and asked with painful tact, "Was it tonight or last night your father was supposed to come?"

"I don't know," I said.

I always felt that something had not been done right, or not done at all, when I heard my grandmother's voice. I felt that our family had failed her. She was still energetic, she looked after her house and yard, she could still carry armchairs upstairs, and she had my great-aunt's company, but she needed something more—more gratitude, more compliance, than she ever got.

"Well, I sat up for him last night, but he didn't come."

"He must be coming tonight then." I did not want to spend time talking to her because I was preparing for my Grade Thirteen exams on which my whole future would depend. (Even now, on cool bright spring evenings, with the leaves just out on the trees, I can feel the stirring of expectation connected with this momentous old event, my ambition roused and quivering like a fresh blade to meet it.)

I told my mother what the call was about and she said, "Oh, you'd better ride up and remind your father, or there'll be trouble."

Whenever she had to deal with the problem of my grandmother's touchiness my mother brightened up, as if she had got back some competence or importance in our family. She had Parkinson's disease. It had been overtaking her for some time with erratic symptoms but had recently been diagnosed and pronounced incurable. Its progress took up more and more of her attention. She could no longer walk or eat or talk normally—her body was stiffening out of her control. But she had a long time yet to live.

When she said something like this about the situation with my grandmother—when she said anything that showed an awareness of other people, or even of the work around the house, I felt my heart soften towards her. But when she finished up with a reference to herself, as she did this time *(and that will upset me)*, I hardened again, angry at her for her abdication, sick of her self-absorption, which seemed so flagrant, so improper in a mother.

I had never been to the Foundry in the two years my father had worked there, and I did not know where to find him. Girls of my age did not hang around men's workplaces. If they did that, if they went for long walks by themselves along the railway track or the river, or if they bicycled alone on the country roads (I did these last two things) they were sometimes said to be *asking for it*.

I did not have much interest in my father's work at the Foundry, anyway. I had never expected the fox farm to make us rich, but at least it made us unique and independent. When I thought of my father working in the Foundry I felt that he had suffered a great defeat. My mother felt the same way. Your father is too *fine* for that, she would say. But instead of agreeing with her I would argue, intimating that she did not like being an ordinary workingman's wife and that she was a snob.

The thing that most upset my mother was receiving the Foundry's Christmas basket of fruit, nuts, and candy. She could not bear to be on the receiving, not the distributing, end of that sort of thing, and the first time it happened we had to put the basket in the car and drive down the road to a family she had picked out as suitable recipients. By the next Christmas her authority had weakened and I broke into the basket, declaring that we needed treats as much as anybody. She wiped away tears at my hard tone, and I ate the chocolate, which was old and brittle and turning gray.

I could not see any light in the Foundry buildings. The windows were painted blue on the inside—perhaps a light would not get through. The office was an old brick house at the end of the long main building, and there I saw a light through the Venetian blinds, and I thought that the manager or one of the office staff must be working late. If I knocked they would tell me where my father was. But when I looked through the little window in the door I saw that it was my father in there. He was alone, and he was scrubbing the floor.

I had not known that scrubbing the office floor every night was one of the watchman's duties. (This does not mean that my father had deliberately kept quiet about it—I might not have been listening.) I was surprised, because I had never seen him doing any work of this sort before. Housework. Now that my mother was sick, such work was my responsibility. He would never have had time. Besides that, there was men's work and there was women's work. I believed this, and so did everybody else I knew.

My father's scrubbing apparatus was unlike anything anybody would have at home. He had two buckets on a stand, on rollers, with attachments on either side to hold various mops and brushes. His scrubbing was vigorous and efficient—it had no resigned and ritualistic, feminine sort of rhythm. He seemed to be in a good humor.

He had to come and unlock the door to let me in.

His face changed when he saw it was me.

"No trouble at home, is there?"

I said no, and he relaxed. "I thought you were Tom."

Tom was the factory manager. All the men called him by his first name.

"Well then. You come up to see if I'm doing this right?"

I gave him the message, and he shook his head.

"I know. I forgot."

I sat on a corner of the desk, swinging my legs up out of his way. He said he was nearly finished here, and that if I wanted to wait he would show me around the Foundry. I said I would wait.

When I say that he was in a good humor here, I don't mean that his humor around home was bad, that he was sullen and irritable there. But he showed a cheerfulness now that at home might have seemed inappropriate. It seemed, in fact, as if there was a weight off him here.

When he had finished the floor to his satisfaction he hooked the mop to the side and rolled the apparatus down a slanting passageway that connected the office with the main building. He opened a door that had a sign on it.

Caretaker.

"My domain."

He emptied the water from the buckets into an iron tub, rinsed and emptied them again, swished the tub clean. There on a shelf above the tub among the tools and rubber hose and fuses and spare window-panes was his lunch bucket, which I packed every day when I got home from school. I filled the thermos with strong black tea and put in a bran muffin with butter and jam and a piece of pie if we had any and three thick sandwiches of fried meat and ketchup. The meat was cottage roll ends or baloney, the cheapest meat you could buy.

He led the way into the main building. The lights burning there were like streetlights—that is, they cast their light at the intersections of the passageways, but didn't light up the whole inside of the building, which was so large and high that I had the sense of being in a forest with thick dark trees, or in a town with tall, even buildings. My father switched on some more lights and things shrank a bit. You could now see the brick walls, blackened on the inside, and the windows not only painted over but covered with black wire mesh. What lined the passageways were stacks of bins, one on top of the other higher than my head, and elaborate, uniform metal trays.

We came on an open area with a great heap of metal lumps on the floor, all disfigured with what looked like warts or barnacles.

"Castings," my father said. "They haven't been cleaned yet. They put them in a contraption called a wheelabrator and it blasts shot at them, takes all the bumps off."

Then a pile of black dust, or fine black sand.

"That looks like coal dust but you know what they call it? Green sand."

"*Green* sand?"

"Use it for molding. It's sand with a bonding agent in it, like clay. Or sometimes it's linseed oil. Are you any way interested in all this?"

I said yes, partly for pride's sake. I didn't want to seem like a stupid girl. And I was interested, but not so much in the particular explanations my father began to provide me with, as in the general effects—the gloom, the fine dust in the air, the idea of there being places like this all over the country, in every town and city. Places with their windows painted over. You passed them in a car or on the train and never gave a thought to what was going on inside. Something that took up the whole of people's lives. A never-ending over-and-over attention-consuming life-consuming process.

"Like a tomb in here," my father said, as if he had picked up some of my thoughts.

But he meant something different.

"Compared to the daytime. The racket then, you can't imagine it. They try to get them to wear earplugs, but they won't do it."

"Why not?"

"I don't know. Too independent. They won't wear the fire aprons either. See here. Here's what they call the cupola."

This was an immense black pipe which did have a cupola on top. He showed me where they made the fire, and the ladles used to carry the molten metal and pour it into the molds. He showed me chunks of metal that were like grotesque stubby limbs, and told me that those were the shapes of the hollows in the castings. The air in the hollows, that is, made solid. He told me these things with a prolonged satisfaction in his voice, as if what he revealed gave him reliable pleasure.

We turned a corner and came on two men working, stripped to their pants and undershirts.

"Now here's a couple of good hard working fellows," my father said. "You know Ferg? You know Geordie?"

I did know them, or at least I knew who they were. Geordie Hall delivered bread, but had to work in the Foundry at night to make extra money, because he had so many children. There was a joke that his wife made him work to keep him away from her. Ferg was a younger man you saw around town. He couldn't get girls because he had a wen on his face.

"She's seeing how us working fellows live," my father said, with a note of humorous apology. Apologizing to them for me, for me to them—light apologies all round. This was his style.

Working carefully together, using long, strong hooks, the two men lifted a heavy casting out of a box of sand.

"That's plenty hot," my father said. "It was cast today. Now they have to work the sand around and get it ready for the next casting. Then do another. It's piecework, you know. Paid by the casting."

We moved away.

"Two of them been together for a while," he said. "They always work together. I do the same job by myself. Heaviest job they've got around here. It took me a while to get used to it, but it doesn't bother me now."

Much that I saw that night was soon to disappear. The cupola, the hand-lifted ladles, the killing dust. (It was truly killing—around town, on the porches of small neat houses, there were always a few yellow-faced, stoical men set out to take the air. Everybody knew and accepted that they were dying of *the foundry disease,* the dust in their lungs.) Many particular skills and dangers were going to go. Many everyday risks, along with much foolhardy pride, and random ingenuity and improvisation. The processes I saw were probably closer to those of the Middle Ages than to those of today.

And I imagine that the special character of the men who worked in the Foundry was going to change, as the processes of the work changed. They would become not so different from the men who worked in the factories, or at other jobs. Up until the time I'm talking about they had seemed stronger and rougher than those other workers; they had more pride and were perhaps more given to self-dramatization than men whose jobs were not so dirty or dangerous. They were too proud to ask for any protection from the hazards they had to undergo, and in fact, as my father had said, they disdained what protection was offered. They were said to be too proud to bother about a union.

Instead, they stole from the Foundry.

"Tell you a story about Geordie," my father said, as we walked along. He was "doing a round" now, and had to punch clocks in various parts of the building. Then he would get down to shaking out his own floors. "Geordie likes to take a bit of lumber and whatnot home with him. A few crates or whatever. Anything he thinks might come in handy to fix the house or build a back shed. So the other night he had a load of stuff, and he went out after dark and put it in the back of his car so it'd be there when he went off work. And he didn't know it, but Tom was in the office and just happened to be standing by the window and watching him. Tom hadn't brought the car, his wife had the car, she'd gone somewhere, and Tom had just walked over to do a little work or pick up something he forgot. Well, he saw what Geordie was up to and he waited around till he saw him coming off work and then he stepped out and said, Hey. He said, hey, wonder if you could give me a lift home. The wife's got the car, he said. So they got in Geordie's car with the other fellows standing around spluttering and Geordie sweating buckets, and Tom never said a word. Sat there whistling while Geordie's trying to get the key in the ignition. He let Geordie drive him home and never said a word. Never turned and looked in the back. Never intended to. Just let him sweat. And told it all over the place next day."

It would be easy to make too much of this story and to suppose that between management and workers there was an easy familiarity, tolerance, even an appreciation of each other's dilemmas. And there was some of that, but it didn't mean there wasn't also plenty of rancor and callousness and of course deceit. But jokes were important. The men who worked in the evenings would gather in my father's little room, the caretaker's room, in most weather—but outside the main door when the evenings were hot—and smoke and talk while they took their unauthorized break. They would tell about jokes that had been played recently and in years past. They talked about jokes played by and upon people now long dead. Sometimes they talked seriously as well. They argued about whether there were ghosts, and talked about who claimed to have seen one. They discussed money—who had it, who'd lost it, who'd expected it and not got it, and where people kept it. My father told me about these talks years later.

One night somebody asked, when is the best time in a man's life?

Some said, it's when you are a kid and can fool around all the time and go down to the river in the summer and play hockey on the road in the winter and that's all you think about, fooling around and having a good time.

Or when you're a young fellow going out and haven't got any responsibilities.

Or when you're first married if you're fond of your wife and a bit later, too, when the children are just little and running around and haven't shown any bad characteristics yet.

My father spoke up and said, "Now. I think maybe now."

They asked him why.

He said because you weren't old yet, with one thing or another collapsing on you, but old enough that you could see that a lot of things you might have wanted out of life you would never get. It was hard to explain how you could be happy in such a situation, but sometimes he thought you were.

When he was telling me about this he said, "I think it was the company I enjoyed. Up till then I'd been so much on my own. They weren't maybe the cream of the crop, but those were some of the best fellows I ever met."

He also told me that one night not long after he had started working at the Foundry he came off work around midnight and found that there was a great snowstorm in progress. The roads were full and the snow blowing so hard and fast that the snowplows would not get out till morning. He had to leave the car where it was—even if he got it shoveled out he couldn't tackle the roads. He started to walk home. It was a distance of about two miles. The walking was heavy, in the freshly drifted snow, and the wind was coming against him from the west. He had done several floors that night, and he was just getting used to the work. He wore a heavy overcoat, an Army greatcoat, which one of our neighbors had given him, having no use for it when he got home from the war. My father did not often wear it either. Usually he wore a windbreaker. He must have put it on that night because the temperature had dropped even below the usual winter cold, and there was no heater in the car. He felt dragged down, pushing against the storm, and about a quarter of a mile from home he found that he wasn't moving. He was standing in the middle of a drift and he could not move his legs. He could hardly stand against the wind. He was worn out. He thought perhaps his heart was giving out. He thought of his death.

He would die leaving a sick crippled wife who could not even take care of herself, an old mother full of disappointment, a younger daughter whose health had always been delicate, an older girl who was strong and bright enough but who often seemed to be self-centered and mysteriously incompetent, a son who promised to be clever and reliable but who was still only a little boy. He would die in debt, and before he had even finished pulling down the pens. They would stand there— drooping wire on the cedar poles that he had cut in the Austins' swamp in the summer of 1927—to show the ruin of his enterprise.

"Was that all you thought about?" I said when he told me this.

"Wasn't that enough?" he said, and went on to tell me how he pulled one leg out of the snow, and then the other: he got out of that drift and then there were no more drifts quite so deep, and before long he was in the shelter of the windbreak of pine trees that he himself had planted the year that I was born. He got home.

But I had meant, didn't he think of himself, of the boy who had trapped along the Blyth Creek, and who went into the store and asked for Signs Snow Paper, didn't he struggle for his own self? I meant, was his life now something only other people had a use for?

My father always said he didn't really grow up till he went to work in the Foundry. He never wanted to talk about the fox farm or the fur business, until he was old and could talk easily about almost anything.

But my mother, walled in by increasing paralysis, was always eager to recall the Pine Tree Hotel, the friends and the money she had made there.

And my father, as it turned out, had another occupation waiting for him. I'm not talking about his raising turkeys, which came after the work at the Foundry and lasted till he was seventy or over, and which may have done damage to his heart, since he would find himself wrestling and hauling around fifty-and sixty-pound birds. It was after giving up such work that he took up writing. He began to write reminiscent pieces and to turn some of them into stories, which were published in an excellent though short-lived local magazine. And not long before his death he completed a novel about pioneer life, called *The Macgregors.*

He told me that writing it had surprised him. He was surprised that he could do such a thing, and surprised that doing it could make him so happy. Just as if there was a future in it for him.

ALISON BECHDEL

The following pages are the first pages of Alison Bechdel's graphic patremoir Fun Home. *Courageously original and lovingly honest,* Fun Home *is a coming of age story—a story of lesbian self-discovery—which also outs the father posthumously as a closeted gay man and a possible suicide. In intertwining her father's story with her own, Bechdel is conscious of being as ruthless as her father was in "his monomaniacal restoration of our old house." She, too, is a Daedalus, who answers "not to the laws of society, but to those of [her] craft." Interviewed in 2006 by* The Guardian's *Oliver Burkeman, Bechdel commented that "I've discovered that there's something inherently hostile about having someone else write about your life, no matter how well-intentioned that other person might be." Talking about* Fun Home, *she went on to say, "It violates their subjectivity. That's the really awful thing about this book: I made my mother and my brothers objects in my version of this story." Bechdel, here, is too hard on herself. In the book, her family's subjectivity is restored through allusive ambiguities and thematic depth—and through the tension between the drawings and the words. Profoundly personal,* Fun Home *is also mythic. From the opening page onward, it is a rich affirmation of Stephen Daedalus's closing words in* A Portrait of the Artist as a Young Man: *"Welcome, O life, I go to encounter for the millionth time the reality of experience and to forge in the smithy of my soul the uncreated conscience of my race. Old father, old artificer, stand me now and ever in good stead." This affirmation is triumphantly validated by "the tricky reverse narration" of* Fun Home's *final panels, in which Bechdel's artistically resurrected, epic father is there to catch and save her child self.*

CHAPTER 1

OLD FATHER, OLD ARTIFICER

LIKE MANY FATHERS, MINE COULD OCCASIONALLY BE PREVAILED ON FOR A SPOT OF "AIRPLANE."

AS HE LAUNCHED ME, MY FULL WEIGHT WOULD FALL ON THE PIVOT POINT BETWEEN HIS FEET AND MY STOMACH.

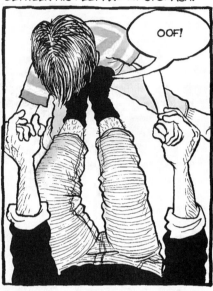

OOF!

IT WAS A DISCOMFORT WELL WORTH THE RARE PHYSICAL CONTACT, AND CERTAINLY WORTH THE MOMENT OF PERFECT BALANCE WHEN I SOARED ABOVE HIM.

IN THE CIRCUS, ACROBATICS WHERE ONE PERSON LIES ON THE FLOOR BALANCING ANOTHER ARE CALLED "ICARIAN GAMES."

CONSIDERING THE FATE OF ICARUS AFTER HE FLOUTED HIS FATHER'S ADVICE AND FLEW SO CLOSE TO THE SUN HIS WINGS MELTED, PERHAPS SOME DARK HUMOR IS INTENDED.

BUT BEFORE HE DID SO, HE MANAGED TO GET QUITE A LOT DONE.

HIS GREATEST ACHIEVEMENT, ARGUABLY, WAS HIS MONOMANIACAL RESTORATION OF OUR OLD HOUSE.

WHEN OTHER CHILDREN CALLED OUR HOUSE A MANSION, I WOULD DEMUR. I RESENTED THE IMPLICATION THAT MY FAMILY WAS RICH, OR UNUSUAL IN ANY WAY.

IN FACT, WE WERE UNUSUAL, THOUGH I WOULDN'T APPRECIATE EXACTLY HOW UNUSUAL UNTIL MUCH LATER. BUT WE WERE NOT RICH.

IT'S JUST A HOUSE.

ALISON!

WHAT?

SEND TAMMI HOME. YOU HAVE WORK TO DO.

THE GILT CORNICES, THE MARBLE FIREPLACE, THE CRYSTAL CHANDELIERS, THE SHELVES OF CALF-BOUND BOOKS--THESE WERE NOT SO MUCH BOUGHT AS PRODUCED FROM THIN AIR BY MY FATHER'S REMARKABLE LEGERDEMAIN.

WASH THESE OLD CURTAINS SO WE CAN PUT UP THE HAND-EMBROIDERED LACE ONES I FOUND IN MRS. STRUMP'S ATTIC.

MY FATHER COULD SPIN GARBAGE...

...INTO GOLD.

HE COULD TRANSFIGURE A ROOM WITH THE SMALLEST OFFHAND FLOURISH.

HE COULD CONJURE AN ENTIRE, FINISHED PERIOD INTERIOR FROM A PAINT CHIP.

HE WAS AN ALCHEMIST OF APPEARANCE, A SAVANT OF SURFACE, A DAEDALUS OF DECOR.

FOR IF MY FATHER WAS ICARUS, HE WAS ALSO DAEDALUS--THAT SKILLFUL ARTIFICER, THAT MAD SCIENTIST WHO BUILT THE WINGS FOR HIS SON AND DESIGNED THE FAMOUS LABYRINTH...

THIS IS THE WALLPAPER FOR MY ROOM?

...AND WHO ANSWERED NOT TO THE LAWS OF SOCIETY, BUT TO THOSE OF HIS CRAFT.

BUT I **HATE** PINK! I **HATE** FLOWERS!

TOUGH TITTY.

HISTORICAL RESTORATION WASN'T HIS JOB.

(TWELFTH-GRADE ENGLISH)

ARCHI-TECTURAL DIGEST

IT WAS HIS PASSION. AND I MEAN PASSION IN EVERY SENSE OF THE WORD.

LIBIDINAL. MANIC. MARTYRED.

OUR GOTHIC REVIVAL HOUSE HAD BEEN BUILT DURING THE SMALL PENNSYLVANIA TOWN'S ONE BRIEF MOMENT OF WEALTH, FROM THE LUMBER INDUSTRY, IN 1867.

BUT LOCAL FORTUNES HAD DECLINED STEADILY FROM THAT POINT, AND WHEN MY PARENTS BOUGHT THE PLACE IN 1962, IT WAS A SHELL OF ITS FORMER SELF.

THE SHUTTERS AND SCROLLWORK WERE GONE. THE CLAPBOARDS HAD BEEN SHEATHED WITH SCABROUS SHINGLES.

THE BARE LIGHTBULBS REVEALED DINGY WARTIME WALLPAPER AND WOODWORK PAINTED PASTEL GREEN.

ALL THAT WAS LEFT OF THE HOUSE'S LUMBER-ERA GLORY WERE THE EXUBERANT FRONT PORCH SUPPORTS.

BUT OVER THE NEXT EIGHTEEN YEARS, MY FATHER WOULD RESTORE THE HOUSE TO ITS ORIGINAL CONDITION, AND THEN SOME.

HE WOULD PERFORM, AS DAEDALUS DID, DAZZLING DISPLAYS OF ARTFULNESS.

HE WOULD CULTIVATE THE BARREN YARD...

...INTO A LUSH, FLOWERING LANDSCAPE.

HE WOULD MANIPULATE FLAGSTONES THAT WEIGHED HALF A TON...

...AND THE THINNEST, QUIVERING LAYERS OF GOLD LEAF.

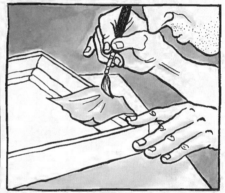

IT COULD HAVE BEEN A ROMANTIC STORY, LIKE IN *IT'S A WONDERFUL LIFE*, WHEN JIMMY STEWART AND DONNA REED FIX UP THAT BIG OLD HOUSE AND RAISE THEIR FAMILY THERE.

HELLO, DARLING!

HELLO, DADDY!

BUT IN THE MOVIE WHEN JIMMY STEWART COMES HOME ONE NIGHT AND STARTS YELLING AT EVERYONE...

...IT'S OUT OF THE ORDINARY.

DAEDALUS, TOO, WAS INDIFFERENT TO THE HUMAN COST OF HIS PROJECTS.

HE BLITHELY BETRAYED THE KING, FOR EXAMPLE, WHEN THE QUEEN ASKED HIM TO BUILD HER A COW DISGUISE SO SHE COULD SEDUCE THE WHITE BULL.

INDEED, THE RESULT OF THAT SCHEME--A HALF-BULL, HALF-MAN MONSTER--INSPIRED DAEDALUS'S GREATEST CREATION YET.

HE HID THE MINOTAUR IN THE LABYRINTH-- A MAZE OF PASSAGES AND ROOMS OPEN- ING ENDLESSLY INTO ONE ANOTHER...

...AND FROM WHICH, AS STRAY YOUTHS AND MAIDENS DISCOVERED TO THEIR PERIL...

...ESCAPE WAS IMPOSSIBLE.

THEN THERE ARE THOSE FAMOUS WINGS. WAS DAEDALUS REALLY STRICKEN WITH GRIEF WHEN ICARUS FELL INTO THE SEA?

OR JUST DISAPPOINTED BY THE DESIGN FAILURE?

SOMETIMES, WHEN THINGS WERE GOING WELL, I THINK MY FATHER ACTUALLY ENJOYED HAVING A FAMILY.

OR AT LEAST, THE AIR OF AUTHENTICITY WE LENT TO HIS EXHIBIT. A SORT OF STILL LIFE WITH CHILDREN.

AND OF COURSE, MY BROTHERS AND I WERE FREE LABOR. DAD CONSIDERED US EXTENSIONS OF HIS OWN BODY, LIKE PRECISION ROBOT ARMS.

PUT HOT, SOAPY WATER IN THE SINK AND GET SOME CLEAN RAGS.

IN THIS REGARD, IT WAS LIKE BEING RAISED NOT BY JIMMY BUT BY MARTHA STEWART.

IN THEORY, HIS ARRANGEMENT WITH MY MOTHER WAS MORE COOPERATIVE.

WHAT DO YOU THINK OF THIS GAS CHANDELIER?

BORDELLO.

AUCTION CATALOG

IN PRACTICE, IT WAS NOT.

BRUCE CHATWIN

Chatwin's essay is an outlier. The approach seems conventional enough, and the spare, ascetic quality of the prose speaks of simplicity and openness. And yet, like so much of Chatwin's work, this essay works by indirection. Of all the essays collected here, this one would least deserve inclusion if the essays included were to be strictly about fathers. Despite the title, and despite the biographical facts, this is not an essay about a father: this is an essay to a father—and to a mother—a message of consolation from a dying child to his parents. To understand this essay you have to make sense of the dead hedgehog's presence, and you also have to believe in miracles. Whereas Kafka pretended to be writing to his father so as to understand himself, the dying Chatwin writes to his parents by pretending to write about them. His reserve is the reserve of emotion.

YOUR FATHER'S EYES ARE BLUE AGAIN

My mother has come back from her cataract operation. For years she has felt hemmed in by the murk. The colours amaze her.

'Your father's eyes are blue again.'

My father has the most beautiful blue eyes I have ever seen in a man. I do not say this because he is my father. They are mariner's eyes, level and steady. On the Malta convoys they scanned the surface of the sea for mines, or the horizon for an enemy warship. They are the eyes of a man who has never known the meaning of dishonesty. They have never tempted him to anything mean or shoddy.

My mother's eyes are brown and lively, with suggestions of Southern ancestry.

When my mother, Margharita, was in hospital he found a photograph I had feared was lost. He had it taken at Hove in 1940 before going to sea. The photo shows the clear blue eyes, that can only be blue, gazing squarely at the camera from under the patent leather peak of his naval officer's cap. My mother kept it by her bedside. I would kiss it before going to bed. My first memory of him is on my third birthday, the 13th of May 1943. He took us bicycling near Flamborough Head, the grey Yorkshire headland that Rimbaud may have seen from a brig and put into his prose-poem *Promontoire*.

He rigged up an improvised saddle for me on his crossbar, with stirrups of purple electric wire. I pointed to a squashed brown thing on the road.

'What's that, daddy?'

'I don't know.'

He did not want me to see something dead.

'Well, it looks to me like a piece of hedgehog.'

My father was not looking in the box of old photos for the one of himself, but for one of his father's yacht, the *Aireymouse*. In the Twenties and Thirties my grandfather, a Birmingham lawyer, owned a vessel of legendary beauty. She was a teak, clipper-bowed ketch built at Fowey in Cornwall in 1898; she had once been rigged as a cutter. An aireymouse is a bat and, under her bowsprit, there was the figurehead of a bat with outstretched wings. The bat had disappeared by my father's day. *Aireymouse* had brown sails dyed with cutchbark, a brass ship's bell, and a gold line from stem to stern.

My grandfather died in 1933, and *Aireymouse* had to be sold. She needed expensive repairs to her stanchions. Neither my father nor his brothers and sister could afford them. They sold her for £200. For my father alone it was the loss of a lover.

He had other boats—the *Nocteluca,* the *Dozmaree*, the *Nereid*, the *Sunquest*—but he shared them with others, and none matched the boat of his dreams.

I do not think he could bring himself to find out what had happened to *Aireymouse*. He heard rumours. In Guernsey a car had driven over the pier and landed on her deck—without doing too much damage. Or she was a rotting house-boat in the mud of a West Country creek. Or an incendiary bomb had hit her in the War. He came to accept that she was gone, but never quite believed it. On our sailing holidays we all believed that one golden evening, off Ushant or in the Race of Alderney, two sails would appear on the horizon and the ethereal craft would heave into view. My father would raise his binoculars and say the words he yearned to say: 'It's *Aireymouse.*'

He became resigned. My parents no longer went to sea. They bought a camping van and travelled all over Europe. My father kept a sailor's log-book of their journeys, and read road-maps as if they were charts.

He had also dreamed of making one trade-wind passage to the West Indies. He never found the time to get away. Too many people depended on his legal advice. He would come home exhausted in the evenings after grappling with the problems of National Health Service hospitals. After his retirement, he had an arthritic hip and I feared he would go into decline. Once the operation had been performed, he was young again.

Four years ago my brother took him on the trade-wind passage. The boat was a modern yacht to be delivered to Antigua. But the owners had made her top-heavy with expensive junk. In a following sea, she did a fifty-degree roll and they had to turn back to the Cape Verde Islands. My father looked younger than ever after his adventure, but it was a disappointment.

Three days before Margharita went to hospital, he found himself talking on the phone to a man who said: 'I've been looking for you for a long time.' Was Charles Chatwin related to the pre-war owners of *Aireymouse*?

'I am,' said my father. 'She was our boat.'

'I've bought her,' the man said.

The man had found her up the River Dart. He fell in love with her and bought her. He took her to a yard in Totnes. The deck was gone. Many of the oak timbers were gone. But the teak hull was in perfect condition.

'I'm going to reconstruct her,' the man said. Could he count on Charles's help?

Charles will be eighty this year.

Let us pray he will sail on *Aireymouse.*

JUDITH ORTIZ COFER

When Odysseus reveals himself to Telemachus, Telemachus, wild with disbelief, breaks out:

No, you're not Odysseus! Not my father!
Just some spirit spellbinding me now—
to make me ache with sorrow all the more....
you seem like a god who rules the skies up there!

To the child, the father can often seem an overwhelming, godlike being. The father of Cofer's poem, however, is not simply a godlike, Odysseus figure. He is a more complex being, compounded of Christian and pagan myth, Odysseus and Jonah both. The prophylactic father-God venerated on the altar of this poem is also "an apparition on leave from a shadow-world," and his presence seems a contingent one, dependent on the prayers and the siren song of the children. Blessing and burden both, his vigilance imposes itself on the children and, as they keep vigil, they are cursed with his course. In another father poem, "Absolution in the New Year," Cofer talks of the father as "a starved spirit / that fed on my dreams," and in her essay "A Prayer, A Candle, and a Notebook" she talks of her father as "a dreamer without hope, an artist without a medium," a man who "directed my goals through his own unfulfilled dreams." Again and again, Cofer's essays, poems and stories are animated by a sense of longing and rejection, of wanting to break free yet hold on. Jonah must be thrown overboard before he can return to prophesy, and the sirens calling to Odysseus are also trying to sing Odysseus to his death.

MY FATHER IN THE NAVY:
A CHILDHOOD MEMORY

Stiff and immaculate
in the white cloth of his uniform
and a round cap on his head like a halo,
he was an apparition on leave from a shadow-world
and only flesh and blood when he rose from below
the waterline where he kept watch over the engines
and dials making sure the ship parted the waters
on a straight course.
Mother, brother and I kept vigil
on the nights and dawns of his arrival,
watching the corner beyond the neon sign of a quasar
for the flash of white, our father like an angel
heralding a new day.
His homecomings were the verses
we composed over the years making up
the siren's song that kept him coming back
from the bellies of iron whales
and into our nights
like the evening prayer.

CLARENCE DAY

Even allowing for its humorous exaggeration, Day's essay strongly demonstrates how fathers are very much of a place, a time, and a culture. There is no mistaking the stockbroking certainties of early 20th century New York in the cut of "Father's Trousers." No other place, time, or environment could have produced such a man, and the successes of Day's stories about his father (whether in vignette, book, play, movie or television form) owe as much to the way in which Day looked back to more certain times as they do to his gentle irony and his triumph in coming to positive terms with such a powerful yet potentially damaging father. Day's items about his father were so important to the early New Yorker *that Harold Ross, legendary founder and publisher, said "If I had never done anything other than publish Clarence Day, I would be satisfied." With respectful wryness and wit, Day not only helped shape* The New Yorker, *he helped shape how Americans perceive their fathers. Like Teddy Roosevelt, he made a positive of "bully."*

FATHER'S OLD TROUSERS

Father didn't care much for jewelry. He disliked the heavy watch-chains which were worn by the men of his time, chains with charms dangling down from the middle. His had none of these things on it; it was strong and handsome but simple. His studs and cuff-links were on the same order, not ornate like those then in fashion. His ring was a solid plain band of gold, set with a rectangular sapphire. All these objects we regarded with a reverence which we felt was their due. There was a special sort of rightness about Father's things, in our eyes, and we had a special respect for them because they were Father's.

Father had had a lighter ring once, with a smaller sapphire, which he had worn as a young man. He had discarded it as less suitable for him, however, as he got on in life, and it had been put away long ago in the safe in our pantry.

Mother didn't like to have it lying idle there, year after year. After I left college, she decided that I had better wear it, so that the family would get some good out of it once more. One afternoon she and I went into the crowded pantry, with its smell of damp washcloths, and she took it out of the safe.

I did not want a ring, but Mother presented this one to me with such affection that I saw no way to get out of accepting it. She put it on my finger and kissed me. I looked at the thing. The sapphire was a beautiful little stone. I thought that after a while I might learn to like it, perhaps. At any rate, there was nothing to get out of order or break.

I soon discovered, however, that this ring was a nuisance—it was such hard work not to lose it. If I had bought and paid for it myself, I suppose I'd have cherished it, but as it had been wished on me, it was only a responsibility. It preyed on my mind. After a little while, I stopped wearing it and put it away.

When Mother noticed that it wasn't on my finger, she spoke out at once. She said there wasn't much point in my having a ring if I merely kept it in my bureau drawer. She reminded me that it was a very handsome ring and I ought to be proud to wear it.

I explained that I couldn't get used to remembering that I was wearing a ring, and had several times left it on public washstands and got it back only by sheer luck. Mother was frightened. She instantly agreed that it would be a terrible thing to lose Father's ring. It went back into the safe in the pantry.

Several years later, it was taken out again, and after another little ceremony it was entrusted to George. He had even more trouble with it than I'd had. He, too, decided that he didn't wish to wear it himself, so, as he had married, he gave it to his wife, who adored it. Everyone was happy for a while until Mother happened to see Father's ring nestling on Wilhelmine's finger. Mother was very fond of Wilhelmine, but this strange sight disturbed her. She felt that the only right and appropriate use for that ring was for it to be worn by one of Father's sons. She asked George to take it away from Wilhelmine and return it. He silently did so, and back it went again to the pantry.

It was a curious fact that everything that Father had ever owned seemed to be permanently a part of him. No matter what happened to it, it remained impressed with his personality. This isn't unusual in the case of a ring, I suppose, but the same thing was true even of Father's old neckties, especially from his point of view. I don't think he cared what became of that ring, the way Mother did, but when he gave me an old necktie or a discarded pair of trousers, they still seemed to him to be his. Not only did he feel that way about it but he made me feel that way, too. He explained to me that he gave things which he didn't care about to the coachman or the Salvation Army, but that when he had a particularly handsome tie which had plenty of wear in it yet, or a pair of trousers which he had been fond of, he saved anything of that sort for me.

A pair of striped trousers which he had worn to church on Sundays for years went up to New Haven with me one Christmas, when I was a junior, and as I was short of clothes at the time, they came in very handy. I had to be careful not to take off my coat while I was wearing them, though. They looked oddly baggy in the seat when exposed to full view—on nights when I was playing billiards in a poolroom, for instance. They also made it harder for me to climb Osborn Hall's iron gate. This gate was ten feet high, with a row of long, sharp spikes at the top, and to get quickly over it in Father's trousers was quite a feat.

There was no point in getting over it quickly. In fact, there was no point in getting over it at all. Osborn Hall was used solely for lectures, and we saw quite enough of it in the daytime without trying to get in there at night. Besides, we couldn't get in anyhow, even after climbing the gate because the big inside doors were locked fast. After standing in the vestibule a minute, between the doors and the gate, there was nothing to do but climb back again and go home to bed. This seemed like a useful or stimulating performance, though, when we had been drinking.

On nights like these, as I was undressing in my bedroom, I sometimes had moral qualms over the way that I was making Father's trousers lead this new kind of life. Once in a while such misgivings would even come over me elsewhere. They were not clear-cut or acute, but they floated around in the back of my mind. Usually I paid little attention to what clothes I had on, but when I did happen to notice that I was wearing those trousers into places which were not respectable, I didn't feel right about it.

Then one week I lent them to a classmate of mine, Jerry Ives, to wear in his role of a fat man in some Psi U play. Father wasn't fat, but he was much more full-bodied than Jerry, and there was plenty of room in his trousers for a pillow and Jerry besides. I thought no more of the matter until the night of the play, but when the curtain went up and I saw Father's Sunday trousers running across the stage pursued by a comic bartender who was yelling "Stop thief!" I felt distinctly uncomfortable.

After that, nothing seemed to go right with them. The fact was, they simply didn't fit into undergraduate life. The night that I most fully realized this, I remember, was when a girl whom Father would have by no means approved of sat on what was my lap but his trousers. Father was a good eighty miles away and safely in bed, but I became so preoccupied and ill at ease that I got up and left.

ANNE SEXTON

"All My Pretty Ones" is informed by the horror inherent in the Shakespearean allusion, and by the inadequacy of language to express Macduff's grief and guilt at the death of his family. The father of this poem is seared by association, as is Sexton's narratorial self in echoing Macduff. On the surface, Sexton's poem is a poem of forgiveness, a poem in which the child exercises her power over the memory of her father, revels in her power, and then chooses to be merciful. The disturbingly incestuous, electrifyingly Oedipal elements found in many of Sexton's other father poems seem to have no place here. Even her father's alcoholic tendency, a tendency which Sexton shared, appears transmuted into a sacramental virtue. On a deeper level, though, Sexton's narratorial "I" follows her mother's path, and the truth about her father is both cloaked and revealed in "all she does not say." The "eyes, as thick as wood," are eyes of concealment, Birnam Wood eyes which make it nearly impossible to discover the real I of the father until the "hurly-burly years" throw the reader back to Macbeth's *"When the hurlyburly's done / When the battle's lost and won," and the consequent, "Fair is foul, and foul is fair." Beyond* Macbeth, *too, lies "the love and legal verbiage of another" Shakespeare play, hints of* Hamlet *with a father's ghost, a too-hasty marriage, murder, incestuous murmurs, madness, the concealment provided by a strange face or "antic disposition," suicide, a mortal coil shuffled off, and disturbing truths unearthed by a sexton's spade. Under the calm, carefully controlled surface of "All My Pretty Ones," beyond the housekeeping and the domestic details of sifting, culling, and classifying, broods a revenge tragedy in miniature, an incestuous tragedy worthy of the English Ford.*

ALL MY PRETTY ONES

Father, this year's jinx rides us apart
where you followed our mother to her cold slumber,
a second shock boiling its stone to your heart,
leaving me here to shuffle and disencumber
you from the residence you could not afford:
a gold key, your half of a woolen mill,
twenty suits from Dunne's, an English Ford,
the love and legal verbiage of another will,
boxes of pictures of people I do not know.
I touch their cardboard faces. They must go.

But the eyes, as thick as wood in this album,
hold me. I stop here, where a small boy
waits in a ruffled dress for someone to come . . .
for this soldier who holds his bugle like a toy
or for this velvet lady who cannot smile.
Is this your father's father, this commodore
in a mailman suit? My father, time meanwhile
has made it unimportant who you are looking for.
I'll never know what these faces are all about.
I lock them into their book and throw them out.

This is the yellow scrapbook that you began
the year I was born; as crackling now and wrinkly
as tobacco leaves: clippings where Hoover outran
the Democrats, wiggling his dry finger at me
and Prohibition; news where the *Hindenburg* went
down and recent years where you went flush
on war. This year, solvent but sick, you meant
to marry that pretty widow in a one-month rush.
But before you had that second chance, I cried
on your fat shoulder. Three days later you died.

These are the snapshots of marriage, stopped in places.
Side by side at the rail toward Nassau now;
here, with the winner's cup at the speedboat races,
here, in tails at the Cotillion, you take a bow,
here, by our kennel of dogs with their pink eyes,
running like show-bred pigs in their chain-link pen;
here, at the horseshow where my sister wins a prize;
and here, standing like a duke among groups of men.
Now I fold you down, my drunkard, my navigator,
my first lost keeper, to love or look at later.

I hold a five-year diary that my mother kept
for three years, telling all she does not say
of your alcoholic tendency. You overslept,
she writes. My God, father, each Christmas Day
with your blood, will I drink down your glass
of wine? The diary of your hurly-burly years
goes to my shelf to wait for my age to pass.
Only in this hoarded span will love persevere.
Whether you are pretty or not, I outlive you,
bend down my strange face to yours and forgive you.

MIRIAM TOEWS

Miriam Toews's essay points to the variety and power of the father genre. Children writing about their father are driven to find original ways to bring out his uniqueness, are challenged to do their best for their father. Indeed, the inventive excellence of the genre is generated by the need to pay proper homage. Emotionally and stylistically, "A Father's Faith" is the most direct and conventional of Toews's several father tributes. In Swing Low: A Life, *Toews recreates her father as a first-person narrator, and his life is movingly, convincingly told through the narrative "I." In her novel,* A Complicated Kindness, *Toews's feisty 16-year-old heroine, Nomi, constantly refers to her gentle, vulnerable father as Ray. In "My Father's Faith," Toews' father is "father" only in the title and in the first paragraph. For the rest of the essay he is "dad." This simple change makes "A Father's Faith" a testament to all that is implied by the word "dad": emotional closeness, and a child's faith. The gentle normalcy of this essay, the quotidian ordinariness, is in stark contrast to the incomprehensible violence of the father's suicide. It is telling that Toews never once uses the word "suicide," even though she is open about the fact. The fact is incontrovertible, but the word is too negative for an essay of celebration and affirmation.*

A FATHER'S FAITH

On the morning on May 13, 1998, my father woke up, had breakfast, got dressed and walked away from the Steinbach Bethesda Hospital, where he had been a patient for two and a half weeks. He walked through his beloved hometown, along Hespeler Road, past the old farmhouse where his mother had lived with her second husband, past the water tower, greeting folks in his loud, friendly voice, wishing them well. He passed the site on First Street where the house in which my sister and I grew up once stood. He walked down Main Street, past the Mennonite church where, throughout his life, he had received countless certificates for perfect attendance, past Elmdale School where he had taught grade six for forty years.

As he walked by his home on Brandt Road, he saw his old neighbour Bill sitting in his lawn chair. He waved and smiled again, then he continued on past the cemetery where his parents were buried, and the high school his daughters had attended, and down Highway 52, out of town, past the Frantz Motor Inn, which is just outside the town limits because it serves alcohol and Steinbach is a dry town. He kept walking until he got too tired, so he hitched a ride with a couple of guys who were on their way to buy a fishing licence in the small village of Woodridge on the edge of the Sandilands Forest.

The sun would have been very warm by the time they dropped him off, and he would have taken off his stylish cap and wiped his brow with the back of his hand. I'm sure he thanked them profusely, perhaps offering them ten dollars for their trouble, and then he walked the short distance to the cafe near the railroad tracks, the place he and my mom would sometimes go for a quiet coffee and a change of scenery. He would have been able to smell the clover growing in the ditches beside the tracks and between the ties. He may have looked down the line and remembered that the train would be coming from Ontario, through Warroad, Minnesota, on its way to Winnipeg.

A beautiful young woman named Stephanie was just beginning her shift and she spoke to him through the screen door at the side of the restaurant. Yes, she said, the train will be here soon. And my dad smiled and thanked her, and mentioned that he could hear the whistle. Moments later, he was dead.

Steinbach is an easy forty-minute drive from Winnipeg, east on the Trans-Canada, then south on Highway 12. On the way into town there's a sign proclaiming "Jesus Saves." On the way back to the city just off Highway 12 there's another that says, "Satan is Real. You Can't Be Neutral. Choose Now." The town has recently become a city of 8,500 people, two-thirds of whom are Mennonite, so it's not surprising that about half of the twenty-four churches are Mennonite and conservative. There is a Catholic church too, but it's new and I'm not sure exactly where it is. A little way down from the bowling alley I can still make out my name on the sidewalk, carved in big bold letters when I was ten and marking my territory.

My town made sense to me then. For me it was a giant playground where my friends and I roamed freely, using the entire town in a game of arrows—something like hide-and-seek—for which my dad, the teacher, provided boxes and boxes of fresh new chalk and invaluable tips. He had, after all, played the same game in the same town many years before.

At six p.m. the siren would go off at the firehall, reminding all the kids to go home for supper, and at nine p.m. it was set off again, reminding us to go home to bed. I had no worries, and no desire ever to leave this place where everyone knew me. If they couldn't remember my name, they knew I was the younger daughter of Mel and Elvira Toews, granddaughter of C.T. Loewen and Henry Toews, from the Kleine Gemeinde congregation, and so on and so on. All the kids in town, other than the church-sponsored Laotians who came over in the seventies, could be traced all the way back to the precise Russian veldt their great-grandparents had emigrated from. They were some of the thousands of Mennonites who came to Manitoba in the late 1800s to escape religious persecution. They were given free land and a promise that they could, essentially, do their own thing without interference. They wanted to keep the world away from their children and their children away from the world. Naturally it was an impossible ideal.

As I grew older, I became suspicious and critical and restless and angry. Every night I plotted my escape. I imagined that Barkman's giant feed mill on Main Street, partially visible from my bedroom window, was a tall ship that would take me away some day. I looked up places like Hollywood and Manhattan and Venice and Montreal in my Childcraft encyclopedias. I begged my sister to play, over and over, the sad songs from her Jacques Brel piano book, and I'd light candles and sing along, wearing a Pioneer Girls tam on my head, using a chopstick as a cigarette holder, pretending I was Jackie Brel, Jacques's long-lost but just as world-weary Mennonite twin. I couldn't believe that I was stuck in a town like Steinbach, where dancing was a sin and serving beer a felony.

There were other things I became aware of as well. That my grandmother was a vanilla alcoholic who believed she was a teetotaller. That seventy-five-year-old women who had borne thirteen children weren't allowed to speak to the church congregation, but that fifteen-year-old boys were. That every family had a secret. And I learned that my dad had been depressed all his life.

I had wondered, when I was a kid, why he spent so much of the weekend in bed and why he didn't talk much at home. Occasionally he'd tell me, sometimes in tears, that he loved me very much and that he wished he were a better father, that he were more involved in my life. But I never felt the need for an apology. It made me happy and a bit envious to know that my dad's students were able to witness his humour and intelligence firsthand, to hear him expound on his favourite subjects: Canadian history, Canadian politics and Canadian newspapers. I remember watching him at work and marvelling at his energy and enthusiasm. I thought he looked very handsome when he rolled up his sleeves and tucked his tie in between the buttons of his shirt, his hands on his hips, all ready for business and hard work.

Teaching school—helping others make sense of the world—was a good profession for a man who was continuously struggling to find meaning in life. I think he needed his students as much as they needed him. By fulfilling his duties, he was also shoring up a psyche at risk of erosion.

Four years before his death he was forced to retire from teaching because of a heart attack and some small strokes. He managed to finish the book he was writing on Canada's prime ministers, but then he seemed to fade away. He spent more and more of his time in bed, in the dark, not getting up even to eat or wash, not interested in watching TV or listening to the radio. Despite our pleading and cajoling, despite the medication and visits to various doctors' offices, appointments he dutifully kept, and despite my mother's unwavering love, we felt we were losing him.

I know about brain chemistry and depression, but there's still a part of me that blames my dad's death on being Mennonite and living in that freaky, austere place where this world isn't good enough and admission into the next one, the perfect one, means everything, where every word and deed gets you closer to or farther away from eternal life. If you don't believe that then nothing Steinbach stands for will make sense. And if life doesn't make sense you lose yourself in it, your spirit decays. That's what I believed had happened to my dad, and that's why I hated my town.

In the weeks and months after his death, my mom and my sister and I tried to piece things together. William Ashdown, the executive director of the Mood Disorders Association of Manitoba, told us the number of mentally ill Mennonites is abnormally high. "We don't know if it's genetic or cultural," he said, "but the Steinbach area is one that we're vitally concerned about."

"It's the way the church delivers the message," says a Mennonite friend of mine, "the message of sin and accountability. To be human, basically, is to be a sinner. So a person, a real believer, starts to get down on himself, and where does it end? They say self-loathing is the cornerstone of depression, right?"

Years ago, the Mennonite Church practised something called "shunning," whereby if you were to leave your husband, or marry outside the Church, or elope, or drink, or in some way contravene the Church's laws or act "out of faith," you could be expelled from the Church and ignored, shunned by the entire community, including your own family. Depression or despair, as it would have been referred to then, was considered to be the result of a lack of faith and therefore could be another reason for shunning.

These days most Mennonites don't officially practise shunning, although William Ashdown claims there are still Mennonites from extreme conservative sects who are being shunned and shamed into silence within their communities for being mentally ill. Certainly Arden Thiessen, the minister of my dad's church, and a long-time friend of his, is aware of the causes of depression and the pain experienced by those who suffer from it. He doesn't see it as a lack of faith, but as an awful sickness.

But I can't help thinking that that history had just a little to do with my alcoholic grandmother's insisting that she was a non-drinker, and my dad's telling his doctors, smiling that beautiful smile of his, that he was fine, just fine.

Not long before he died my dad told me about the time he was five and was having his tonsils out. Just before the operation began he was knocked out with ether and he had a dream that he was somersaulting through the hospital walls, right through, easily, he said, moving his hands in circles through the air. It was wonderful. He told me he would never forget that feeling.

But mostly, the world was a sad and unsafe place for him, and his town provided shelter from it. Maybe he saw this as a gift, while I came to see it as oppression. He could peel back the layers of hypocrisy and intolerance and see what was good, and I couldn't. He believed that it mattered what he did in life, and he believed in the next world, one that's better. He kept the faith of his Mennonite forebears to the very end, or what he might call the beginning, and removed himself from this world entirely.

Stephanie, the waitress in the cafe in Woodridge, told my mother that my dad was calm and polite when he spoke to her, as if he were about to sit down to a cup of tea. She told her that he hadn't seemed at all afraid. But why would you be if you believed you were going to a place where there is no more sadness?

My dad never talked to us about God or religion. We didn't have family devotion like everybody else. He never quoted out loud from the Bible or lectured us about not going to church. In fact his only two pieces of advice to me were "Be yourself" and "You can do anything."

But he still went to church. It didn't matter how low he felt, or how cold it was outside. He would put on his suit and tie and stylish cap and walk the seven or eight blocks to church. He always walked, through searing heat or sub-arctic chill. If he was away on holidays he would find a church and go to it. At the lake he drove forty miles down gravel roads to attend an outdoor church in the bush. I think he needed church like a junkie needs a fix: to get him through another day in a world of pain.

What I love about my town is that it gave my dad the faith that stopped him from being afraid in those last violent seconds he spent on earth. And the place in my mind where we meet is on the front steps of my dad's church, the big one on Main Street across from Don's Bakery and the Goodwill store. We smile and talk for a few minutes outside, basking in the warmth of the summer sun he loved so much. Then he goes in and I stay outside, and we're both happy where we are.

ANNE CARSON

"Let us be gentle when we question our fathers," says Anne Carson in Plainwater: Essays and Poetry, *as her narrative self prepares for pilgrimage into a foreign country. Certainly, as Carson attempts the task of trying to understand a Mosaic father, the questioning in "Father's Old Blue Cardigan" is cloaked in gentleness. In putting on his old blue cardigan her narrator seeks solace and comfort, looks for protection against the cold and the shadows associated with the father. Inside the cardigan, she looks past his laws and the subsequent dementia—the dementia which elsewhere in* Plainwater *she says is "continuous with sanity"—to see the small boy protected against the potential rigours of a lengthy journey by a solicitous aunt. There is gentleness as Carson assumes the protective cardigan to follow her father back into a childhood where the imagination made frightening fingers of innocent haystack shadows. Her father's laws, like the cardigan, were donned for protection and are therefore excusable. By gentle questioning, the father can be forgiven his stern coldness and the madness brought on by imagination. By gentle questioning, too, "The cold paring down from the moonbone in the sky" yields meaning as it resists it, meaning found in the opposition of the cold to the July heat, in the diminishment of the paring, in the realization that père is father in French and that the cold comes fathering down from the moonbone, and always remembering, too, that the moon is female in her madness. Imagination may lead to madness, and yet without it there can be no understanding fathers, no understanding poetry.*

FATHER'S OLD BLUE CARDIGAN

Now it hangs on the back of the kitchen chair
where I always sit, as it did
on the back of the kitchen chair where he always sat.

I put it on whenever I come in,
as he did, stamping
the snow from his boots.

I put it on and sit in the dark.
He would not have done this.
Coldness comes paring down from the moonbone in the sky.

His laws were a secret.
But I remember the moment at which I knew
he was going mad inside his laws.

He was standing at the turn of the driveway when I arrived.
He had on the blue cardigan with the buttons done up all the way
    to the top.
Not only because it was a hot July afternoon

but the look on his face—
as a small child who has been dressed by some aunt early in the
    morning
for a long trip

on cold trains and windy platforms
will sit very straight at the edge of his seat
while the shadows like long fingers

over the haystacks that sweep past
keep shocking him
because he is riding backwards.

EDMUND GOSSE # 1

Like Winston Churchill after him, Edmund Gosse's first attempt to write about his father took the form of an official biography. Written shortly after his father's death on August 23rd 1888—a harrowing, protracted death from cancer which, if Edmund's version of events is to be believed, saw the tortured, disillusioned and blaspheming father die in the arms of his son and daughter-in-law—the Life of Philip Henry Gosse *was admired by Henry James as "a singularly clever, skilful, vivid, well-done biography . . . very happy in proportion, tact and talent." At least two readers—John Addington Symons and George Moore—suggested Gosse be more autobiographical and explore the father-son relationship further. It was, however, to be almost twenty years before Gosse unburdened himself of his deeply conflicted masterpiece,* Father and Son. *Though the book was an immediate success and reviews were largely enthusiastic, the reviewer of the* Academy *had reservations about the "close anatomisation by a son of a father," and the* Times Literary Supplement *raised the question of "how far in the interests of popular edification or amusement it is legitimate to expose the weaknesses and inconsistencies of a good man who is also one's father." Perhaps not always fortunately, subsequent writers, far more frank and confessional, showed far fewer qualms in writing about their fathers.*

epilogue from *FATHER AND SON*

This narrative, however, must not be allowed to close with the Son in the foreground of the piece. If it has a value, that value consists in what light it may contrive to throw upon the unique and noble figure of the Father. With the advance of years, the characteristics of this figure became more severely outlined, more rigorously confined within settled limits. In relation to the Son—who presently departed, at a very immature age, for the new life in London—the attitude of the Father continued to be one of extreme solicitude, deepening by degrees into disappointment and disenchantment. He abated no jot or tittle of his demands upon human frailty. He kept the spiritual cord drawn tight; the Biblical bearing-rein was incessantly busy, jerking into position the head of the dejected neophyte. That young soul, removed from the Father's personal inspection, began to blossom forth crudely and irregularly enough, into new provinces of thought, through fresh layers of experience. To the painful mentor at home in the West, the centre of anxiety was still the meek and docile heart, dedicated to the Lord's service, which must, at all hazards and with all defiance of the rules of life, be kept unspotted from the world.

The torment of a postal inquisition began directly I was settled in my London lodgings. To my Father—with his ample leisure, his palpitating apprehension, his ready pen—the flow of correspondence offered no trouble at all; it was a grave but gratifying occupation. To me the almost daily letter of exhortation, with its string of questions about conduct, its series of warnings, grew to be a burden which could hardly be borne, particularly because it involved a reply as punctual and if possible as full as itself. At the age of seventeen, the metaphysics of the soul are shadowy, and it is a dreadful thing to be forced to define the exact outline of what is so undulating and so shapeless. To my Father there seemed no reason why I should hesitate to give answers of full metallic ring to his hard and oft-repeated questions; but to me this correspondence was torture. When I feebly expostulated, when I begged to be left a little to myself, these appeals of mine automatically stimulated, and indeed blew up into fierce flames, the ardour of my Father's alarm.

The letter, the only too-confidently expected letter, would lie on the table as I descended to breakfast. It would commonly be, of course, my only letter, unless tempered by a cosy and chatty note from my dear and comfortable stepmother, dealing with such perfectly tranquillizing subjects as the harvest of roses in the garden or the state of health of various neighbours. But the other, the solitary letter, in its threatening whiteness, with its exquisitely penned address—there it would lie awaiting me, destroying the taste of the bacon, reducing the flavour of the tea to insipidity. I might fatuously dally with it, I might pretend not to observe it, but there it lay. Before the morning's exercise began, I knew that it had to be read, and what was worse, that it had to be answered. Useless the effort to conceal from myself what it contained. Like all its precursors, like all its followers, it would insist, with every variety of appeal, on a reiterated declaration that I still fully intended, as in the days of my earliest childhood, 'to be on the Lord's side' in everything.

In my replies, I would sometimes answer precisely as I was desired to answer; sometimes I would evade the queries, and write about other things; sometimes I would turn upon the tormentor, and urge that my tender youth might be let alone. It little mattered what form of weakness I put forth by way of baffling my Father's direct, firm, unflinching strength. To an appeal against the bondage of a correspondence of such unbroken solemnity I would receive—with what a paralysing promptitude!—such a reply as this:—

Let me say that the 'solemnity' you complain of has only been the expression of tender anxiousness of a father's heart, that his only child, just turned out upon the world, and very far out of his sight and hearing, should be walking in God's way. Recollect that it is not now as it was when you were at school, when we had personal communication with you at intervals of five days:—we now know absolutely nothing of you, save from your letters, and if they do not indicate your spiritual prosperity, the deepest solicitudes of our hearts have nothing to feed on. But I will try henceforth to trust you, and lay aside my fears; for you are worthy of my confidence; and your own God and your father's God will hold you with His right hand.

Over such letters as these I am not ashamed to say that I sometimes wept; the old paper I have just been copying shows traces of tears shed upon it more than forty years ago, tears commingled of despair at my own feebleness, distraction, at my want of will, pity for my Father's manifest and pathetic distress. He would 'try henceforth to trust' me, he said. Alas! the effort would be in vain; after a day or two, after a hollow attempt to write of other things, the importunate subject would recur; there would intrude again the inevitable questions about the Atonement and the Means of Grace, the old anxious fears lest I was 'yielding' my intimacy to agreeable companions who were not 'one with me in Christ', fresh passionate entreaties to be assured, in every letter, that I was walking in the clear light of God's presence.

It seems to me now profoundly strange, although I knew too little of the world to remark it at the time, that these incessant exhortations dealt, not with conduct, but with faith. Earlier in this narrative I have noted how disdainfully, with what an austere pride, my Father refused to entertain the subject of personal shortcomings in my behaviour. There were enough of them to blame, Heaven knows, but he was too lofty-minded a gentleman to dwell upon them, and, though by nature deeply suspicious of the possibility of frequent moral lapses, even in the very elect, he refused to stoop to anything like espionage.

I owe him a deep debt of gratitude for his beautiful faith in me in this respect, and now that I was alone in London, at this tender time of life, 'exposed', as they say, to all sorts of dangers, as defenceless as a fledgling that has been turned out of its nest, yet my Father did not, in his uplifted Quixotism, allow himself to fancy me guilty of any moral misbehaviour, but concentrated his fears entirely upon my faith.

'Let me know more of your inner light. Does the candle of the Lord shine on your soul?' This would be the ceaseless inquiry. Or, again, 'Do you get any spiritual companionship with young men? You passed over last Sunday without even a word, yet this day is the most interesting to me in your whole week. Do you find the ministry of the Word pleasant, and, above all, profitable? Does it bring your soul into exercise before God? The Coming of Christ draweth nigh. Watch, therefore and pray always, that you may be counted worthy to stand before the Son of Man.'

If I quote such passages as this from my Father's letters to me, it is not that I seek entertainment in a contrast between his earnestness and the casuistical inattention and provoked distractedness of a young man to whom the real world now offered its irritating and stimulating scenes of animal and intellectual life, but to call out sympathy, and perhaps wonder, at the spectacle of so blind a Roman firmness as my Father's spiritual attitude displayed.

His aspirations were individual and metaphysical. At the present hour, so complete is the revolution which has overturned the puritanism of which he was perhaps the latest surviving type, that all classes of religious persons combine in placing philanthropic activity, the objective attitude, in the foreground. It is extraordinary how far-reaching the change has been, so that nowadays a religion which does not combine with its subjective faith a strenuous labour for the good of others is hardly held to possess any religious principle worth proclaiming.

This propaganda of beneficence, this constant attention to the moral and physical improvement of persons who have been neglected, is quite recent as a leading feature of religion, though indeed it seems to have formed some part of the Saviour's original design. It was unknown to the great preachers of the seventeenth century, whether Catholic or Protestant, and it offered but a shadowy attraction to my Father, who was the last of their disciples. When Bossuet desired his hearers to listen to the *cri de misère a l'entour de nous, qui devrait nous fondre le coeur*, he started a new thing in the world of theology. We may search the famous 'Rule and Exercises of Holy Living' from cover to cover, and not learn that Jeremy Taylor would have thought that any activity of the district-visitor or the Salvation lassie came within the category of saintliness.

My Father, then, like an old divine, concentrated on thoughts upon the intellectual part of faith. In his obsession about me, he believed that if my brain could be kept unaffected by any of the seductive errors of the age, and my heart centred in the adoring love of God, all would be well with me in perpetuity. He was still convinced that by intensely directing my thoughts, he could compel them to flow in a certain channel, since he had not begun to learn the lesson, so mournful for saintly men of his complexion, that 'virtue would not be virtue, could it be given by one fellow creature to another'. He had recognized, with reluctance, that holiness was not hereditary, but he continued to hope that it might be compulsive. I was still 'the child of many prayers', and it was not to be conceded that these prayers could remain unanswered.

The great panacea was now, as always, the study of the Bible, and this my Father never ceased to urge upon me. He presented to me a copy of Dean Alford's edition of the Greek New Testament, in four great volumes, and these he had had so magnificently bound in full morocco that the work shone on my poor shelf of sixpenny poets like a duchess among dairy maids. He extracted from me a written promise that I would translate and meditate upon a portion of the Greek text every morning before I started for business. This promise I presently failed to keep, my good intentions being undermined by an invincible *ennui*; I concealed the dereliction from him, and the sense that I was deceiving my Father ate into my conscience like a canker. But the dilemma was now before me that I must either deceive my Father in such things or paralyse my own character.

My growing distaste for the Holy Scriptures began to occupy my thoughts, and to surprise as much as it scandalized me. My desire was to continue to delight in those sacred pages, for which I still had an instinctive veneration. Yet I could not but observe the difference between the zeal with which I snatched at a volume of Carlyle or Ruskin—since these magicians were now first revealing themselves to me—and the increasing languor with which I took up Alford for my daily 'passage'. Of course, although I did not know it, and believed my reluctance to be sinful, the real reason why I now found the Bible so difficult to read was my familiarity with its contents. These had the colourless triteness of a story retold a hundred times. I longed for something new, something that would gratify curiosity and excite surprise. Whether the facts and doctrines contained in the Bible were true or false was not the question that appealed to me; it was rather that they had been presented to me so often and had sunken into me so far that, as someone has said, they 'lay bedridden in the dormitory of the soul', and made no impression of any kind upon me.

It often amazed me, and I am still unable to understand the fact, that my Father, through his long life—or until nearly the close of it—continued to take an eager pleasure in the text of the Bible. As I think I have already said, before he reached middle life, he had committed practically the whole of it to memory, and if started anywhere, even in a Minor Prophet, he could go on without a break as long as ever he was inclined for that exercise. He, therefore, at no time can have been assailed by the satiety of which I have spoken, and that it came so soon to me I must take simply as an indication of difference of temperament. It was not possible, even through the dark glass of correspondence, to deceive his eagle eye in this matter, and his suspicions accordingly took another turn. He conceived me to have become, or to be becoming, a victim of 'the infidelity of the age.'

In this new difficulty, he appealed to forms of modern literature by the side of which the least attractive pages of Leviticus or Deuteronomy struck me as even thrilling. In particular, he urged upon me a work, then just published, called *The Continuity of Scripture* by William Page Wood, afterwards Lord Chancellor Hatherley. I do not know why he supposed that the lucubrations of an exemplary lawyer, delivered in a style that was like the trickling of sawdust, would succeed in rousing emotions which the glorious rhetoric of the Orient had failed to awaken; but Page Wood had been a Sunday School teacher for thirty years, and my Father was always unduly impressed by the acumen of pious barristers.

As time went on, and I grew older and more independent in mind, my Father's anxiety about what he called 'the pitfalls and snares which surround on every hand the thoughtless giddy youth of London' became extremely painful to himself. By harping in private upon these 'pitfalls'—which brought to my imagination a funny rough woodcut in an old edition of Bunyan, where a devil was seen capering over a sort of box let neatly into the ground—he worked himself up into a frame of mind which was not a little irritating to his hapless correspondent, who was now 'snared' indeed, limed by the pen like a bird by the feet, and could not by any means escape. To a peck or a flutter from the bird the implacable fowler would reply:

You charge me with being suspicious, and I fear I cannot deny the charge. But I can appeal to your own sensitive and thoughtful mind for a considerable allowance. My deep and tender love for you; your youth and inexperience; the examples of other young men; your distance from parental counsel; our absolute and painful ignorance of all the details of your daily life, except what you yourself tell us:—try to throw yourself into the standing of a parent, and say if my suspiciousness is unreasonable. I rejoicingly acknowledge that from all I see you are pursuing a virtuous, steady, worthy course. One good thing my suspiciousness does:—ever and anon it brings out from you assurances, which greatly refresh and comfort me. And again, it carries me ever to God's Throne of Grace on your behalf. Holy Job *suspected* that his sons might have sinned, and cursed God in their heart. Was not his suspicion much like mine, grounded on the same reasons and productive of the same results? For it drove him to God in intercession. I have adduced the example of this Patriarch before, and he will endure being looked at again.

In fact, Holy Job continued to be frequently looked at, and for this Patriarch I came to experience a hatred which was as venomous as it was undeserved. But what youth of eighteen would willingly be compared with the sons of Job? And indeed, for my part, I felt much more like that justly exasperated character, Elihu the Buzite, of the kindred of Ram.

As time went on, the peculiar strain of inquisition was relaxed, and I endured fewer and fewer of the torments of religious correspondence. Nothing abides in one tense projection, and my Father, resolute as he was, had other preoccupations. His orchids, his microscope, his physiological researches, his interpretations of prophecy, filled up the hours of his active and strenuous life, and, out of his sight, I became not indeed out of his mind, but no longer ceaselessly in the painful foreground of it. Yet, although the reiteration of his anxiety might weary him a little as it had wearied me well nigh to groans of despair, there was not the slightest change in his real attitude towards the subject or towards me.

I have already had occasion to say that he had nothing of the mystic or the visionary about him. At certain times and on certain points, he greatly desired that signs and wonders, such as had astonished and encouraged the infancy of the Christian Church, might again be vouchsafed to it, but he did not pretend to see such miracles himself, nor give the slightest credence to others who asserted that they did. He often congratulated himself on the fact that although his mind dwelt so constantly on spiritual matters it was never betrayed into any suspension of the rational functions.

Cross-examination by letter slackened, but on occasion of my brief and usually summer visits to Devonshire I suffered acutely from my Father's dialectical appetites. He was surrounded by peasants, on whom the teeth of his arguments could find no purchase. To him, in that intellectual Abdera, even an unwilling youth from London offered opportunities of pleasant contest. He would declare himself ready, nay eager, for argument. With his mental sleeves turned up, he would adopt a fighting attitude, and challenge me to a round on any portion of the Scheme of Grace. His alacrity was dreadful to me, his well-aimed blows fell on what was rather a bladder or a pillow than a vivid antagonist.

He was, indeed, most unfairly handicapped,—I was naked, he in a suit of chain armour,—for he had adopted a method which I thought, and must still think, exceedingly unfair. He assumed that he had private knowledge of the Divine Will, and he would meet my temporizing arguments by asseverations,—'So sure as my God liveth!' or by appeals to a higher authority,—'But what does *my* Lord tell me in Paul's Letter to the Philippians?' It was the prerogative of his faith to know, and of his character to overpower objection; between these two millstones I was rapidly ground to powder.

These 'discussions', as they were rather ironically called, invariably ended for me in disaster. I was driven out of my *papier-mâché* fastnesses, my canvas walls rocked at the first peal from my Father's clarion, and the foe pursued me across the plains of Jericho until I lay down ignominiously and covered my face. I seemed to be pushed with horns of iron, such as those which Zedekiah the son of Chenaanah prepared for the encouragement of Ahab.

When I acknowledged defeat and cried for quarter, my Father would become radiant, and I still seem to hear the sound of his full voice, so thrilling, so warm, so painful to my overstrained nerves, bursting forth in a sort of benediction at the end of each of these one-sided contentions, with 'I bow my knees unto the Father of our Lord Jesus Christ, that He would grant you, according to the riches of His glory, to be strengthened with might by His Spirit in the inner man; that Christ may dwell in your heart by faith; that you, being rooted and grounded in love, may be able to comprehend with all saints what is the breadth, and length, and depth, and height, and to know the love of Christ which passeth knowledge, that you might be filled with the fullness of God.'

Thus solemn and thus ceremonious was my Father apt to become, without a moment's warning, on plain and domestic occasions; abruptly brimming over with emotion like a basin which an unseen flow of water has filled and over-filled.

I earnestly desire that no trace of that absurd self-pity which is apt to taint recollections of this nature should give falsity to mine. My Father, let me say once more, had other interests than those of his religion. In particular, at this time, he took to painting in water- colours in the open air, and he resumed the assiduous study of botany. He was no fanatical monomaniac. Nevertheless, there was, in everything he did and said, the central purpose present. He acknowledged it plainly; 'with me,' he confessed, 'every question assumes a Divine standpoint and is not adequately answered if the judgement-seat of Christ is not kept in sight.'

This was maintained whether the subject under discussion was poetry, or society, or the Prussian war with Austria, or the stamen of a wild flower. Once, at least, he was himself conscious of the fatiguing effect on my temper of this insistency, for, raising his great brown eyes with a flash of laughter in them, he closed the Bible suddenly after a very lengthy disquisition, and quoted his Virgil to startling effect:—

Claudite jam rivos, pueri: Sat prata biberunt.

The insistency of his religious conversation was, probably, the less incomprehensible to me on account of the evangelical training to which I had been so systematically subjected. It was, however, none the less intolerably irksome, and would have been exasperating, I believe, even to a nature in which a powerful and genuine piety was inherent. To my own, in which a feeble and imitative faith was expiring, it was deeply vexatious. It led, alas! to a great deal of bowing in the house of Rimmon, to much hypocritical ingenuity in drawing my Father's attention away, if possible, as the terrible subject was seen to be looming and approaching. In this my stepmother would aid and abet, sometimes producing incongruous themes, likely to attract my Father aside, with a skill worthy of a parlour conjurer, and much to my admiration. If, however, she was not unwilling to come, in this way, to the support of my feebleness, there was no open collusion between us. She always described my Father, when she was alone with me, admiringly, as one 'whose trumpet gave no uncertain sound'. There was not a tinge of infidelity upon her candid mind, but she was human, and I think that now and then she was extremely bored.

My Father was entirely devoid of the prudence which turns away its eyes and passes as rapidly as possible in the opposite direction. The peculiar kind of drama in which every sort of social discomfort is welcomed rather than that the characters should be happy when guilty of 'acting a lie', was not invented in those days, and there can hardly be imagined a figure more remote from my Father than Ibsen. Yet when I came, at a far later date, to read *The Wild Duck*, memories of the embarrassing household of my infancy helped me to realize Gregers Werle, with his determination to pull the veil of illusion away from every compromise that makes life bearable.

I was docile, I was plausible, I was anything but combative; if my Father could have persuaded himself to let me alone, if he could merely have been willing to leave my subterfuges and my explanations unanalysed, all would have been well. But he refused to see any difference in temperament between a lad of twenty and a sage of sixty. He had no vital sympathy for youth, which in itself had no charm for him. He had no compassion for the weaknesses of immaturity, and his one and only anxiety was to be at the end of his spiritual journey, safe with me in the house where there are many mansions. The incidents of human life upon the road to glory were less than nothing to him.

My Father was very fond of defining what was his own attitude at this time, and he was never tired of urging the same ambition upon me. He regarded himself as the faithful steward of a Master who might return at any moment, and who would require to find everything ready for his convenience. That master was God, with whom my Father seriously believed himself to be in relations much more confidential than those vouchsafed to ordinary pious persons. He awaited, with anxious hope, 'the coming of the Lord', an event which he still frequently believed to be imminent. He would calculate, by reference to prophecies in the Old and New Testament, the exact date of this event; the date would pass, without the expected Advent, and he would be more than disappointed,—he would be incensed. Then he would understand that he must have made some slight error in calculation, and the pleasures of anticipation would recommence.

Me in all this he used as a kind of inferior coadjutor, much as a responsible and upper servant might use a footboy. I, also, must be watching; it was not important that I should be seriously engaged in any affairs of my own. I must be ready for the Master's coming; and my Father's incessant cross-examination was made in the spirit of a responsible servant who fidgets lest some humble but essential piece of household work has been neglected.

My holidays, however, and all my personal relations with my Father were poisoned by this insistency. I was never at my ease in his company; I never knew when I might not be subjected to a series of searching questions which I should not be allowed to evade. Meanwhile, on every other stage of experience I was gaining the reliance upon self and the respect for the opinion of others which come naturally to a young man of sober habits who earns his own living and lives his own life. For this kind of independence my Father had no respect or consideration, when questions of religion were introduced, although he handsomely conceded it on other points. And now first there occurred to me the reflection, which in years to come I was to repeat over and over, with an ever sadder emphasis,—what a charming companion, what a delightful parent, what a courteous and engaging friend my Father would have been, and would pre-eminently have been to me, if it had not been for this stringent piety which ruined it all.

Let me speak plainly. After my long experience, after my patience and forbearance, I have surely the right to protest against the untruth (would that I could apply to it any other word!) that evangelical religion, or any religion in a violent form, is a wholesome or valuable or desirable adjunct to human life. It divides heart from heart. It sets up a vain, chimerical ideal, in the barren pursuit of which all the tender, indulgent affections, all the genial play of life, all the exquisite pleasures and soft resignations of the body, all that enlarges and calms the soul are exchanged for what is harsh and void and negative. It encourages a stern and ignorant spirit of condemnation; it throws altogether out of gear the healthy movement of the conscience; it invents virtues which are sterile and cruel; it invents sins which are no sins at all, but which darken the heaven of innocent joy with futile clouds of remorse. There is something horrible, if we will bring ourselves to face it, in the fanaticism that can do nothing with this pathetic and fugitive existence of ours but treat it as if it were the uncomfortable ante-chamber to a palace which no one has explored and of the plan of which we know absolutely nothing. My Father, it is true, believed that he was intimately acquainted with the form and furniture of this habitation, and he wished me to think of nothing else but of the advantages of an eternal residence in it.

Then came a moment when my self-sufficiency revolted against the police-inspection to which my 'views' were incessantly subjected. There was a morning, in the hot-house at home, among the gorgeous waxen orchids which reminded my Father of the tropics in his youth, when my forbearance or my timidity gave way. The enervated air, soaked with the intoxicating perfumes of all those voluptuous flowers, may have been partly responsible for my outburst. My Father had once more put to me the customary interrogatory. Was I 'walking closely with God'? Was my sense of the efficacy of the Atonement clear and sound? Had the Holy Scriptures still their full authority with me? My replies on this occasion were violent and hysterical. I have no clear recollection what it was that I said,—I desire not to recall the whimpering sentences in which I begged to be let alone, in which I demanded the right to think for myself, in which I repudiated the idea that my Father was responsible to God for my secret thoughts and my most intimate convictions.

He made no answer; I broke from the odorous furnace of the conservatory, and buried my face in the cold grass upon the lawn. My visit to Devonshire, already near its close, was hurried to an end. I had scarcely arrived in London before the following letter, furiously despatched in the track of the fugitive, buried itself like an arrow in my heart:

When your sainted Mother died, she not only tenderly committed you to God, but left you also as a solemn charge to me, to bring you up in the nurture and admonition of the Lord. That responsibility I have sought constantly to keep before me: I can truly aver that it *has* been ever before me—in my choice of a housekeeper, in my choice of a school, in my ordering of your holidays, in my choice of a second wife, in my choice of an occupation for you, in my choice of a residence for you; and in multitudes of lesser things—I have sought to act for you, not in the light of this present world, but with a view to Eternity.

Before your childhood was past, there seemed God's manifest blessing on our care; for you seemed truly converted to Him; you confessed, in solemn baptism, that you had died and had been raised with Christ; and you were received with joy into the bosom of the Church of God, as one alive from the dead.

All this filled my heart with thankfulness and joy, whenever I thought of you:—how could it do otherwise? And when I left you in London, on that dreary winter evening, my heart, full of sorrowing love, found its refuge and its resource in this thought,—that you were one of the lambs of Christ's flock; sealed with the Holy Spirit as His; renewed in heart to holiness, in the image of God.

For a while, all appeared to go on fairly well: we yearned, indeed, to discover more of heart in your allusions to religious matters, but your expressions towards us were filial and affectionate; your conduct, so far as we could see, was moral and becoming; you mingled with the people of God, spoke of occasional delight and profit in His ordinances; and employed your talents in service to Him.

But of late, and specially during the past year, there has become manifest a rapid progress towards evil. (I must beg you here to pause, and again to look to God for grace to weigh what I am about to say; or else wrath will rise.)

When you came to us in the summer, the heavy blow fell full upon me; and I discovered how very far you had departed from God. It was not that you had yielded to the strong tide of youthful blood, and had fallen a victim to fleshly lusts; in that case, however sad, your enlightened conscience would have spoken loudly, and you would have found your way back to the blood which cleanseth us from all sin, to humble confession and self- abasement, to forgiveness and to recommunion with God. It was not this; it was worse. It was that horrid, insidious infidelity, which had already worked in your mind and heart with terrible energy. Far worse, I say, because this was sapping the very foundations of faith, on which all true godliness, all real religion, must rest.

Nothing seemed left to which I could appeal. We had, I found, no common ground. The Holy Scriptures had no longer any authority: you had taught yourself to evade their inspiration. Any particular Oracle of God which pressed you, you could easily explain away; even the very character of God you weighed in your balance of fallen reason, and fashioned it accordingly. You were thus sailing down the rapid tide of time towards Eternity, without a single authoritative guide (having cast your chart overboard), except what you might fashion and forge on your own anvil,—except what you might *guess*, in fact.

Do not think I am speaking in passion, and using unwarrantable strength of words. If the written Word is not absolutely authoritative, what do we know of God? What more than we can infer, that is, guess,—as the thoughtful heathens guessed,—Plato, Socrates, Cicero,—from dim and mute surrounding phenomena? What do we know of Eternity? Of our relations to God? Especially of the relations of a *sinner* to God? What of reconciliation? What of the capital question—How can a God of perfect spotless rectitude deal with me, a corrupt sinner, who have trampled on those of His laws which were even written on my conscience? . . .

This dreadful conduct of yours I had intended, after much prayer, to pass by in entire silence; but your apparently sincere inquiries after the cause of my sorrow have led me to go to the root of the matter, and I could not stop short of the development contained in this letter. It is with pain, not in anger, that I send it; hoping that you may be induced to review the whole course, of which this is only a stage, before God. If this grace were granted to you, oh! how joyfully should I bury all the past, and again have sweet and tender fellowship with my beloved Son, as of old.

The reader who has done me the favour to follow this record of the clash of two temperaments will not fail to perceive the crowning importance of the letter from which I have just made a long quotation. It sums up, with the closer logic, the whole history of the situation, and I may leave it to form the epigraph of this little book.

All that I need further say is to point out that when such defiance is offered to the intelligence of a thoughtful and honest young man with the normal impulses of his twenty-one years, there are but two alternatives. Either he must cease to think for himself; or his individualism must be instantly confirmed, and the necessity of religious independence must be emphasized.

No compromise, it is seen, was offered; no proposal of a truce would have been acceptable. It was a case of 'Everything or Nothing'; and thus desperately challenged, the young man's conscience threw off once for all the yoke of his 'dedication', and, as respectfully as he could, without parade or remonstrance, he took a human being's privilege to fashion his inner life for himself.

THOMAS HARDY

On November 14, 1907, Thomas Hardy wrote a brief note to his old friend Edmund Gosse to tell him he had just finished reading Father and Son *and that he thought it "Very striking & unique; & beautifully told." Ten years after writing these words, and some fifteen years after the death of his own father, the now 76-year-old Hardy published "To My Father's Violin." Though the introduction to this anthology hails Gosse as father of the patremoir, and as having made possible the writing of candid essays and poems about fathers, Hardy would almost certainly have written a similar poem even if Gosse's book had never been published. After all, many of Hardy's best poems, poems such as "Old Furniture" or "Logs on the Hearth," use objects or settings to unlock strong emotional associations. Many, too, use simple language, tight rhyme schemes, and classical or literary allusions to maintain dignity and reserve while revealing personal feelings. While the complexity of rhyme and meter in "My Father's Violin," with the interplay between the quick trimeter lines and the longer pentameter, serves to heighten the contrast between the "psalm of duty" and the "trill of pleasure," much of the poem's power comes from the way Thomas Hardy son and poet overlaps with Thomas Hardy musician and father. The father's music lives on in the aging son's poem. The "tangled wreck" of the strings is reminiscent of the "Darkling Thrush" in which "The tangled bine-stems scored the sky / Like strings of broken lyres." Even if no bird "thrills the shades" in "My Father's Violin," the aging, childless Hardy—remembering his father and contemplating mortality—becomes his own darkling thrush. Incidentally, the violin described in this poem was restored by John Dike of Sherborne in 1988 and was used by the Yetties to record music loved and played by Hardy and his father. The recording, still available, is entitled "The Musical Heritage of Thomas Hardy," and the violin now rests in the Dorset County Museum.*

TO MY FATHER'S VIOLIN

Does he want you down there
In the Nether Glooms where
The hours may be a dragging load upon him,
As he hears the axle grind
Round and round
Of the great world, in the blind
Still profound
Of the night-time? He might liven at the sound
Of your string, revealing you had not forgone him.

In the gallery west the nave,
But a few yards from his grave,
Did you, tucked beneath his chin, to his bowing
Guide the homely harmony
Of the quire
Who for long years strenuously -
Son and sire -
Caught the strains that at his fingering low or higher
From your four thin threads and eff-holes came outflowing.

And, too, what merry tunes
He would bow at nights or noons
That chanced to find him bent to lute a measure,
When he made you speak his heart
As in dream,
Without book or music-chart,
On some theme
Elusive as a jack-o'-lanthorn's gleam,
And the psalm of duty shelved for trill of pleasure.

Well, you can not, alas,
The barrier overpass
That screens him in those Mournful Meads hereunder,
Where no fiddling can be heard
In the glades
Of silentness, no bird
Thrills the shades;
Where no viol is touched for songs or serenades,
No bowing wakes a congregation's wonder.

He must do without you now,
Stir you no more anyhow
To yearning concords taught you in your glory;
While, your strings a tangled wreck,
Once smart drawn,
Ten worm-wounds in your neck,
Purflings wan
With dust-hoar, here alone I sadly con
Your present dumbness, shape your olden story.

E.B. WHITE

Despite its romantic wealth of nostalgic detail and loving tenderness, this is the most masculine essay in this anthology. "Once More to the Lake" celebrates the father-son relationship, and mother and daughter have no place in this communion. This is an essay for all good Christians to ponder, an essay to help them rethink the relationship between God the Father, God the Son, and God the Holy Ghost. White is the Holy Ghost of this essay, the "I" straddling the Father and the Son. To approach the piece from a devilishly different direction, White is also a Shakespearean witch who shows us the succession of generations, "the line stretched out to the crack of doom." Particulars such as "the dead helgramite, the wisps of moss, the rusty fishhook, the dried blood of yesterday's catch" are powerful ingredients in an incantation to annihilate time and reveal deeper truths. Norman Rockwell on the surface, White has Edward Hopper depths. Not surprisingly, this is one of the most anthologized— one of the most deservedly anthologized—essays in the English language.

ONCE MORE TO THE LAKE

One summer, along about 1904, my father rented a camp on a lake in Maine and took us all there for the month of August. We all got ringworm from some kittens and had to rub Pond's Extract on our arms and legs night and morning, and my father rolled over in a canoe with all his clothes on; but outside of that the vacation was a success and from then on none of us ever thought there was any place in the world like that lake in Maine. We returned summer after summer—always on August 1st for one month. I have since become a salt-water man, but sometimes in summer there are days when the restlessness of the tides and the fearful cold of the sea water and the incessant wind which blows across the afternoon and into the evening make me wish for the placidity of a lake in the woods. A few weeks ago this feeling got so strong I bought myself a couple of bass hooks and a spinner and returned to the lake where we used to go, for a week's fishing and to revisit old haunts.

I took along my son, who had never had any fresh water up his nose and who had seen lily pads only from train windows. On the journey over to the lake I began to wonder what it would be like. I wondered how time would have marred this unique, this holy spot—the coves and streams, the hills that the sun set behind, the camps and the paths behind the camps. I was sure that the tarred road would have found it out and I wondered in what other ways it would be desolated. It is strange how much you can remember about places like that once you allow your mind to return into the grooves which lead back. You remember one thing, and that suddenly reminds you of another thing. I guess I remembered clearest of all the early mornings, when the lake was cool and motionless, remembered how the bedroom smelled of the lumber it was made of and of the wet woods whose scent entered through the screen. The partitions in the camp were thin and did not extend clear to the top of the rooms, and as I was always the first up I would dress softly so as not to wake the others, and sneak out into the sweet outdoors and start out in the canoe, keeping close along the shore in the long shadows of the pines. I remembered being very careful never to rub my paddle against the gunwale for fear of disturbing the stillness of the cathedral.

The lake had never been what you would call a wild lake. There were cottages sprinkled around the shores, and it was in farming country although the shores of the lake were quite heavily wooded. Some of the cottages were owned by nearby farmers, and you would live at the shore and eat your meals at the farmhouse. That's what our family did. But although it wasn't wild, it was a fairly large and undisturbed lake and there were places in it which, to a child at least, seemed infinitely remote and primeval.

I was right about the tar: it led to within half a mile of the shore. But when I got back there, with my boy, and we settled into a camp near a farmhouse and into the kind of summertime I had known, I could tell that it was going to be pretty much the same as it had been before—I knew it, lying in bed the first morning, smelling the bedroom, and hearing the boy sneak quietly out and go off along the shore in a boat. I began to sustain the illusion that he was I, and therefore, by simple transposition, that I was my father. This sensation persisted, kept cropping up all the time we were there. It was not an entirely new feeling, but in this setting it grew much stronger. I seemed to be living a dual existence. I would be in the middle of some simple act, I would be picking up a bait box or laying down a table fork, or I would be saying something, and suddenly it would be not I but my father who was saying the words or making the gesture. It gave me a creepy sensation.

We went fishing the first morning. I felt the same damp moss covering the worms in the bait can, and saw the dragonfly alight on the tip of my rod as it hovered a few inches from the surface of the water. It was the arrival of this fly that convinced me beyond any doubt that everything was as it always had been, that the years were a mirage and there had been no years. The small waves were the same, chucking the rowboat under the chin as we fished at anchor, and the boat was the same boat, the same color green and the ribs broken in the same places, and under the floor-boards the same freshwater leavings and débris—the dead helgramite, the wisps of moss, the rusty discarded fishhook, the dried blood from yesterday's catch. We stared silently at the tips of our rods, at the dragonflies that came and went. I lowered the tip of mine into the water, tentatively, pensively dislodging the fly, which darted two feet away, poised, darted two feet back, and came to rest again a little farther up the rod. There had been no years between the ducking of this dragonfly and the other one—the one that was part of memory. I looked at the boy, who was silently watching his fly, and it was my hands that held his rod, my eyes watching. I felt dizzy and didn't know which rod I was at the end of.

We caught two bass, hauling them in briskly as though they were mackerel, pulling them over the side of the boat in a businesslike manner without any landing net, and stunning them with a blow on the back of the head. When we got back for a swim before lunch, the lake was exactly where we had left it, the same number of inches from the dock, and there was only the merest suggestion of a breeze. This seemed an utterly enchanted sea, this lake you could leave to its own devices for a few hours and come back to, and find that it had not stirred, this constant and trustworthy body of water. In the shallows, the dark, water-soaked sticks and twigs, smooth and old, were undulating in clusters on the bottom against the clean ribbed sand, and the track of the mussel was plain. A school of minnows swam by, each minnow with its small, individual shadow, doubling the attendance, so clear and sharp in the sunlight. Some of the other campers were in swimming, along the shore, one of them with a cake of soap, and the water felt thin and clear and insubstantial. Over the years there had been this person with the cake of soap, this cultist, and here he was. There had been no years.

Up to the farmhouse to dinner through the teeming, dusty field, the road under our sneakers was only a two-track road. The middle track was missing, the one with the marks of the hooves and the splotches of dried, flaky manure. There had always been three tracks to choose from in choosing which track to walk in; now the choice was narrowed down to two. For a moment I missed terribly the middle alternative. But the way led past the tennis court, and something about the way it lay there in the sun reassured me; the tape had loosened along the backline, the alleys were green with plantains and other weeds, and the net (installed in June and removed in September) sagged in the dry noon, and the whole place steamed with midday heat and hunger and emptiness. There was a choice of pie for dessert, and one was blueberry and one was apple, and the waitresses were the same country girls, there having been no passage of time, only the illusion of it as in a dropped curtain—the waitresses were still fifteen; their hair had been washed, that was the only difference—they had been to the movies and seen the pretty girls with the clean hair.

Summertime, oh summertime, pattern of life indelible, the fade proof lake, the woods unshatterable, the pasture with the sweet fern and the juniper forever and ever, summer without end; this was the background, and the life along the shore was the design, the cottages with their innocent and tranquil design, their tiny docks with the flagpole and the American flag floating against the white clouds in the blue sky, the little paths over the roots of the trees leading from camp to camp and the paths leading back to the outhouses and the can of lime for sprinkling, and at the souvenir counters at the store the miniature birch-bark canoes and the post cards that showed things looking a little better than they looked. This was the American family at play, escaping the city heat, wondering whether the newcomers at the camp at the head of the cove were "common" or "nice," wondering whether it was true that the people who drove up for Sunday dinner at the farmhouse were turned away because there wasn't enough chicken.

It seemed to me, as I kept remembering all this, that those times and those summers had been infinitely precious and worth saving. There had been jollity and peace and goodness. The arriving (at the beginning of August) had been so big a business in itself, at the railway station the farm wagon drawn up, the first smell of the pine-laden air, the first glimpse of the smiling farmer, and the great importance of the trunks and your father's enormous authority in such matters, and the feel of the wagon under you for the long ten-mile haul, and at the top of the last long hill catching the first view of the lake after eleven months of not seeing this cherished body of water. The shouts and cries of the other campers when they saw you, and the trunks to be unpacked, to give up their rich burden. (Arriving was less exciting nowadays, when you sneaked up in your car and parked it under a tree near the camp and took out the bags and in five minutes it was all over, no fuss, no loud wonderful fuss about trunks.)

Peace and goodness and jollity. The only thing that was wrong now, really, was the sound of the place, an unfamiliar nervous sound of the outboard motors. This was the note that jarred, the one thing that would sometimes break the illusion and set the years moving. In those other summertimes, all motors were inboard; and when they were at a little distance, the noise they made was a sedative, an ingredient of summer sleep. They were one-cylinder and two-cylinder engines, and some were make-and-break and some were jump-spark, but they all made a sleepy sound across the lake. The one-lungers throbbed and fluttered, and the twin-cylinder ones purred and purred, and that was a quiet sound too. But now the campers all had outboards. In the daytime, in the hot mornings, these motors made a petulant, irritable sound; at night, in the still evening when the afterglow lit the water, they whined about one's ears like mosquitoes. My boy loved our rented outboard, and his great desire was to achieve single-handed mastery over it, and authority, and he soon learned the trick of choking it a little (but not too much), and the adjustment of the needle valve. Watching him I would remember the things you could do with the old one-cylinder engine with the heavy flywheel, how you could have it eating out of your hand if you got really close to it spiritually. Motor boats in those days didn't have clutches, and you would make a landing by shutting off the motor at the proper time and coasting in with a dead rudder. But there was a way of reversing them, if you learned the trick, by cutting the switch and putting it on again exactly on the final dying revolution of the flywheel, so that it would kick back against compression and begin reversing. Approaching a dock in a strong following breeze, it was difficult to slow up sufficiently by the ordinary coasting method, and if a boy felt he had complete mastery over his motor, he was tempted to keep it running beyond its time and then reverse it a few feet from the dock. It took a cool nerve, because if you threw the switch a twentieth of a second too soon you would catch the flywheel when it still had speed enough to go up past center, and the boat would leap ahead, charging bull-fashion at the dock.

We had a good week at the camp. The bass were biting well and the sun shone endlessly, day after day. We would be tired at night and lie down in the accumulated heat of the little bedrooms after the long hot day and the breeze would stir almost imperceptibly outside and the smell of the swamp drift in through the rusty screens. Sleep would come easily and in the morning the red squirrel would be on the roof, tapping out his gay routine. I kept remembering everything, lying in bed in the mornings—the small steamboat that had a long rounded stern like the lip of a Ubangi, and how quietly she ran on the moonlight sails, when the older boys played their mandolins and the girls sang and we ate doughnuts dipped in sugar, and how sweet the music was on the water in the shining night, and what it had felt like to think about girls then. After breakfast we would go up to the store and the things were in the same place—the minnows in a bottle, the plugs and spinners disarranged and pawed over by the youngsters from the boys' camp, the fig newtons and the Beeman's gum. Outside, the road was tarred and cars stood in front of the store. Inside, all was just as it had always been, except there was more Coca-Cola and not so much Moxie and root beer and birch beer and sarsaparilla. We would walk out with a bottle of pop apiece and sometimes the pop would backfire up our noses and hurt. We explored the streams, quietly, where the turtles slid off the sunny logs and dug their way into the soft bottom; and we lay on the town wharf and fed worms to the tame bass. Everywhere we went I had trouble making out which was I, the one walking at my side, the one walking in my pants.

One afternoon while we were there at that lake a thunderstorm came up. It was like the revival of an old melodrama that I had seen long ago with childish awe. The second-act climax of the drama of the electrical disturbance over a lake in America had not changed in any important respect. This was the big scene, still the big scene. The whole thing was so familiar, the first feeling of oppression and heat and a general air around camp of not wanting to go very far away. In midafternoon (it was all the same) a curious darkening of the sky, and a lull in everything that had made life tick; and then the way the boats suddenly swung the other way at their moorings with the coming of a breeze out of the new quarter, and the premonitory rumble. Then the kettle drum, then the snare, then the bass drum and cymbals, then crackling light against the dark, and the gods grinning and licking their chops in the hills. Afterward the calm, the rain steadily rustling in the calm lake, the return of light and hope and spirits, and the campers running out in joy and relief to go swimming in the rain, their bright cries perpetuating the deathless joke about how they were getting simply drenched, and the children screaming with delight at the new sensation of bathing in the rain, and the joke about getting drenched linking the generations in a strong indestructible chain. And the comedian who waded in carrying an umbrella.

When the others went swimming my son said he was going in too. He pulled his dripping trunks from the line where they had hung all through the shower, and wrung them out. Languidly, and with no thought of going in, I watched him, his hard little body, skinny and bare, saw him wince slightly as he pulled up around his vitals the small, soggy, icy garment. As he buckled the swollen belt suddenly my groin felt the chill of death.

JOHN BERRYMAN

In "Dream Song 384," Berryman opposes puns and allusiveness to tragedy and stark horror. This, the penultimate of Berryman's Dream Songs, returns to the first dream song, in which Henry, one of Berryman's alter egos, struggles with the consequences of his father's suicide. In "384" we see Henry "heft the ax once more, his final card, / and fell it on the start." "Fell" is evil, as well as the past of fall. Poetry is Berryman's ax, and with it he shapes his own father's suicide as both productive and destructive. "384" skilfully echoes the Civil War classic, "John Brown's Body," and John Smith's body becomes one with John Brown, who "lies a-mouldering in the grave / but his soul goes marching on." To "tear apart / the mouldering grave clothes" is to try to free himself from the molding confines of his father's suicide. However, one reading of "the start" is Berryman himself, and punning logic also makes "384" a suicide note. Berryman/Henry uses the play of language and of poetry in his wish to scrabble scribble right down and bury himself under the obscuring surfaces of life and death. Yet in the Dream Song sequence, the final card or final song which Berryman lets fall upon the start is "Dream Song 385," which begins and ends with his daughter, "my heavy daughter." What better ax to let fall on his father's suicide, what better rebuttal, than the growth of his daughter! The rebuttal is all the more powerful in that while the daughter can be seen as real—Martha Berryman, born December 2, 1962—she is also symbolic of the heavy leaves of the Dream Songs themselves. Poetry and fathering are answers to the father's mortality; never mind that Berryman himself committed suicide on January 7th, 1972, just six and a half months after the birth of a second daughter.

DREAM SONG 384

The marker slants, flowerless, day's almost done,
I stand above my father's grave with rage,
often, often before
I've made this awful pilgrimage to one
who cannot visit me, who tore his page
out: I come back for more,

I spit upon this dreadful banker's grave
who shot his heart out in a Florida dawn
O ho alas alas
When will indifference come, I moan & rave
I'd like to scrabble till I got right down
away down under the grass

and ax the casket open ha to see
just how he's taking it, which he sought so hard
we'll tear apart
the mouldering grave clothes ha & then Henry
will heft the ax once more, his final card,
and fell it on the start.

FRANZ KAFKA

The pages that follow are only the first 17 of a 47-page scream. Kafka was 36 years old when he wrote this document, and his father was 67. Supposedly a letter to the father, it is thought never to have been delivered, though Kafka did give it to his mother and also shared it with Milena Jesenská, the young Czech translator of his work with whom he developed an intimate correspondence and relationship shortly after the letter was written. Kafka biographer Friedrich Karl has pointed out how this letter "must not be viewed as a 'letter' . . . but as a fictional representation of Kafka's perceptions." This document is a true Montaigne essaie, an exploration of human nature, an attempt to know or shape oneself, and as such, it should perhaps be read with this Montaigne dictum in mind: "I have never seen a greater monster or miracle than myself." In this letter Kafka reveals himself as a monster of neediness, a miracle of introspection. The relentless sense of grievance, the constant recrimination, the incessant whining would be easy to dismiss as raw hysteria if the consummate artistry of the letter weren't so evident. The letter, as Kafka wrote to Milena, is also a "lawyer's letter," full of "lawyer's tricks." It is a courtroom in which Kafka puts his father on trial, and acts as prosecuting attorney, judge, jury, and sentence. In this Kafkaesque trial, the very composition of the letter itself becomes the most damning piece of evidence, and in the end Kafka's father is convicted of the crime of having made Kafka who he is by not appreciating who he was. Perhaps Montaigne again supplies the best explanation for this tortuous piece of logic: "My life has been filled with terrible misfortune; most of which never happened."

LETTER TO HIS FATHER

Dearest Father,

You recently asked me why I claim to fear you. As usual, I didn't know what to answer you, partly because of the fear I have of you, partly because this fear is grounded in too many particulars for me to state even half of them coherently. And even this attempt to answer you in writing will be very incomplete because this fear and its consequences hinder me and because the scope of the undertaking greatly exceeds my thoughts and understanding.

The matter has always seemed very simple to you, at least as far as you've spoken about it to me and—indiscriminately—to many others. To you, things seem somewhat as follows: you've worked hard all your life for your children, for me above all, and consequently I have lived in the lap of luxury, with complete freedom to learn whatever I wanted, without having to worry about food or anything else. You haven't demanded gratitude for this, knowing the thanklessness of children, but hoped at least for some response, some sign of sympathy; instead of which, I have always withdrawn, to my room, my books, my crazy friends, my farfetched ideas; I've never talked to you openly, I never came to you in the Temple, I never visited you in Franzensbad, never had a sense of family, never worried about the business or any of your other concerns; I burdened you with the factory and then abandoned you, I supported Ottla in her willfulness and while I won't even lift a finger for you (I don't even get you theatre tickets), I'll do anything for my friends. When you muster your judgment against me, it seems that you don't exactly reproach me anything inappropriate or wicked (with the possible exception of my recent intentions of marriage), except coldness, distance, and ingratitude. And you even make your reproaches as if it were my fault, as if I could have steered everything differently, while you are completely faultless, other than of having been too good to me.

I only believe this usual interpretation of yours to be true insofar as I too believe that you are totally blameless in our estrangement. However, I am equally blameless. If I could bring you to recognize this, then it would be possible to have—not perhaps a new life, as we are both much too old for that, but at least a kind of truce—not a cessation, but at least a softening of your endless reproaches.

Remarkably, you have some kind of inkling of what I want to say. For example, you recently told me, "I always liked you, even if outwardly I didn't behave towards you as other fathers tend to do, exactly because I can't pretend the way others do." Well, father, on the whole I have never doubted your kindness towards me, but I do hold this observation to be incorrect. You can't pretend, that's true, but only on this basis to maintain that other fathers dissemble is either pure, indiscussable righteousness or it is—and this is what I really believe it to be—the cloaked expression of the fact that something is wrong between us, and that you have unwittingly contributed to this situation. If you truly mean this, then we are in agreement.

Naturally, I'm not saying that I am who I am only because of your influence. That would be severe exaggeration (and I am inclined to this exaggeration). It is very easily possible that I, even if I had grown up totally free of your influence, still could not have became a man after your own heart. I probably still would have become a weak, fearful, hesitant, restless person, neither Robert Kafka not Karl Herman, but still completely other than I am now, and we could have gotten along wonderfully well. I would have been happy to have you as friend, boss, uncle, grandfather, or even (though more hesitantly) as step-father. Only as father were you too strong for me, especially as my brothers died young, my sisters only arrived long after, and therefore I had to sustain the first shock all alone, for which I was much too weak.

Compare the two of us: I, to express things concisely, am a Lowy with a certain Kafka core, which however is not set in motion by the

Kafka drive for life, business and conquest, rather by a Lowy impulse which works more secretly and shyly in another direction and often even fails. You, on the other hand, a true Kafka in strength, health, appetite, loudness, eloquence, self-satisfaction, confidence, stamina, presence of mind, knowledge of people, a certain largesse; naturally also with all the flaws and weaknesses which belong to these advantages and into which your temperament and your irascibility sometimes drive you. Compared to Uncles Philip, Ludwig, and Heinrich, you are, as far as I can determine, perhaps not quite a Kafka in your general world view. That is surprising, and here also I don't quite see clearly. After all, they were all merrier, fresher, more natural, more easygoing, and less severe than you. (Besides, in this I have also inherited a lot from you, maintaining the inheritance far too well, without however, as you do, having the necessary counterweights in my Nature.) On the other hand, you too have undergone various difficult times in this regard. You were maybe happier before your children, me in particular, disappointed and depressed you at home (when visitors came, you were certainly different), and perhaps you have again become happier, now that the grandchildren and your son-in-law give you some of that love which your children, even Valli possibly, couldn't give. Anyhow, we were so different and this difference was so mutually dangerous that if anyone had wanted to calculate how I, the slowly developing child and you, the finished man, would relate to each other, they would have had to assume that you would simply crush me so that nothing of me would remain. That simply hasn't happened—life can't be calculated—but maybe worse has happened. In saying this I continue to ask you not to forget that I never in the slightest believe in a fault on your part. You acted on me as you had to act, but you must stop maintaining it a particular vice in me that I succumbed to this action.

I was an anxious child; despite that, I was also certainly stubborn, as children are. Certainly Mother also spoiled me, but I can't believe that

I was particularly hard to manage; I can't believe that a friendly word, a quiet taking by the hand, a kind glance couldn't have exacted from me everything wanted. Now you are basically a good and gentle man (the following won't contradict that, as I am only talking about how you appeared to the child). But not every child has the stamina and the fearlessness to seek long enough to reach the kindness. You can only handle a child the way you yourself are constituted, with force, noise and temper, and in this case it also seemed to you to be very suitable because you wanted to raise a strong, brave, young man.

Naturally I can't now describe your earliest child raising methods directly, but I can somewhat imagine them by referring to later years and also to your treatment of Felix. What sharpens the impression is that you were younger then, therefore fresher, wilder, more primitive, and less preoccupied than you are now, and that as well you were completely tied to the business, and could hardly show yourself to me once a day, and therefore made a much deeper impression on me, one hardly ever smoothed to habit.

I only have a direct memory of one incident from the early years. You may remember it, too. Once in the night I whimpered continually for water, certainly not out of thirst, probably instead partly to annoy, partly to entertain myself. After a few strong threats hadn't helped, you took me out of bed, carried me to the balcony, and let me stand there a while, in front of the closed door, alone in my nightshirt. I won't say this was wrong—maybe there was really no other way of getting peace for the night—yet by this incident I want to characterize your educational methods and their effect on me. I was then afterwards certainly properly obedient, yet I was inwardly damaged. I could never properly connect the, for me, natural action of mindlessly begging for water and the extraordinary horror of being carried out. Years later, I still suffered from the torturing thought that the huge man, my father, the ultimate authority, might come in the night almost for no reason to take me from my bed out to the balcony, and that I therefore was such a nonentity for him.

That was only a small beginning, but the feeling of being nothing which often masters me (in other respects, also a noble and fruitful feeling) in many ways stems from your influence. I could have used a little encouragement, a little friendliness, a little clearing of my path, instead of which you blocked it for me, though of course with the good intention that I should go another way. But I wasn't suited to that. For example, when I saluted or marched briskly, you encouraged me, but I wasn't a future soldier; or you encouraged me when I was able to eat heartily or even drink beer with my food, or when I uncomprehendingly sang songs, or parroted your favourite expressions, but nothing of all that belonged to my future. And it is significant that even today you really only encourage me in something when you yourself are drawn into sympathy, when it concerns your own feelings, which I injure (for example, through my intentions to marry) or which are injured in me (when, for example, Pepa scolds me). Then I am encouraged, reminded of my worth, the matches I would be justified in making are pointed out, and Pepa is totally condemned. But even allowing for the fact that I am almost too old for encouragement, of what use is it when it is only given when it really isn't about me?

At that time, and particularly at that time, I could have used the encouragement. I was already oppressed by your sheer physical presence. I remember, for example, how we often undressed together in a bath hut. I scrawny, weak, small, you strong, big and large. Already in the hut, I felt myself to be pitiable, and not just in front of you, but in front of the whole world, for you were to me the measure of all things. If we then stepped out of the hut and in front of people, I holding on to your hand, a small skeleton, insecure, barefoot on the boards, in fear of the water, incapable of imitating your strokes, which you indeed with the best of intentions, but to my deepest shame, always demonstrated, then I despaired greatly and in such moments all my bad experiences in all disciplines combined massively together. I felt best when you sometimes undressed first, and I could stay alone in the hut and delay the shame of the public appearance, until finally you came to check up on me and drove me out of the hut. I was grateful to you for not seeming to notice my distress, and I was also proud of my father's body. Moreover, this difference still exists between us in a similar way today.

Further, your intellectual domination followed from this: you had raised yourself so high through you own efforts, and consequently you had an unlimited trust in your own opinion. As a child this was not nearly as blinding for me, as it was later on as a developing young man. You ruled the world from your armchair. Your opinion was right, every other opinion was crazy, farfetched, *meshugge*, not normal. And with that, your self-confidence was so great that you didn't need to be consistent, and you would still not cease from being right. It could also happen that you had absolutely no opinion on a topic, and consequently all possible opinions on the subject had, without exception, to be false. You could, for instance, complain about the Czechs, then the Germans, then the Jews, and not just in specifics but in every respect, and finally nobody else was left except you. You became for me the conundrum of all tyrants whose rights are based on their person and not on reason. At least, it seemed so to me.

With respect to me you were, in fact, amazingly often right; not only, as was natural, in conversation, since it rarely came to conversation, yet also in reality. Even that wasn't particularly incomprehensible: I was after all in all my thinking under your heavy pressure, even in thinking, especially in thinking which did not coincide with yours. All these seemingly independent thoughts were from the very beginning burdened with your negative judgments; it was almost impossible to bear those until the complete and lasting expression of an idea. I'm not speaking here of any lofty, so much as any small childhood enterprise. One needed only to be happy about something, to be filled with it, to come, and to speak of it, and the answer was an ironic sigh, a head shaking, a tapping of the fingers on the table: "I've seen better," or "Wish I had your worries," or "My mind's not calm enough for that," or "What will that get you?" or "Big deal." Naturally, when you lived in stress and worry, I couldn't expect enthusiasm for every childish triviality. It was rather a matter of your repeatedly and thoroughly preparing such disappointments for a child because of your contradictory nature; further this contradictoriness was constantly strengthened by the piling up of examples so that it finally became habit; and even if for once you were of the same opinion as me, and even if these disappointments of the child were not disappointments of ordinary life, since they concerned you as the measure of all things, they struck to the core. Courage, determination, confidence, joy at this or that did not last when you were against it or even when your opposition could just be assumed, and it could be assumed at almost everything I did.

That applied to people as well as to thoughts. It was enough for me to have a little interest in someone—because of my nature this didn't happen very often—for you, without consideration for my feelings or respect for my opinions, to barge in with insults, calumnies, and denigration. Innocent, childish people, as for example the Yiddish actor Löwy, had to suffer that. Without knowing him, you compared him in a horrifying way, in a way I have already forgotten, to vermin, and as so often with people whom I liked, you automatically produced the proverb about the dog and its fleas. I particularly remember the actor now because at the time I noted your remarks about him as follows: "This is how my father speaks about my friend (whom he doesn't even know), only because he is my friend. I will always be able to hold this against him when he reproaches me with lack of filial love and gratitude." What was always incomprehensible to me was your total insensitivity as to the harm and shame you could create with your words and judgments, as if you had no conception of your power. I too have certainly often wounded you with words, but I always knew it and it hurt me that I couldn't control myself and withhold the words. I regretted them as I spoke. You, however, struck out with your words without ado; you felt sorry for no one, not during, not after, and one was defenceless against you.

But your whole method of upbringing was like that. You have, I believe, a talent for raising children; your methods would certainly have benefited a child which resembled you; it would have seen the sense of what you said; it would not have worried about anything else, and it would have quietly done what was asked. However, for me as a child everything you counseled was a direct command from Heaven; I never forgot it, and it remained the most important means of judging the world, above all of judging you, and there you failed utterly. Since I as a child was chiefly with you at meals, your teachings for the most part were lessons in tablemanners. What came to the table had to be eaten, and the quality of the meal could not be discussed—but you often found the meal unappetizing, called it "the swill," said the "cow" (the cook) had ruined it. Because you, according to your strong appetite and your particular likings, ate everything quickly, hot and in large bites, the child had to hurry; there was barren silence at table, broken by admonitions: "Eat first, then speak," "Faster, faster, faster," or "See, I finished long ago." Bones couldn't be chewed—except by you: vinegar couldn't be slurped—except by you. The main thing was to cut the bread straight; that you did so with a knife dripping with sauce was unimportant. One had to watch that no scraps fell on the floor; in the end, most lay under your chair. Only eating was allowed at table, but you cleaned and cut your nails, sharpened pencils, cleaned your ears with a toothpick. Please, father, understand me correctly: in themselves these were meaningless particulars. They only became depressing for me because you, the awesome measure of all things, did not yourself obey the commandments which you lay upon me. Through this the world for me became divided into three parts: one in which I, the slave, lived under laws which were only invented for me and which I, without knowing why, could never completely comply to; a second world, endlessly distant from mine, in which you lived, busy with ruling, with the issuing of decrees, and with the anger at lack of compliance; and finally a third world in which everyone else lived happily, free from orders and the need to obey. I was always in disgrace; if I followed your orders that was a disgrace, as they were after all only meant for me; if I was defiant that was a disgrace, because how could I dare defy you; or the biggest disgrace of all was if I failed to follow you, even though you took my compliance for granted, because, for instance, I lacked your strength, your appetite, your skill. In this fashion flowed not the thoughts but the feelings of the child.

My situation at the time becomes clearer, maybe, if I compare it with Felix's now. You also handle him in a similar fashion, even using a particularly frightening child rearing method against him, in which you, whenever he does something improper at meals, amuse yourself, as you did back then with me, by saying, "You're a big pig," and you also add, "A real Hermann," or "Exactly like your father." Now maybe—more than maybe can't be determined—this doesn't damage Felix essentially, because for him you happen to be only a particularly significant grandfather, yet not "everything" as you were for me; and besides, Felix has a calmer, already to a certain extent more manly personality, one which may be taken aback by a thunderous voice, but which won't, over the long haul, allow itself to be dominated. Above all, he is only relatively seldom together with you, has other influences, and you are more a beloved curiousity from which he can chose what to take. You were no curiousity for me; I couldn't choose; I had to accept everything.

And this even without being able to object to it, because it has never been possible for you to speak calmly about something with which you don't agree or which simply doesn't originate with you;

your dominating temperament won't allow it. In recent years you attributed this to your heart condition. I don't know that you were ever any different; at most your heart condition is a means to more strictly assert your domination, as the very thought of it must suffocate the slightest contradiction in others. Naturally this is not a reproach; just a statement of fact. As, for instance, with Ottla, when you say "One can't even talk to her; she always flies right at your face," yet in reality she doesn't fly at you at all; you confuse the thing with the person; the thing flies in your face, and you decide it immediately without listening to the person; what is brought up afterwards can only irritate you, never convince you. Then all one hears from you is, "Do what you want. You're free as far as I'm concerned. You're grown up, I don't have to give you any advice," and all of that in a dreadful, hoarse undertone of anger and total condemnation, at which I only tremble less today than in my childhood, because the child's exclusive feeling of guilt is partly replaced by an insight into our mutual helplessness.

The impossibility of a calm exchange also had a further, quite natural consequence: I lost the ability to speak. Probably I would not, in any case, have become a great speaker, but I would have mastered the normal flow of human conversation. You, however, very early forbade me speech. Your threat, "Not a word of contradiction," and with it the raised hand, have always accompanied me. What I got from you—and you are, as soon as it concerns your interests, an exceptional speaker—was a halting, stammering form of speech. Even that was too much for you; finally I was silent, at first maybe out of defiance, then because I could neither think nor speak in front of you. And because you were actually the one who raised me, this stayed with me throughout my life. It is indeed a remarkable error, if you believe I never showed compliance. "Always contrary" is not, as you believe and reproach me, really my mantra with respect to you. Quite the opposite: you would have been happier with me if I had obeyed you less. As it is, all your educational methods hit the mark exactly; I didn't evade a single move; I am who I am (except, of course, for my innate qualities and for life's influences) as a result of your upbringing and my obedience. That this result is nevertheless painful for you, that you unconsciously refuse to acknowledge it as the result of your child rearing methods lies in the fact that your hand and my substance were so foreign to each other. You said, "Not a word of backtalk," thinking thereby to silence the unpleasant oppositional forces in me; but the effect was too strong for me, I was too obedient, I became totally mute, I cringed away from you, and only dared to move when I was far enough from you that your might couldn't reach, at least not directly. You, however, stood in front of this, and everything again seemed contrary to you, while it was only the natural consequence of your strength and my weakness.

Your extremely effective—for me, at least, infallible—rhetorical methods of upbringing were: abuse, threats, irony, spiteful laughter, and—most amazingly—self-pity. I can't remember that you ever scolded me directly and with openly abusive words. It also wasn't necessary; you had so many other means; besides, at home and especially at work, the abusive words aimed at others flew around me in such numbers, that I as a little boy was sometimes almost deafened by them, and had no grounds not to apply them to myself as well, since the people you were abusing certainly weren't worse than I, and you certainly weren't more displeased with them than with me. And here, too, was again your puzzling innocence and unassailability: you swore without having any second thoughts about it, yet you condemned swearing in others and forbade it.

You reinforced the abuse with threats, and those also applied to me. For instance, your "I'll rip you apart like a fish" was terrifying for me; even though I knew that nothing worse would ensue (however, as a small child I didn't know that); it almost corresponded with my conception of your might that you would also have been capable of such a thing. It was also terrifying when you ran yelling around the table to grab at someone, clearly not really intending to grab, yet pretending to do so, until mother finally came to the rescue, or so it seemed. One had once again, so it seemed to the child, kept one's life through your mercy and carried it on as an undeserved gift from you. To these instances also belong the threats about the consequences of disobedience. When I began to do something that didn't please you, and you threatened me with failure, my awe of your opinion was so great that the failure became inevitable, even if perhaps it didn't happen until a later date. I lost confidence in my own abilities. I was unsettled, doubtful. The older I got, the greater the material at your disposal to prove my worthlessness; gradually you became in a certain sense right. Again, I guard against maintaining that I only became this way because of you; you only strengthened what already existed, but you strengthened it greatly, simply because you were very powerful with respect to me and because you used all your power to that end.

You put special trust in using irony to raise children; this also best suited your superiority over me. A caution from you generally took this form: "Can't you do that such-and-such a way?"; "That's too much for you, I suppose."; "Naturally, you don't have the time for it," and so on. As well, every such question was accompanied by a nasty laugh and a grimace. One was to a certain extent already punished before one even knew that one had done something wrong. Also irritating were those rebukes in which one was treated in the third person, thus not even dignified with abusive direct address; where you would speak somewhat formally to mother, though actually to me, sitting right there; for example, "Naturally, one can't have that from his lordship," and the like. (That had the consequence that I, for example, didn't dare and, from habit, later never even thought to question you directly when mother was near. It was far less dangerous for the child to question the mother sitting next to you; and therefore one asked mother, "How is father?" and insured oneself against surprises.) Naturally, there were also cases where one was in full agreement with the nastiest irony, namely when it applied to someone else; Elli, for instance, with whom I fought for years. It was a feast of spite and *schadenfreude* for me when, almost before every meal, it was said, "She has to sit ten meters back from the table, the fat lass," and when you then sat nastily in your armchair, a bitter enemy, without the slightest trace of friendliness or affect, exaggeratedly attempting to imitate how utterly repulsively for your taste she sat there. How often must this and similar scenes have been repeated; how little did you truly achieve with them. I think the failure lay in the fact that the use of scorn and nastiness did not seem in any right relationship to the incident itself, one didn't feel that the scorn was provoked by the triviality of this Sitting-Far-From-The- Table, instead that it was, in its full measure, already to hand, and only accidentally had taken precisely this incident as a pretext to burst out. Since one was convinced that a pretext would anyhow be found, one didn't particularly get a hold of oneself; also one's feelings were dulled by the ongoing threats; one had gradually become almost sure that one wouldn't get a hiding. One became a sulky, inattentive, disobedient child, always thinking of flight—usually an inward one. Thus you suffered, and thus we suffered. From your viewpoint you were completely right when you, with clenched teeth and that gurgling laugh which had given the child its first notions of hell, bitterly used to say (as just latterly because of a letter from Constantinople), "What a fine crowd that is!"

This posture towards your children seemed quite unbearable when you, as often happened, openly complained. I admit that I as a child (possibly later) had no empathy for that and couldn't understand how you could possibly expect to find sympathy. You were in every respect so gigantic; what could our sympathy matter to you, or even our help? You must actually scorn it, as you so often did us. I therefore didn't believe your complaints, and I tried to find secret motives behind them.

Only later did I comprehend that you truly suffered greatly through your children; at that time, though, when under different circumstances the complaints might have met with a childlike spirit—open, unhesitating, ready to offer any help—for me they could again only too clearly be methods of childrearing and humiliation; as such, not so strong, yet with the damaging side effect that the child got used to not taking seriously the very things which it should have.

Fortunately, there were exceptions to this as well, especially when you suffered silently and love and kindness with all their strength overcame all obstacles and seized me directly. It was certainly rare, yet it was wonderful. Perhaps, earlier, it was when I saw you exhausted, your elbow on the desk, sleeping a little in the hot summer afternoon after eating at work; or when you, worn out, joined us on Sundays in the cool of the summer; or when you, when mother was gravely ill, clutched the bookcase while shaking with tears; or when during my latest illness you came quietly to me in Ottla's room, stayed at the sill, stretched out your neck to see me in the bed, and out of consideration only greeted me with a wave. At such times one lay down and wept with bliss, and one weeps yet again as one writes.

You also have a particularly lovely, very rare way of quietly, contentedly, warmly smiling, a way of smiling which can make the recipient most happy. I can't remember that I ever expressly received this smile in my childhood, but it must have happened, since why would you have refused it to me, as I then still seemed blameless to you and was your great hope. Yet such friendly impressions achieved nothing over time, except to increase my sense of guilt and to make the world even less comprehensible to me.

SYLVIA PLATH

What we make of our fathers need not bear much resemblance to what they are or who they were. Of all the responses to fathers in this anthology, Plath's is easily the most extreme in its distortions, made all the more powerful by the carefully calculated mythic ambiguities of her style. Even allowing for hyperbole and black humour, the violent strokes of her caricature are deliberately childish in their tone and in their passionate unfairness. Fathers, often, are primal figures, hard to approach with objectivity. Her "Daddy" is a deliberate incantation, a ritual chant to exorcise the demon father. The wisps of biographical fact—her father's death when she was eight, his Polish origins, his German ancestry, his physical appearance—are savagely shaped into a terrifying voodoo doll of irrational hate. Her father is too much part of herself, and her attack on him—a desperate and conflicted attempt to free herself of her obsessions and to reclaim a saner self—is, in retrospect, an inexorable step towards the suicide which took place four months after the completion of this poem.

DADDY

You do not do, you do not do
Any more, black shoe
In which I have lived like a foot
For thirty years, poor and white,
Barely daring to breathe or Achoo.

Daddy, I have had to kill you.
You died before I had time—
Marble-heavy, a bag full of God,
Ghastly statue with one gray toe
Big as a Frisco seal

And a head in the freakish Atlantic
Where it pours bean green over blue
In the waters off beautiful Nauset.
I used to pray to recover you.
Ach, du.

In the German tongue, in the Polish town
Scraped flat by the roller
Of wars, wars, wars.
But the name of the town is common.
My Polack friend

Says there are a dozen or two.
So I never could tell where you
Put your foot, your root,
I never could talk to you.
The tongue stuck in my jaw.

It stuck in a barb wire snare.
Ich, ich, ich, ich,
I could hardly speak.
I thought every German was you.
And the language obscene

An engine, an engine
Chuffing me off like a Jew.
A Jew to Dachau, Auschwitz, Belsen.
I began to talk like a Jew.
I think I may well be a Jew.

The snows of the Tyrol, the clear beer of Vienna
Are not very pure or true.
With my gipsy ancestress and my weird luck
And my Taroc pack and my Taroc pack
I may be a bit of a Jew.

I have always been scared of *you*,
With your Luftwaffe, your gobbledygoo.
And your neat mustache
And your Aryan eye, bright blue.
Panzer-man, panzer-man, O You—

Not God but a swastika
So black no sky could squeak through.
Every woman adores a Fascist,
The boot in the face, the brute
Brute heart of a brute like you.

You stand at the blackboard, daddy,
In the picture I have of you,
A cleft in your chin instead of your foot
But no less a devil for that, no not
Any less the black man who

Bit my pretty red heart in two.
I was ten when they buried you.
At twenty I tried to die
And get back, back, back to you.
I thought even the bones would do.

But they pulled me out of the sack,
And they stuck me together with glue.
And then I knew what to do.
I made a model of you,
A man in black with a Meinkampf look

And a love of the rack and the screw.
And I said I do, I do.
So daddy, I'm finally through.
The black telephone's off at the root,
The voices just can't worm through.

If I've killed one man, I've killed two—
The vampire who said he was you
And drank my blood for a year,
Seven years, if you want to know.
Daddy, you can lie back now.

There's a stake in your fat black heart
And the villagers never liked you.
They are dancing and stamping on you.
They always knew it was you.
Daddy, daddy, you bastard, I'm through.

MARY GORDON

In 1996, thirty-nine years after her father's death, Mary Gordon published The Shadow Man, *the 'patremoir' to which this essay forms the introduction. In the course of investigating her father's life and of reflecting on the motives for her search, Gordon had her father's bones dug up and reburied. The intensity of her obsession with her father, who died when she was only seven, is terrifying—yet readily understandable. The father of her childhood, after all, was not a real human being. He was a fairy-tale father, an Angela Carter father, a "magic uncle," a Pied Piper strewing candy and trailing kids. In trying to find her "real" father, in trying to come to terms with the lies her father told her, Gordon confesses that "I have done things to my father. I have remembered him, researched him, investigated him, exposed him, invented him." The one thing she could not do was exorcise him. Gordon is a spiritual sister to Sylvia Plath—Plath who lost her father when she was eight—and despite Gordon's ironies, her literary inventiveness and distancing techniques, she cannot escape the curse of victimhood which her father's early death bequeathed her.*

excerpt from *THE SHADOW MAN*

It is a winter afternoon. March 25, 1994. I am in a dark room, a windowless room in lower Manhattan. Varick and Houston streets, the National Archives and Records Administration—Northeast Region. I am looking at the census for the years 1900 and 1910, looking for facts about my father and his family. I'm doing it out of some impulse of studiousness, or thoroughness, an impulse whose source is not desire, even the desire to know, but a rote habit. The habit of doing things as they should be done. In this case it is an unfriendly habit, because in this dark room, illumined by the silver light of the screens of the microfilm readers, at the age of forty-four, I discover I am not the person I thought I was.

This was only the last and perhaps most obvious stop on a journey of discovery and loss, of loss and re-creation, of the shedding of illusion and the taking on of what might be another illusion, but one of my own. I was looking for my father. I always understood that in looking for him, I might find things that I wished I hadn't, but I didn't know the extent to which this would be the case. And I didn't know that some of the things I'd thought most essential to my idea of who I was would have to be given up.

My father died when I was seven years old. I've always thought that was the most important thing anyone could know about me. I've told his story hundreds of times, because I thought his life was extraordinarily interesting, extraordinarily complex, and in telling his story, I took on the luster of having an interesting and complex father. No one could know me very well without knowing some of the high points of his history: His riotous youth at Harvard, then in Paris and Oxford in the twenties. His career as the king of Cleveland soft porn, the editor of a "humor" magazine called *Hot Dog*. His conversion, in the thirties, from Judaism to Catholicism, his turn at that time to the political right; his becoming a Francoist, a Coughlinite.

I am primarily a writer of fiction, but I knew I couldn't present him as a fictional character because the details of his life, presented as fiction, would be too bizarre to be believed. I did use some elements of his life in some of my characters: the father in *Final Payments* has his politics; the artist in *Men and Angels* meets someone like him in France. But why did it take me so long to get around to writing his life as biography, or memoir, or some nonfiction genre whose proper name hasn't yet been found? I've been a writer for as long as I have conscious memory, or perhaps it is better to say I have no conscious memory of myself as not a writer. Now I am forty-six. Why did I wait so long to write this book?

This isn't the first book I've written about my father. When I was ten, and he'd been dead only three years, I attempted his biography. It began, "My father is the greatest man I have ever known."

For many years I believed it. Well into my adulthood, he was the untouched figure of romance. He was so much more compelling than other people's fathers. He was a writer, and a convert. While he was still alive, I'd watch him walking to the station on his way to work in the city, wearing a hat and hard brown shoes, holding a thin leather briefcase. Unlike other children's fathers, who wore caps and carried lunchpails. On his way home from the train station, he would fill his pockets with candy and walk down the street giving sweets to all the children on the block. "Thanks, Mr. Gordon," they would say, the children who didn't speak to me and to whom I had no wish to speak. No wish and no need. Why should I talk to children? I had him.

But the whole enterprise was a charade, a costume drama. He wasn't going to work. His "work" was a series of schemes to get rich men to bankroll him and his magazines. Occasionally he was successful, but not for long. Never long enough for him to support us. It was my mother's money that bought the candy for the children; he was the Pied Piper on her salary. And his gifts didn't make the children stop taunting me with the information their parents had given them: "We know your father doesn't have a job."

I was ashamed that he didn't have that thing that seemed so meaningful to them, a job, but I was proud of his going off, wherever it was he went off to. I watched him walking up the street, urbane, elegant, his long strides eating up the sidewalk, eating my heart because all day we would be separated. He was the handsomest man in the world, as handsome as the movie stars I loved: Jimmy Stewart, Fred Astaire.

But when I look now at pictures of him, he doesn't look at all handsome. In the photo on my desk, he's slumped on the couch. He looks awful: old, sick, and miserable. In another picture, in which I must be only a few days old, he's holding me, enraged. A new father should be smiling, not enraged. I don't remember an enraged father. In almost all the pictures, he's toothless. How can the glamorous father of my memory be a man who doesn't put his teeth in when he knows he's being photographed?

How can my Fred Astaire, my Jimmy Stewart, have a pot belly that sticks out over his belt? Looking at the pictures, I remember the slit he made in the waistband of his pants so he could fit into them, and my mother telling him he couldn't go out on the street like that. I remember her saying he couldn't wear the shoes he did, shoes whose toes curled up like Persian slippers because they were too big (he said he liked them big; his feet sweat in the summer). These are not the accoutrements of a glamorous man.

My adult life with my father has been marked by reversals and undoings, moments of frozen incomprehension, shutting my eyes, turning away. Finding and then hiding the evidence that says my childhood image is not one I can live by now. When I suggested naming my son after him, my husband said, "That would be fine, but you'd be naming him after a madman." I told him I thought that was rather strong. My father was unusual, eccentric, but mad? Not my father. Not *mine*.

My husband reminded me of a manuscript I'd shown him before we were married. I'd shown it to him because I was ashamed of it and I felt he needed to know about it, as I would have felt I had to tell him about a murder in the family, or a tendency to albinism or club feet.

The manuscript was a biography my father wrote about the conservative French Catholic poet Paul Claudel. Or, rather, my father called it a biography; there are almost no details of Claudel's life. It's really a diatribe against André Gide, against Modernism, against the infection of the Jews. "The Jew Proust. The Jew Bergson. The Jew Masoch, the Jew Leon Blum," my father wrote.

My father, born a Jew in the last year of the nineteenth century, wrote this ten years after six million of his blood were murdered. I remember the look on my husband's face when he read it. Sorrow clouded the blue of his Protestant eyes, furrowed his midwestern forehead. "But this is mad," he said. I refused to absorb his interpretation. I said it was not mad but evil.

This is not a happy position for a loving daughter to be in: to be forced to choose between seeing something her father wrote as mad and seeing it as evil. I chose the second. I chose as my father's daughter. He would have considered it a cowardly evasion to call something mad that was quite possibly evil. So I called his manuscript evil, then forgot about it. I named my son for him, adding the middle name—Dess—of my husband's mother, a happy woman whose fulfilled life ended at the age of ninety-six. I thought her goodness and normalcy could cleanse my father's curse, and what would be left to my son was his grandfather's brilliance, his inventiveness, his passionate heart.

For I have always known that I lived at the center of the heart of a passionate man. My desire not to move from that place led to a kind of memorializing that amounted to entombment. The construction of a mausoleum made up of desire and need, snippets of events or reports of events, lyrics of songs, lines from stories. Made up, too, of forgetfulness, refusal of evidence, misplacing of crucial things or precious information, denial of facts.

I needed this mausoleum in order to be myself. His death was a great shock, an early death for me, the death of my childhood and the death of a way of life that included pleasure and play. My father was a man who loved children. Before I happened to him, he adopted families. He became a magic uncle to his friends' children, people now in their fifties or sixties, who remember him as indulgent and imaginative, rescuing them from ordinary life. He liked large families. But I was born when my mother was forty-one and he fifty-five. She, a polio victim, gave birth in an aura of miracle. So there were no more children, and that was too bad. He would have been wonderful with a lot of money, a lot of children. He should have been able to open the door of a large, untidy house and make his way over children sprawling all over the floor, his own children and the friends of his own. But for me, his only child, he distilled all his abstract love for children into the hard diamond of adoration and devotion. "I love you more than God," he once told me. This was serious; he was a religious man. I didn't know, and still don't, if he meant he loved me more than he loved God or more than God loved me. It almost doesn't matter. It was a serious thing to say and it scared me. Whichever he meant, he was right.

He was a jumpy, almost hysterical man, but with me he was unfailingly patient. Only now that I have children of my own do I realize the extent of his patience. But no child realizes an adult is being patient with her: even if she did, the idea would be meaningless to her, one of the arcana of adulthood, like the fear of aging or the desire for money in the bank.

He understood how much children love the ordinary domestic life that adults have access to and from which they are barred. Marriage, cocktails, are to children as exotic as dragons. So every night, when he told me a story before I went to sleep, he gave me a choice of four situations: I could hear a story about a mean old woman and a nice old man, a nice old woman and a mean old man, a mean young woman and a nice young man, or a nice young woman and a mean young man. In these stories, someone was always degraded and always in conflict. But it seemed to me that these couples simply went about the business of their simple lives, and their lives enthralled me.

When he died, my mother and I moved in with my grandmother and my aunt. My aunt was a polio victim like my mother; my grandmother was seventy-eight. I was the only able-bodied person in the house. A house of pious and severely law-abiding laborers who thought that life was difficult and that my dreamy ways were something it was their responsibility to "knock out of me." I think they believed they were doing it for my own good, but it was a joyless experience, and I grieved for my father all the more because not only he, but joy, had been lost from my life.

I turned to religion, to reading and writing. I did what he wanted me to do: I prayed. I read and wrote. What was he bringing me up to be? What could he have imagined, insisting I grow up in a working-class neighborhood but teaching me to read at three, having me memorize, at five, the Latin of the Mass?

He was bringing me up to be his partner: someone who would get his jokes and help him with his work.

For a large part of my life I believed that such a life would have been the best of all possible lives. It would have been, I thought, a life without dullness, without bourgeois responsibility, without excess and slowness. We would spend our time in the great cities of Europe; I would always wear classic, beyond-the-fashion clothes. I would be known as my father's daughter.

I have not become that woman. Just as there is much about my father's life that horrifies me, there is much about me he would have hated. He didn't want a daughter who was a feminist, a leftist, divorced and remarried, the media's usual suspect when they need the insiders' rap sheet on the Catholic hierarchy or the pope.

I did, though, become a writer. Would he have liked it if he'd known I'd be writing about him? What would he think of my writing this book?

People ask me, "Why are you able to write it now?" I think they're looking for some answer appropriate for a TV talk show. They expect me to say, "I can do it now because I am a mother. Because I have a solid body of work. " The answer is more mysterious. In a way, it happened by accident.

In 1984, Sara Bershtell, then of Pantheon, asked me to contribute to a volume called *Fathers*. Rather easily and quickly, I wrote a piece called "David." It lays out the facts of my father's biography, of the difficulties of it, but it ends with a promise of "love that passes understanding." In a way, I now see, it was a refusal to go further. A desire to be not the writer exploring my father but his loving child.

At that time, I was finishing my novel *Men and Angels*, after which I began another novel, *The Other Side*. I didn't write any more about my father for a while. Then, in 1991, I was seized by the image of the lawn outside my aunt's house, and then by memories of my grandmother's furniture. This led to a meditation on my father's death, called "The Important Houses," which was published in *The New Yorker*. My childhood, as a subject, was beginning to seep into my bones. I wrote another meditation on the strong presence of death in my childhood, called "The Other Deaths," published in *Salmagundi*.

I had a lot of pages about my father. It seemed I was writing a book. It seemed that it was time to go on a journey to try to find—something. My father was with me all the time. I began writing him a long letter. I had scores of folders, labeled "Fathers," "Daughters," "Memory," "Loss," "Fascism," "Kafka," "Proust," "Anti-Semitism," and so on. I wanted to tell him everything I thought.

I entered the cave of memory, which nowadays seems like a tourist trap in high season. Everyone's talking about memory: French intellectuals, historians of the Holocaust, victims of child abuse, alleged abusers. It's a subject of conversation in the academy and on morning chat shows—even on A.M. radio. As I began to explore my memories, I was caught up in the impossibility of memory as a reliable source. What I had trusted as a text to live by began to seem as malleable as last week's gossip, and as undependable. This loss of faith in memory was the first of the losses that came to me as a result of writing this book.

My memories weren't my only way of knowing my father. He was a writer, a published writer. I could learn about him by reading what he wrote. I had a box full of his articles and poems, which I had read from time to time, sometimes appalled, sometimes refusing to take in the content and concentrating on what I called his felicity of style. But I'd never studied his writing, using the training I have as a literary critic. I never read what he wrote as a text. I'd never used the resources at my disposal to try to find if there was anything he had published that I hadn't already found. I know that I read him so cursorily because I was afraid that some things he'd written might be distressing to me. But it was only when I read him carefully, over and over, in the way that one must when one is writing about something, that I experienced the anguish I'd tried to forestall. Reading him as a professional reader and writer, I tried to understand him not as a father but as someone who had written the words I had to interpret. I saw not only the horror of his ideas, but the weakness of his style. I lost another father: the father of the brilliant sentence, the brilliantly shaped phrase.

After I felt satisfied that I'd read everything of his that I could find, and had read it thoroughly, I went to public records. I asked the help of historian friends of mine, and they pointed me in the direction of government offices, archives, and libraries. I contacted genealogists, Jewish historians, the Mormons, passport offices, military records, death certificates, and wills. I traveled to my father's hometown, Lorain, Ohio, where I had never been before. I spoke to people in the community and possible relatives. I learned less than what I'd hoped, but enough so that I understood that his life had been made up of lies, some tragic, some pathetic, all of them leaving me with the feeling that I'd been stolen from. I had lost him as the figure in history I thought he was; I had lost my place in America.

I couldn't even try to verify any of what I'd learned with my mother. At the very time that I was engaging in this project of memory and discovery, my mother, in her late eighties, was losing her memory, and losing her grip on her present life. I was losing both the father and the mother of my childhood at the same time. I had to come to terms with this both in my life and in my writing about my life. I had to learn that with some things it is impossible to come to terms.

Or that I had to come to terms using methods I never would have dreamed of. I became a storyteller to my father, and then a detective in the department of magic realism. Finally, it was only by turning my father into a fictional character after all, by understanding that I could never know him except as an invention of my own mind and heart, that I could make a place for him in my life.

But perhaps this is true of all of us. Perhaps that is what it is to grow up: to understand that the parent of your childhood is your invention, that if such a person ever lived, he or she is no longer living. That the living parent of your adulthood is not the reconstituted giant of the child's mind and heart.

The psychoanalyst Hans Loewald says that an analysis is successful if it succeeds in transforming ghosts into ancestors. Perhaps if we substitute "maturation" for "analysis," the statement remains true. My father was a beloved and a looming ghost. If the process of transforming ghosts into ancestors is a grueling one for everybody, I believe it was especially intense in the case of my father and me. His love for me was so extravagant; he was more than ordinarily engaging to my imagination; his contradictions are more than ordinarily extreme. Nevertheless, in the process of transforming him from the looming ghost determining my every breath into the benevolent ancestor at my shoulder, I have done what everyone who wishes to make peace with his or her parents must do. Or, at least, I have begun to do it. I even had his remains moved from the grave of my mother's family to a new grave, where he can be a patriarch, the head of a family he never saw.

This book is a chronicle of my attempts to transform myself and my father. It's also a book about America. My father's family came to America in the great wave of immigration at the end of the nineteenth and the beginning of the twentieth century. He lived the dark side of the American immigrant's story, the one that isn't usually told: He was a Jew in a time of pervasive anti-Semitism. He was a young man at a time when it seemed endlessly possible for young men to make and remake themselves. When the fire that fed the melting pot burned at a very high flame. When the pressure to pick up the dominant tone of the American tuning fork was both great and unquestioned. I have always liked to think of my father as absolutely unique, but this is another idea I've had to give up. He was a man of his place and time.

IDEALLY, the writer should follow the example of Saint Augustine, who begins his *Confessions* with only the lightest of directions to the reader: "*Tolle, lege.*" Take and read.

I haven't been able to do that. I don't know whether it's a fault of character or a fault of the age, this need to explain myself, to be a visible partner in the reader's enterprise. Perhaps anyone writing about herself at such length must fight the impulse to apologize. The terror that no one will care. So I approach you, the reader, in a way I wouldn't ordinarily, asking indulgence and attention. But is it you, really, whose indulgence I ask? Or is it my father, whom I lost, and found again, whom I both metaphorically and literally unburied and reburied in the course of writing this book.

When I ask myself if I'm glad I've pursued this project or wish I'd never begun it, I feel as if I'm in a scene from one of those science-fiction movies in which one scientist tries to discourage another from going forward. The mustachioed man in the impeccable suit says to his wild-haired colleague, "There are some things, Dr. Poliakoff, which are better not known."

Certainly, much of what I learned involved pain and loss. But I haven't lost my father. He's still *there*; occasionally he still overwhelms me. He's like a wave that breaks over me, involves me, overturns me, exhilarates me, carries me, then disappears, leaving only a trace of itself in the sand, the print of a tongue, a lip. I have freed him to live among the dead, in a place I will no longer join him. Now he must come to me. We are together in a new place now, among the living. Each year at Rosh Hashanah, Jews pray, "May you be inscribed in the book of life." This is what I've tried to do. To place or re-place both my father and myself in the book of life. The book of the living.

Now I know that whether I am in silence or listening to music, in a dark room or walking through New York streets, swimming in the ocean, about to fall asleep in a strange bed in a foreign city, talking about Flaubert or Joyce to students, beating eggs or stirring soup, feeding my children or listening to their stories, making love beneath the body of a man he could not even have imagined, I am always my father's daughter. Having lost him, once, twice, I will have him forever. He is always with me, always mine.

MARGARET ATWOOD

There is an illusion of plain precision in this poem. In some of her other father poems, Atwood is a druid priestess decorating green holly wreaths with red berries of pain, a Cordelia with a love "like salt" for her father's dying Lear, or a curatorial, forensic archaeologist scraping a slide clear of "little / flowers of crystallizing earth" to recover an ancestral Otzi-like echo of her father in his youth. Here, Atwood garlands the painful banality of death in an institution with the flowers of her verse; snipping them off with clinical care, while at the same time turning her narratorial self into a flower girl who, with her epithamalium, eases the turtle father out of the deathbed shell, helping him to transform the institution into a ship and the nurses into "plump muscular angels" to shift him on his way. Her wordflowers are placed in the prosaic pickle jar of her poem in an attempt to preserve the memory of "the same father I knew before," the naturalist father who first took her into the Canadian wilderness and taught her how to look "hard and up close at the small details." In the end, however, "Flowers" acknowledges the pain of helplessness: not flowers, sorrow, anger, nor even memory can save the father or the self from inevitable death. Part of Atwood's power lies in her willingness to recognize the limitations of language.

FLOWERS

Right now I am the flower girl.
I bring fresh flowers,
dump out the old ones, the greenish water
that smells like dirty teeth
into the bathroom sink, snip off the stem ends
with surgical scissors I borrowed
from the nursing station,
put them into a jar
I brought from home, because they don't have vases
in this hotel for the ill,
place them on the table beside my father
where he can't see them
because he won't open his eyes.

He lies flattened under the white sheet.
He says he is on a ship,
and I can see it—
the functional white walls, the minimal windows,
the little bells, the rubbery footsteps of strangers,
the whispering all around
of the air-conditioner, or else the ocean,
and he is on a ship:
he's giving us up, giving up everything
but the breath going in
and out of his diminished body:
minute by minute he's sailing slowly away,
away from us and our waving hands
that do not wave.

The women come in, two of them, in blue;
it's no use being kind in here,
if you don't have hands like theirs—
large and capable, the hands
of plump muscular angels,
the ones that blow trumpets and lift swords.
They shift him carefully, tuck in the corners.
It hurts, but as little as possible.
Pain is their lore. The rest of us
are helpless amateurs.

A suffering you can neither cure nor enter—
there are worse things, but not many.
After a while it makes us impatient.
Can't we do anything but feel sorry?

I sit there, watching the flowers
in their pickle jar. He is asleep, or not.
I think: He looks like a turtle.
Or: He looks erased.
But somewhere in there, at the far end of the tunnel
of pain and forgetting he's trapped in
is the same father I knew before,
the one who carried the green canoe
over the portage, the painter trailing,
myself with the fishing rods, slipping
on the wet boulders and slapping flies.
That was the last time we went there.

There will be a last time for this also,
bringing cut flowers to this white room.
Sooner or later I too
will have to give everything up,
even the sorrow that comes with these flowers,
even the anger,
even the memory of how I brought them
from a garden I will no longer have by then,
and put them beside my dying father,
hoping I could still save him.

VIRGINIA WOOLF #1

*"Leslie Stephen" forms a fitting bookend to Doris Lessing's "My Father,"
if only because a comparison of the two pieces shows unsuspected timidity
in Virginia Woolf. In her brilliant yet scathing tribute to Edmund Gosse,
Woolf mistook his discretion for cowardice and wrongly accused him "of
dipping and ducking, fingering and faltering upon the surface." Dipping
and ducking, fingering and faltering are terms more properly applicable
to her when, as one of the first to practice the new writing Gosse had made
possible, she was so atypically cautious and guarded in writing about her
father. Skilful and moving as the essay is, there is much of the wax effigy
about "Leslie Stephen," the eccentricities of her father are all too
respectfully recorded or dutifully minimized. For deeper truth and a
living picture of Leslie Stephen, we must look to Mr. Ramsey in* To the
Lighthouse, *not to "Leslie Stephen." Even with Gosse to lean on,
Virginia Woolf, brave and honest in many other areas of her writing,
fingered and faltered in attempting an honest public exhibition of her
father's private self.*

LESLIE STEPHEN

By the time that his children were growing up the great days of my
father's life were over. His feats on the river and on the mountains had
been won before they were born. Relics of them were to be found lying
about the house—the silver cup on the study mantelpiece; the rusty
alpenstocks that leant against the bookcase in the corner; and to the
end of his days he would speak of great climbers and explorers with a
peculiar mixture of admiration and envy. But his own years of activity
were over, and my father had to content himself with pottering about
the Swiss valleys or taking a stroll across the Cornish moors.

That to potter and to stroll meant more on his lips than on other people's is becoming obvious now that some of his friends have given their own version of those expeditions. He would start off after breakfast alone, or with one companion. Shortly before dinner he would return. If the walk had been successful, he would have out his great map and commemorate a new short cut in red ink. And he was quite capable, it appears, of striding all day across the moors without speaking more than a word or two to his companion. By that time, too, he had written the *History of English Thought in the Eighteenth Century,* which is said by some to be his masterpiece; and the *Science of Ethics*—the book which interested him most; and *The Playground of Europe*, in which is to be found "The Sunset on Mont Blanc"—in his opinion the best thing he ever wrote.

He still wrote daily and methodically, though never for long at a time. In London he wrote in the large room with three long windows at the top of the house. He wrote lying almost recumbent in a low rocking chair which he tipped to and fro as he wrote, like a cradle, and as he wrote he smoked a short clay pipe, and he scattered books round him in a circle. The thud of a book dropped on the floor could be heard in the room beneath. And often as he mounted the stairs to his study with his firm, regular tread he would burst, not into song, for he was entirely unmusical, but into a strange rhythmical chant, for verse of all kinds, both "utter trash," as he called it, and the most sublime words of Milton and Wordsworth stuck in his memory, and the act of walking or climbing seemed to inspire him to recite whichever it was that came uppermost or suited his mood.

But it was his dexterity with his fingers that delighted his children before they could potter along the lanes at his heels or read his books. He would twist a sheet of paper beneath a pair of scissors and out would drop an elephant, a stag, or a monkey with trunks, horns, and tails delicately and exactly formed. Or, taking a pencil, he would draw beast after beast—an art that he practised almost unconsciously as he read, so that the fly-leaves of his books swarm with owls and donkeys as if to illustrate the "Oh, you ass!" or "Conceited dunce," that he was wont to scribble impatiently in the margin. Such brief comments, in which one may find the germ of the more temperate statements of his essays, recall some of the characteristics of his talk. He could be very silent, as his friends have testified. But his remarks, made suddenly in a low voice between the puffs of his pipe, were extremely effective. Sometimes with one word—but his one word was accompanied by a gesture of the hand—he would dispose of the tissue of exaggerations which his own sobriety seemed to provoke. "There are 40,000,000 unmarried women in London alone!" Lady Ritchie once informed him. "Oh, Annie, Annie!" my father exclaimed in tones of horrified but affectionate rebuke. But Lady Ritchie, as if she enjoyed being rebuked, would pile it up even higher next time she came.

The stories he told to amuse his children of adventures in the Alps—but accidents only happened, he would explain, if you were so foolish as to disobey your guides—or of those long walks, after one of which, from Cambridge to London on a hot day, "I drank, I am sorry to say, rather more than was good for me," were told very briefly, but with a curious power to impress the scene. The things that he did not say were always there in the background. So, too, though he seldom told anecdotes, and his memory for facts was bad, when he described a person—and he had known many people, both famous and obscure—he would convey exactly what he thought of him in two or three words. And what he thought might be the opposite of what other people thought. He had a way of upsetting established reputations and disregarding conventional values that could be disconcerting, and sometimes perhaps wounding, though no one was more respectful of any feeling that seemed to him genuine. But when, suddenly opening his bright blue eyes, and rousing himself from what had seemed complete abstraction, he gave his opinion, it was difficult to disregard it. It was a habit, especially when deafness made him unaware that this opinion could be heard, that had its inconveniences.

"I am the most easily bored of men," he wrote, truthfully as usual: and when, as was inevitable in a large family, some visitor threatened to stay not merely for tea but also for dinner, my father would express his anguish at first by twisting and untwisting a certain lock of hair. Then he would burst out, half to himself, half to the powers above, but quite audibly, "Why can't he go? Why can't he go?" Yet such is the charm of simplicity—and did he not say, also truthfully, that "bores are the salt of the earth"?—that the bores seldom went, or, if they did, forgave him and came again.

Too much, perhaps, has been said of his silence; too much stress has been laid upon his reserve. He loved clear thinking; he hated sentimentality and gush; but this by no means meant that he was cold and unemotional, perpetually critical and condemnatory in daily life. On the contrary, it was his power of feeling strongly and of expressing his feeling with vigour that made him sometimes so alarming as a companion. A lady, for instance, complained of the wet summer that was spoiling her tour in Cornwall. But to my father, though he never called himself a democrat, the rain meant that the corn was being laid; some poor man was being ruined; and the energy with which he expressed his sympathy—not with the lady—left her discomfited. He had something of the same respect for farmers and fishermen that he had for climbers and explorers. So, too, he talked little of patriotism, but during the South African War—and all wars were hateful to him—he lay awake thinking that he heard the guns on the battlefield. Again, neither his reason nor his cold common sense helped to convince him that a child could be late for dinner without having been maimed or killed in an accident. And not all his mathematics, together with a bank balance which he insisted must be ample in the extreme, could persuade him, when it came to signing a cheque, that the whole family was not "shooting Niagara to ruin," as he put it. The pictures that he would draw of old age and the bankruptcy court, of ruined men of letters who have to support large families in small houses at Wimbledon (he owned a very small house at Wimbledon) might have convinced those who complain of his understatements that hyperbole was well within his reach had he chosen.

Yet the unreasonable mood was superficial, as the rapidity with which it vanished would prove. The chequebook was shut; Wimbledon and the workhouse were forgotten. Some thought of a humorous kind made him chuckle. Taking his hat and his stick, calling for his dog and his daughter, he would stride off into Kensington Gardens, where he had walked as a little boy, where his brother Fitzjames and he had made beautiful bows to young Queen Victoria and she had swept them a curtsey, and so, round the Serpentine, to Hyde Park Corner, where he had once saluted the great Duke himself; and so home. He was not then in the least "alarming"; he was very simple, very confiding; and his silence, though one might last unbroken from the Round Pond to the Marble Arch, was curiously full of meaning, as if he were thinking half aloud, about poetry and philosophy and people he had known.

He himself was the most abstemious of men. He smoked a pipe perpetually, but never a cigar. He wore his clothes until they were too shabby to be tolerable; and he held old-fashioned and rather puritanical views as to the vice of luxury and the sin of idleness. The relations between parents and children today have a freedom that would have been impossible with my father. He expected a certain standard of behaviour, even of ceremony, in family life. Yet if freedom means the right to think one's own thoughts and to follow one's own pursuits, then no one respected and indeed insisted upon freedom more completely than he did. His sons, with the exception of the Army and Navy, should follow whatever professions they chose; his daughters, though he cared little enough for the higher education of women, should have the same liberty. If at one moment he rebuked a daughter sharply for smoking a cigarette—smoking was not in his opinion a nice habit in the other sex—she had only to ask him if she might become a painter, and he assured her that so long as she took her work seriously he would give her all the help he could. He had no special love for painting; but he kept his word. Freedom of that sort was worth thousands of cigarettes.

It was the same with the perhaps more difficult problem of literature. Even today there may be parents who would doubt the wisdom of allowing a girl of fifteen the free run of a large and quite unexpurgated library. But my father allowed it. There were certain facts—very briefly, very shyly he referred to them. Yet "Read what you like," he said, and all his books, "mangy and worthless," as he called them, but certainly they were many and various, were to be had without asking. To read what one liked because one liked it, never to pretend to admire what one did not—that was his only lesson in the art of reading. To write in the fewest possible words, as clearly as possible, exactly what one meant—that was his only lesson in the art of writing. All the rest must be learnt for oneself. Yet a child must have been childish in the extreme not to feel that such was the teaching of a man of great learning and wide experience, though he would never impose his own views or parade his own knowledge. For, as his tailor remarked when he saw my father walk past his shop up Bond Street, "There goes a gentleman that wears good clothes without knowing it."

In those last years, grown solitary and very deaf, he would sometimes call himself a failure as a writer; he had been "jack of all trades, and master of none." But whether he failed or succeeded as a writer, it is permissible to believe that he left a distinct impression of himself on the minds of his friends. Meredith saw him as "Phoebus Apollo turned fasting friar" in his earlier days; Thomas Hardy, years later, looked at the "spare and desolate figure" of the Schreckhorn and thought of him,

Who scaled its horn with ventured life and limb,
Drawn on by vague imaginings, maybe,
Of semblance to his personality
In its quaint glooms, keen lights, and rugged trim.

But the praise he would have valued most, for though he was an agnostic nobody believed more profoundly in the worth of human relationships, was Meredith's tribute after his death: "He was the one man to my knowledge worthy to have married your mother." And Lowell, when he called him "L.S., the most lovable of men," has best described the quality that makes him, after all these years, unforgettable.

E.E. CUMMINGS

Looking back on his life, Cummings saw this poem—a poem completed in 1939, almost thirteen years after the death of his father—as a poem which "doomed me to a moral life." Writing the poem resulted in "a sense of freedom and exileration [sic]—a feeling that I was developing a newer deeper dimension." In "my father moved through dooms of love," Cummings presents his father as a God-like figure, one who is both God the Father and God the Son, one who sings the world into being and, in the concluding couplet, one whose existence redeems the imperfections of the world. By attributing God-like characteristics to his father, Cummings was only doing unto his father what his father had done unto him. In his introduction to The Enormous Room, *a book which he had commissioned and chivied E. E. into writing, the senior Cummings described his son in Christ-like terms. This was not entirely literary play on his part. Several years before, after a farcical misadventure involving his car, his son, and a prostitute, Edward Cummings had, in melodramatic disillusionment, cried out, "I thought I'd given birth to a God." "Dooms of love" is all too apt a phrase to describe the enormous burden placed on Cummings by the warped intensity of his father's love. Joyful, redemptive, and celebratory as this poem is, features such as the connotations of "doom" and the ambiguities of "through" hint at the life-long difficulty Cummings had in just coming to terms with the pressures of his father's love.*

my father moved through dooms of love

my father moved through dooms of love
through sames of am through haves of give,
singing each morning out of each night
my father moved through depths of height

this motionless forgetful where
turned at his glance to shining here;
that if(so timid air is firm)
under his eyes would stir and squirm

newly as from unburied which
floats the first who,his april touch
drove sleeping selves to swarm their fates
woke dreamers to their ghostly roots

and should some why completely weep
my father's fingers brought her sleep:
vainly no smallest voice might cry
for he could feel the mountains grow.

Lifting the valleys of the sea
my father moved through griefs of joy;
praising a forehead called the moon
singing desire into begin

joy was his song and joy so pure
a heart of star by him could steer
and pure so now and now so yes
the wrists of twilight would rejoice

keen as midsummer's keen beyond
conceiving mind of sun will stand,
so strictly(over utmost him
so hugely)stood my father's dream

his flesh was flesh his blood was blood:
no hungry man but wished him food;
no cripple wouldn't creep one mile
uphill to only see him smile.

Scorning the pomp of must and shall
my father moved through dooms of feel;
his anger was as right as rain
his pity was as green as grain

septembering arms of year extend
less humbly wealth to foe and friend
than he to foolish and to wise
offered immeasurable is

proudly and(by octobering flame
beckoned)as earth will downward climb,
so naked for immortal work
his shoulders marched against the dark

his sorrow was as true as bread:
no liar looked him in the head;
if every friend became his foe
he'd laugh and build a world with snow.

My father moved through theys of we,
singing each new leaf out of each tree
(and every child was sure that spring
danced when she heard my father sing)

then let men kill which cannot share,
let blood and flesh be mud and mire,
scheming imagine, passion willed,
freedom a drug that's bought and sold

giving to steal and cruel kind,
a heart to fear, to doubt a mind,
to differ a disease of same,
conform the pinnacle of am

though dull were all we taste as bright,
bitter all utterly things sweet,
maggoty minus and dumb death
all we inherit,all bequeath

and nothing quite so least as truth
—i say though hate were why men breathe—
because my father lived his soul
love is the whole and more than all

CODA

Though the original impetus for this book was the subject of fathers, along the way it has also become an Alan Bennett-type compendium book, a rattle bag, whose curious and eclectic items are intended to lure you, the reader, to further explorations. While not thrown together with the same serendipitous courage as Seamus Heaney and Ted Hughes's wonder-full *The Rattle Bag*—instead, tenuous nodes of organization are embedded here and there in the structure of *Fathers*—this anthology is meant to surprise and tempt you to further knowledge and deeper wisdom. Interestingly, Ann Thwaite also used the compendium book conceit in choosing the title and frontispiece for *Glimpses of the Wonderful,* her biography of Philip Henry Gosse, Edmund's father. Philip Henry had himself published a compendium book of that name, detailing all sorts of natural wonders.

Two final essays remain, neither one of them father essays. A further purpose of this anthology is to share some of the excitement, some of the sense of exploration and discovery that goes with such a project. Books like Patrick Lane's *There is A Season* and Alan Bennett's *Untold Stories* were unlooked for surprises, serendipitous treasures, stumbled across in pursuit of a theme. The hope is that many of the pieces and introductions in this anthology will be starting points for readers to begin their own explorations. While not an *Odyssey* or an *Odyssey* translation, *Fathers* is intended to stimulate Keatsian excitement, "to reveal new planets" and spark "wild surmise." The essays "Edmund Gosse" and "Leslie Stephen," both found in the course of doing background research, have been added to advance that goal.

VIRGINIA WOOLF #2

When this anthology was started, Edmund Gosse was nowhere on the horizon. Once discovered, though, he quickly became more and more central. Although in his age he was a major figure, today he is almost forgotten, except by the highly literate or those with an interest in the late-Victorian period. The following essay is included to recall his importance and to provide a little historical background. It is also included because it is such a brilliant, edgy essay. Though not as subtly crafted and polished as "Leslie Stephen," "Edmund Gosse" shows what the former could and should have been. This essay also shows why people were afraid of Virginia Woolf. Some of Woolf's aggressiveness here may be fuelled by what Harold Bloom has called "anxiety of influence," and a good case might be made that, at least in the field of literary criticism and biographical writings, Woolf is attacking a literary father. Also, Virginia may have been upset because Gosse had preceded her in writing an essay about her father. Incidentally, rich and rewarding alternatives to Virginia's Gosse and Edmund's Philip are offered by Ann Thwaite's Edmund Gosse: A Literary Landscape *and* Glimpses of the Wonderful. *These biographies of Gosse son and Gosse father reveal just how misleading patremoiric writings can be.*

EDMUND GOSSE

When famous writers die it is remarkable how frequently they are credited with one particular virtue—the virtue of kindness to the young and obscure. Every newspaper has lately contained that eulogy upon Arnold Bennett. And here is the same tribute paid to another writer who differed in every possible way from Arnold Bennett—Sir Edmund Gosse. He too, it is said, was generous to the young and obscure. Of Bennett it was certainly, although on some occasions rather obliquely, true. He might, that is to say, have formed a very low opinion of a book; he might have expressed that opinion as his habit was, bluntly and emphatically in print; and yet if he met the writer his sincerity, his concern, his assumption that both cared equally for the craft of letters made it perfectly easy for that unfortunate person to say, "It is all true, and more than true, Mr. Bennett; but if you hate my books, I can't tell you how completely I loathe yours"—after which a frank discussion of fiction and its nature was possible; and a very obscure novelist was left with the feeling that a very famous one was indeed the kindest of men.

But what would have happened if, taking advantage of Sir Edmund's generosity, and assuming a common respect for letters, one had said, "But you can't hate my books, Sir Edmund, more than I hate yours"? Instant annihilation would have been the only and the happiest solution of the situation. But nobody who had ever seen Sir Edmund in the flesh would have risked such folly. Bristling and brilliant, formal but uneasy, he radiated even from a distance all the susceptibilities that make young writers draw in their horns. Generous was not the adjective that sprang to the lips at the sight of him, nor is it one that frequently occurs on reading the life of him by Mr. Charteris. He could be as touchy as a housemaid and as suspicious as a governess. He could smell out an offence where none was meant, and hoard a grievance for years. He could quarrel permanently because a lamp wick was snuffed out too vigorously at a table under his nose. Hostile reviews threw him into paroxysms of rage and despair. His letters are full of phrases like "Mr. Clement Shorter, in terms of unexampled insolence, speaks of me as 'the so-called critic'. . . If that insolent notice in *The Times* is true . . . it is better I should know it . . . I feel I shall never have the heart to write another sentence." It seems possible that one severe review by Churton Collins gave him more pain than he suffered from any private or public sorrow in the course of seventy-nine years. All this must have made him the most prickly of companions, and the young must have been possessed of greater tact than the young usually possess to reach the kindness that no doubt lay hid behind the thorns. For the great merit of the present biography is that it does not attempt to conceal the fact that Sir Edmund was a complex character composed of many different strains. Plain virtue was not a sure passport to his affection. He could disregard genius and ignore merit if they trod too clumsily upon his toes. On the other hand the House of Lords possessed a distinct glamour for him; the rigours of high society delighted him; and to see the words "Marlborough Club" at the head of his notepaper did, it seems, shed a certain lustre upon the page.

But these foibles, amusing and annoying as they are, become at once more interesting and less irritating when we learn that there lay behind them a very good cause—his education, his childhood. "Far more than might be supposed of his conduct in life", writes Mr. Charteris, "was due to unconscious protest against . . . the things which darkened his childhood." Readers of *Father and Son* know well what those things were—the narrowness, the ugliness of his upbringing; the almost insane religious mania of his father; the absence from his home of culture, beauty, urbanity, graciousness—in fact, of all those elements in life to which Edmund Gosse turned as instinctively and needed as profoundly as a flower the sun. What could be more than that the flower, once transplanted, should turn, almost violently, the other way, should climb too high, should twine too lavishly, should—to drop these metaphors—order clothes in Savile Row and emerge from behind the form of Dr. Fog uttering what appear at this distance of time rather excessive praises of the now little known Danish poet, Paludin Müller?—a surly poet who objected to visitors. But young Edmund Gosse triumphed. "Slowly, the poet murmured, 'You flatter me too much, but thank you.' The most stubborn of all the citadels had capitulated."

Few people can have been pitchforked, as Mr. Charteris calls it, into the world by a more violent propulsion than that which Gosse was given by the bleakness of his upbringing. It was no wonder that he overshot the mark, never quite got his equilibrium at parties which he loved, required to know the maiden names of married guests, and observed formalities punctiliously which are taken as a matter of course by those who have never lived in dread of the instant coming of the Lord, and have ordered their clothes for generations in Savile Row. But the impulse itself was generous, and the tokens of kindling and expansion more admirable than ridiculous. The "sensual sufficiency in life" delighted one who had been starved of it. Happiness formed the staple of what he would certainly not have called his creed. "To feel so saturated with the love of things", to enjoy life and "suck it as a wasp drains a peach", to "roll the moments on one's tongue and keep the flavour of them"; above all, to cherish friendship and exalt the ideals of friendship—such were the enjoyments that his nature, long repressed, stretched out to, generously, naturally, spontaneously. And yet . . .

Those who are acquainted with Sir Edmund's lively portraits know what demure but devastating qualifications he was able to insinuate after those two small words. "He possessed the truth and answered to the heavenly calling," he wrote of Andrew Lang, "and yet . . ." Such expansion was natural, was right, was creditable, and yet, we echo, how much better Gosse would have been as a writer, how much more important he would have been as a man if only he had given freer rein to his impulses, if only his pagan and sensual joy had not been dashed by perpetual caution! The peculiarity which Mr. Charteris notes in his walk—"curiously suggestive at once of eagerness and caution"—runs through his life and limits his intelligence. He hints, he qualifies, he insinuates, he suggests, but he never speaks out, for all the world as if some austere Plymouth Brother were lying in wait to make him do penance for his audacity. Yet it seems possible, given the nature of his gifts, that if only he had possessed greater boldness, if only he had pushed his curiosity further, had incurred wrath instead of irritation, and complete confusion instead of some petty social tribulation, he might have rivalled the great Boswell himself. When we read how young Edmund Gosse insinuated himself under cover of Dr. Fog into the presence of an irascible poet and won the day by the adroitness of his flattery, we are reminded of the methods of Boswell in pursuit of Paoli or Voltaire or Johnson. Both men were irresistibly attracted by genius. Both had "a medium-like" power of drawing other people's confidences into the open. Both were astonishingly adept at reporting the talk and describing the appearance of their friends. But where Boswell is drawn headlong by the momentum of his hero and his own veneration beyond discretion, beyond vanity, beyond his fear of what people will say, down into the depths, Gosse is kept by his respect for decorum, by his decency and his timidity, dipping and ducking, fingering and faltering upon the surface. Thus where Boswell left us that profound and moving masterpiece the *Life of Johnson*, Gosse left us *Father and Son,* a classic doubtless, as Mr. Charteris claims, certainly a most original and entertaining book, but how little and light, how dapper and superficial Gosse's portraits appear if we compare them with the portraits left by Boswell himself! Fear seems always to dog his footsteps. He dips his fingers with astonishing agility and speed into character, but if he finds something hot or gets hold of something large, he drops it and withdraws with the agility of a scalded cat. Thus we never know his sitters intimately; we never plunge into the depths of their minds or into the more profound regions of their hearts. But we know all that can be known by someone who is always a little afraid of being found out.

But if Gosse's masterpiece and his portraits suffer from his innate regard for caution, much of the fault must be laid upon his age. Even the most superficial student of letters must be aware that in the nineteenth century literature had become, for one reason or another, a profession rather than a vocation, a married woman rather than a lady of easy virtue. It had its organisation, its functions, its emoluments, and a host of people, not primarily writers, were attached to its service. Among them Gosse, of course, was one of the most eminent. ". . . No public dinner where literature was involved", writes Mr. Charteris, "was complete without Gosse to propose or to return thanks for the cause." He welcomed strangers, addressed bodies, celebrated centenaries, presented prizes, and represented letters on all occasions and with the highest delight in the function. Then, again, some intellectual curiosity had risen in the nineties and ardent if uninstructed ladies wished to be enlightened. Here again Gosse was invaluable. By an odd irony, while Churton Collins, his deadly foe, was lecturing in St. James's Square, Gosse was serving up Matthew Arnold to "some of the smartest women in London" in Bruton Street. After this, says Mr. Charteris, he became "a much more frequent guest in Mayfair" and his appetite for social life was whetted. Nothing would be more foolish than to sneer at a natural love of ceremony or a natural respect for the aristocracy, and yet it seems possible that this concern with the ritual of literature, this scrupulous observance of the rites of society encouraged Edmund Gosse in his growing decorum. Friendship had been his ideal; nobody can question the warmth of his youthful affection for Hamo Thornycroft; and yet when one of his friends, Robert Ross, was involved in a famous scandal he could write "I miss your charming company in which I have always delighted . . . I would say to you—be calm, be reasonable, turn for consolation to the infinite resources of literature . . . Write to me when you feel inclined, and however busy I am I will write in reply, and in a more happy season you must come back and be truly welcomed in this house." Is that the voice of friendship, disinterested, fearless, sincere, or the voice of an uneasy man of letters, who is terribly afraid that dear Lady C. will not ask him to dine, or that divine being the Countess of D. will not invite him for the week-end if they suspect him of harbouring Robert Ross, the friend of Oscar Wilde? And later his decorum seems to have drawn a film over his wonted perspicacity as a critic. M. Gide, for example, thought it well to mention certain facts openly in the third volume of his memoirs. "Was it wise? Was it necessary? Is it useful?" Sir Edmund cried, in "painful perplexity." And he was terribly shocked by an incident in E. M. Forster's *Howards End.* "I should like to know", he wrote to Mr. Marsh, "what you think of the new craze for introducing into fiction the high-born maiden who has had a baby? . . . I do not know how an Englishman can calmly write of such a disgusting thing, with such *sang-froid* . . . I cannot help hoping that you may be induced to say something that will redeem him." But when Sir Edmund goes on to say that no high-bred maiden has ever had a baby illegitimately in a French novel one can only suppose that he was thinking, not unnaturally, of the House of Lords.

But if Gosse was no Boswell and still less a St. Francis, he was able to fill a place and create a legend, and perhaps we have no right to demand more. To be oneself is, after all, an achievement of some rarity, and Gosse, as everybody must agree, achieved it, both in literature and in life. As a writer he expressed himself in book after book of history, of biography, of criticism. For over fifty years he was busily concerned, as he put it, with "the literary character and the literary craft". There is scarcely a figure of any distinction, or a book of any importance in modern letters, upon which we cannot have Gosse's opinion if we wish for it. For instance, one may have a curiosity about Disraeli's novels and hesitate which to begin upon. Let us consult Gosse. Gosse advises on the whole that we shall try *Coningsby.* He gives his reasons. He rouses us with a suggestive remark. He defines Disraeli's quality by comparing him with Bulwer, with Mrs. Gore and Plumer Read. He tells an anecdote about Disraeli that was told him by his friend the Duke of Rutland. He breaks off a phrase here and there for our amusement or admiration. All this he does with perfect suavity and precision, so that by the time he has done, Disraeli is left glowing and mantling like an old picture lit up by a dozen bright candles. To illumine, to make visible and desirable, was his aim as a critic. Literature to him was an incomparable mistress and it was his delight "to dress her chaims and make her more beloved". Lovers of course sometimes go further and a child is the result. Critics too sometimes love literature creatively and the fruit of their devotion has a toughness and a fibre that the smooth strains of Sir Edmund's platonic devotion are entirely without. Like all critics who persist in judging without creating he forgets the risk and agony of child-birth. His criticism becomes more and more a criticism of the finished article, and not of the article in the making. The smoothness, the craftsmanship of the work rouse his appreciation and he directs our attention only to its more superficial aspects. In other words, he is a critic for those who read rather than for those who write. But then no creator possesses Gosse's impartiality, or his width of reading, or his lightness and freedom of mind, so that if we want to hold a candle to some dark face in the long portrait gallery of literature there is no better illuminant than Edmund Gosse.

As for his own face, his own idiosyncrasy, only those who saw him at home among his books, or heard him, mimicking, remembering, in one of those club corners that he made, so characteristically, his own, can bring the odds and ends of this excitable but timid, this enthusiastic but worldly, this kindly but spiteful man into one complete synthesis. It was only in talk that he completely expressed himself. "I was not born for solitude", he wrote. Neither was he born for old age and meditation. "You speak of 'the peace which the years bring', but they bring no peace for me", he wrote. Thought and the ardours and agonies of life were not for him. "I have no idea", he said, "how the spiritual world would look to me, for I have never glanced at it since I was a child and gorged with it." It is a cruel fate that makes those who only come into being when they talk fall silent. It is a harsh necessity that brings these warm and mobile characters into the narrow confines of the grave. Sir Edmund was not in the least anxious to depart and leave a world which, with the solitary exception of Churton Collins, had showered upon him so many delightful gifts for seventy-nine years.

DIANA DER—HOVANESSIAN

Its emphasis on the Armenian father aside, "Shifting the Sun" is hardly a personal poem. Indeed, most of its appeal lies in its aphoristic universality. It seems to belong to the timeless world of folk wisdom. It deals in generalities rather than in specifics. It allows perspective. This sense of perspective and affectionate humour make "Shifting the Sun" an appropriate poem for the coda to this book. To the seeming desperation, rage, and anger of poems like Thomas' "Do Not Go Gentle" or Plath's "Daddy," it opposes serenity, acceptance, and gratitude.

SHIFTING THE SUN

When your father dies, say the Irish,
you lose your umbrella against bad weather.
May his sun be your light, say the Armenians.

When your father dies, say the Welsh,
you sink a foot deeper into the earth.
May you inherit his light, say the Armenians.

When your father dies, say the Canadians,
you run out of excuses.
May you inherit his sun, say the Armenians.

When your father dies, say the French,
you become your own father.
May you stand up in his light, say the Armenians.

When your father dies, say the Indians,
he comes back as the thunder.
May you inherit his light, say the Armenians.

When your father dies, say the Russians,
he takes your childhood with him.
May you inherit his light, say the Armenians.

When your father dies, say the English,
you join his club you vowed you wouldn't.
May you inherit his sun, say the Armenians.

When your father dies, say the Armenians,
your sun shifts forever.
And you walk in his light.

EDMUND GOSSE #2

This anthology ends with a dying fall. Like most of the other forgotten essays in Edmund Gosse's long out of print Silhouettes, *"Leslie Stephen" is chatty, rambling, slightly pompous, and stylistically dated. Despite these failings, the intellectual pleasures offered by this piece justify including it. There is, first of all, the pleasure of seeing how Woolf's and Gosse's versions of Leslie Stephen compare. There is also the pleasure of collating their versions and trying to reconstitute the man. As well, there is the pleasure of finding reasons for Virginia Woolf's mordant delight in doing unto Edmund as he had done unto Leslie four years before. Did she take umbrage at the picture he painted of her father, or did his remarks about the negligence of the Woolfs rankle? Further, there is the pleasure of seeing how Gosse transcended himself in writing* Father and Son, *of how inferior the style of the essay is to the moving immediacy and passion of the book. Lastly, there is the pleasure, the deep delight, to be found in getting a truer appreciation of the shadings and highlights Virginia Woolf cast upon her father's portrait, the pleasure of appreciating how much power the father essay gives to the child.*

And power, of course, is the greatest source of inspiration. Ever since Edmund set pen to paper in 1906, children have had many reasons for following his example: Regret. Anger. Affection. Power. Curiosity. Pride. Disgust. Wonder. Self-knowledge. Self-Pity. Pain. Revenge. Fame. Gratitude. Spite—yet the greatest of these is Power. To write about the father is to have power over him. No matter how much the child may rebel against or transcend the father, chronology (Zeus's rebellion against Chronus notwithstanding) dictates that the father has the power of authority in the father-child relationship. The child always has to look back to the father, always has to acknowledge his primacy. Yet if chronology bestows the power of primacy upon the father, to the child it offers the bittersweet

consolation that the child will outlive the father and thus triumph over him.
In writing about the father, the child can savour that power to the fullest; in
writing about the father, the child can have the last word.
Enough digression. Time for Gosse to have another word.

LESLIE STEPHEN

Of all the remarkable men whom has it been my privilege to know during my long life, there is not one on whom I look back with more respect than I do on Leslie Stephen. He was the "very perfect knight" of literature, temperate in judgment, strenuous without ostentation, affectionate without sentimentality. When he died, twenty-one years ago, it was generally admitted that we had lost our most distinguished living critic, and, in width of range if not in height, our leading man of letters. Moreover, Leslie Stephen as the editor of a variety of very important composite publications had come into contact with a larger number of persons than any other contemporary author. His personal influence was universal, and his sympathy extended on all sides of him. It is, therefore, as surprising to me as it is painful to find his genius strangely neglected by the current generation. He is not attacked, but he is not mentioned, which is worse. His sane and courageous opinions are seldom referred to, his delicate humour seems no longer to raise a smile, and clever young men dispute about rationalism in the eighteenth century as though the "History of English Thought" had never been written. I hope that I exaggerate this neglect, and that the publication by the Hogarth Press of "Some Early Impressions" may have the effect of recalling serious readers to a noble figure which is worthy of all their attention and all their homage.

Leslie Stephen, who was born in 1832, was seventy-one years of age when he committed these recollections to paper. Mr. and Mrs. Woolf, who have published the little volume, supply no further information.

Leslie Stephen's admirable biographer, F. W. Maitland, who had seen the notes when he wrote his "Life" in 1906, expressed a hope that they would some day be given to the public, and here they are.

In the summer of 1903 Leslie Stephen was already a dying man, though dying slowly. He had undergone a dangerous operation and had found relief, but his weakness grew upon him steadily, and on the 5th of February, 1904, he passed away. I suppose that these "Impressions" represent almost his latest thoughts. In writing to an American friend he had said: "The trouble with me is that I do not reminisce. I marvel at my tendency to oblivion of all details. I agreed to write—because one does agree. But instead of reminiscences proper, I have really confined myself to general observations. Therefore, I don't expect to startle the readers."

In fact, he does not "startle" us; and it may be admitted that these "Early Impressions" betray some languor. They are beautiful in their serene simplicity, and to those who are familiar with the temper of Leslie Stephen, and delight in it, they are precious, but the shades of evening press upon them a little. They have the "sober colouring" of which Wordsworth spoke; they come from a mind that "hath kept watch o'er man's mortality," that is ready to depart, and that no longer cares for precise touches of detail. It was my sad privilege at this very time, the autumn of 1903, to be summoned, as were so many other friends, to say farewell to Stephen in the house which had been taken for him in a Wiltshire village. He was still just able to be dressed, and to lie in a long chair, very weak and wasted, and with haggard eyes. I should hesitate after twenty years to speak of so sacred a memory if it were not that my thoughts dwell less on the shrunken features, the withered hands, the wild hair and flowing beard, no longer red but grey; and far more on the dignity, the tenderness, the marvellous spiritual repose. Leslie Stephen, with the sunset light upon his face, uncomplaining, patient, even humorous still in a manner almost heart-rending to those on whom he smiled—that is a vision which will abide with me till I too descend "behind the white wave."

Maitland tells us that his famous father, Sir James Stephen, described Leslie as "a sensitive plant grafted on a Norwegian pine." The illustration offers some botanical difficulty, but describes picturesquely enough the mixture of roughness with delicacy which was so characteristic. The roughness was mainly physical. His bony and attenuated frame, with its incalculable length of limb, gave an impression of something saturnine, and not easily or safely to be approached. I think it was he himself who admitted that when he was climbing in the Alps he was "frequently flattened out against the rock like a beast of ill-repute nailed to a barn." Mr. Thomas Hardy, in a sonnet which he never ventured to show to Leslie Stephen, compared him with the Schreckhorn, that inviolate mountain which he had been the first to conquer, and saw in it a

semblance to his personality.
In its quaint glooms, keen lights, and rugged trim.

Gaunt and difficult in his exterior Stephen indubitably was, and formidable in his silences, which were Alpine in their desolation. But underneath this rugged shell there existed a being tremulous in its sensitiveness to every kind of emotion; and, to speak bluntly, what seemed like gruffness proved to be mostly shyness.

As is natural in those who turn to the retrospect of youth in old age, Leslie Stephen dwells fondly on his university days in these last recollections. He was not one of those great men, like Gibbon or Dryden, who look back upon their *alma mater* only to abuse her. He had a passionate and lasting love for Cambridge, which found frequent expression in his writings and is vocal here. We read of Professor Smyth's lectures which always drew an audience, although they were repeated annually, because it was known that at a certain moment the lecturer would burst into tears upon mentioning the sad fate of Marie Antoinette. Leslie Stephen remarks that this was a spectacle worth taking some trouble to witness. He observes that in his own undergraduate days there was no Carlyle or Emerson or Newman at Cambridge to rouse the slumbering intellect and persuade the undergraduate that he had a soul. Leslie Stephen characteristically asserts that this was no defect, but an advantage, since "spiritual guides are very impressive but sometimes very mischievous persons." There was nothing Stephen deprecated more than the formation of prigs, and perhaps we may perceive something of his eighteenth-century bent of mind in his life-long suspicion of religious "enthusiasm.". His advice to students was the purely commonsense one, "Stick to your triposes, grind at your mill, and don't set the universe in order till you have taken your bachelor's degree." This does not preclude an interest in the moral and intellectual questions of the day, which it would be doing the generation of Leslie Stephen a gross injustice to pretend that they neglected.

The impact of one of the greatest of the sons of Cambridge does not, if I remember right, find a record in Maitland's "Life." The following passage, therefore, in the present "Early Impressions" has great value :—

"In my day, the most famous member of the [so-called] 'Apostles' was Clerk-Maxwell, the great physicist, whose mathematical genius was already recognised. He was a fascinating object to me: propounding quaint paradoxes in a broad Scottish accent; capable of writing humorous lampoons upon the dons; and turning his knowledge of dynamics to account by contriving new varieties of 'headers' into the Cam."

Stephen speaks of the eminent professor of experimental physics as though he belonged to an older generation. In fact, Clerk-Maxwell was only by a few months his senior, but he had been extraordinarily precocious from the age of fifteen onwards, and had developed far earlier than his admirer. Clerk-Maxwell died comparatively young in 1879. Stephen was very anxious to be elected into the society of the Apostles, but was "not thought worthy of initiation," he tells us. This appears to have been the keenest of his university disappointments, but the probability is that his shyness and apparent gruffness had most to do with it, in addition to the fact that he was not a Trinity man.

It is impossible to think of Leslie Stephen without a vision of Swiss peaks towering behind him. He says here that "Nature has not qualified me for athletic excellence," but that is surely a mistake; he may have had no aptitude for the conventional "games" now so extended as to be the mechanical tyranny of school life, but his nervous alertness and muscular endurance were very remarkable. Even in middle life, his feats as a pedestrian were famous. I recollect a walk with him—I think, in 1885—when he was living at St. Ives, which was like a nightmare. I was asked whether I would like to go over to Redruth to see the annual meeting of Cornish wrestlers, and, of course, I said that I should. But the implacable long legs of my companion, like a pair of brass compasses, with the fierce sweep of red beard at my side, reduced me to a sad condition before we reached the arena.

It was in the Alpine Club, of which Stephen was, I think, an original member, that he distinguished himself first as a climber, and the earliest of his publications was "The Ascent of the Allelein Horn"; it is notable that he had reached his thirtieth year by that time, and that "The Playground of Europe," his first literary success, dates from his fortieth. He grew up very slowly as a man of letters. He speaks of himself and his Cambridge friends as a set of men, no longer quite young, who "undoubtedly had both legs and stomachs." At the same time, there was no lack of really intellectual intercourse, and in the case of Leslie Stephen himself, if younger geniuses seemed to be racing ahead of him, he was slowly preparing himself for the highest honours by sedulous reading and thinking.

The great body of Leslie Stephen's public work belongs to his middle years. His literary criticism practically opened with the first series of "Hours in a Library" in 1874, his ethical and philosophical criticism with the "History of English Thought in the Eighteenth Century" in 1876. As a biographer, his "Samuel Johnson" in 1878 displayed a power and an adroitness which infinite experience continued to strengthen and polish till they produced the "Studies" of 1898. By the side of all this personal activity, there has to be borne in mind the various editorial work in which Leslie Stephen expended an infinitude of labour. From 1871 onwards he conducted the "Cornhill Magazine"; in 1885 he planned and opened that vast undertaking, the "Dictionary of National Biography." Meanwhile, he was superintending endless ventures, exploiting the provinces of literature, philosophy, and athletics, in all which he delighted. The importance of the little 1878 volume cannot be exaggerated; the enforced study of the character of Samuel Johnson to which he had not hitherto been much attracted, revealed to Leslie Stephen his own native bias. He discovered his close kinship to the great eighteenth-century men of letters, and his subsequent career as a critic was consistent with his attitude towards Johnson, Swift, and Pope. He did not care much for kings in the abstract, but he liked to feel that George III was round the corner.

The rather long and close apology which he put into Gibbon's mouth in the first volume of "Studies of a Biographer" should be read with care. It is Leslie Stephen's own analysis and defence of his attitude to life and literature. The great men of the eighteenth century help us appreciate the source of Stephen's charm, which was not brilliance of expression, though he was often brilliant, and was neither dazzlement of intuition nor novelty of approach, since of each of these he was suspicious. As a biographical critic, he is not luxuriant, nor romantic; his style is apt, on the contrary, to seem bare of ornament, while his perception of beauty is keen on the moral and seldom on the physical side. He was the associate of Ruskin and Symonds and Carlyle, but his soul was pre-Revolution.

In these hectic days of ours, when so much incense is burned on the altars of strange gods, it cannot but be salutary to be reminded of a genius so honest and sober as that of Leslie Stephen. I hope that a wide circle of readers will be tempted by the gracious simplicity of these "Early Impressions" to acquaint themselves with the principal works of the author. They will find all that accompanies ripeness of judgment and severity of taste in the writings of a man who is ever ready to temper those qualities with grace and humour. They will find genuine learning, moving with ease under its apparatus; the impassioned love of truth, anxious on all occasions to discern clearly and think directly; a resolute freedom from prejudice which includes some scorn for the intellectual weakness of the half-hearted. One with whom I was associated in our acquaintance with him as an editor fifty years ago, Robert Louis Stevenson, said of him: "I think it is always wholesome to read Leslie Stephen"; and George Meredith, whose style was at the antipodes of his, considered Stephen's essays as containing "the profoundest and the most sober criticism we have had in our time." I would entreat our youngest pundits to turn to "Hours in a Library" and see whether they cannot recapture for themselves the charm of Leslie Stephen.

ANDRÉ GÉRARD

The final entry in this anthology is included, in part, as a pretext to draw back the gauze curtain of editorial impersonality. Born a twin in 1953, son of a German mother and a Belgian father, I grew up far from Würzburg and from Liège, among the forests and lakes of the coastal pulp and paper town of Powell River, B.C. Lover of endives and sauerkraut, lebkuchen and rice pie, I have a BSc. ('74) and a BA. ('76) from University of British Columbia, and a Master's of English Literature from the University of Washington ('77), and over the years I have worked as broke hustler, green chain hand, postal employee, commercial fisherman, apartment manager, and tutor. The idea for this anthology came to me some five years ago, and although I tried to resist, the idea would not go away. I am, after all, the father of two teenage children, and some of my thoughts were forged in the fiery smithy of experience. Part of the impetus, too, came from seeing how "astronaut kids," children with fathers half a world away, responded to reading personal essays and poems about fathers. A gift for all my children, biological and emotional, this anthology was compiled as an act of affirmation. Despite being an agnostic—one who lacks the certainty to be an atheist—I believe passionately in the power of friendship, loving-kindness, and literature to give meaning to our lives.

One last poem; not necessarily great, certainly personal. Beyond power, there is love. In and beyond love, there is meaning. This last poem and this anthology are expressions of love. They are assertions of meaning, and this meaning would not exist without my mother and my father. Many of the values embodied in this enterprise are their values. Both poem and anthology are acts of faith. They are my myths to live by. Mind you, my Catholic father is no more Adam, or Lot, than my possibly atheistic mother was Persephone. My father's mythic power lies in daily details. His power lies in love and loyalty. It lies in the death of an older sister when he was five years old. It lies in compulsory military service, the fall of Eben Emael, and the death of his mother at the outbreak of World War II. It lies in losing his pregnant girlfriend to the twisted lies of his gendarme father. It lies in serving on military tribunals after the war and in subsequently trying to drink himself to death. It lies in emigrating to Canada as a farm worker and, in 1951, meeting my mother in Ocean Falls. It lies in enduring life as a factory worker so as to feed a family of six. It lies in a marriage of over 50 years. It lies in several painful years of lovingly caring for my mother, as Alzheimer's disease stripped her of memory and all but an infant-like shell of identity. It lies in the chimney fires of my childhood and in my mother's epitaph. It lies in all of this, and in so much more; and, ultimately, it rises up in values transmitted.

"SAUVEZ VOUS, LES ENFANTS!"

Though the epitaph
Has not yet
Been carved into
The grey granite,
I remember
The crackling pipes of the tin chimney,
Darkly glowing red,
And the mirth of the firemen
At her panicked screams.

In the Cranberry cemetery,
Under a black umbrella
With a broken rib,
Despite the hail
My father seeps salt
And says Hail Marys
For my faithless mother;
Whilst I,
Equally bereft,
Far away in my own house
Turn to poetry.

ENVOI

The end, and yet, of course, it's not the end; nor can it be, as long as there are fathers, and children who write about them. Late in my anthology journey, I sought out William New, poet and colleague and close personal friend of Bill Messenger. Bill Messenger, by way of reminder, is one of the four people mentioned in the dedication to this anthology. He was a literature professor at the University of British Columbia—the best kind of professor, rigorous, demanding and inspirational.

Bill New and I met over coffee, and for two hours we shared stories about Bill Messenger, and we talked poems and literature. In our conversation, Bill asked whether or not I had included any Asian-American poems in the anthology. I told him that, no, I had not, though there was one such poem I would dearly have loved to include.

If you look to the following page, you will see that the goad of Bill's question has now spurred me to include that poem. Unfortunately, lack of time, strength, cash, patience and space prevent me from adding other pieces I would dearly love to include. Joyce Carol Oates, Scott Russell Sanders, Anne Boston, and Native-American writer Sherman Alexie—to name a few of the more prominent—are for you to explore on your own. I leave it to you to "sail beyond the sunset."

EATING TOGETHER

In the steamer is the trout
seasoned with slivers of ginger,
two sprigs of green onion, and sesame oil.
We shall eat it with rice for lunch,
brothers, sister, my mother who will
taste the sweetest meat of the head,
holding it between her fingers
deftly, the way my father did
weeks ago. Then he lay down
to sleep like a snow-covered road
winding through pines older than him,
without any travelers, and lonely for no one.

—*Li-Young Lee*

LIST OF NOTABLE
PATREMOIRS

The following list is far from comprehensive. It consists only of some of the more imaginative and interesting patremoirs found while assembling this anthology.

1. Abad, Hector. *Oblivion: A Memoir* (2010)
2. Ackerley, J. R. *My Father and Myself* (1968).
3. Auster, Paul. *The Invention of Solitude* (1982).
4. Blaise, Clark. *I had a Father: A Post-Modern Autobiography* (1993).
5. Bechdel, Allison. *Fun Home* (2006). Graphic novel.
6. Broyard, Bliss. *One Drop: My Father, His Family, and an Unusual Inheritance* (2007)
7. Burnside, John. *A Lie About My Father: A Memoir* (2006).
8. Burroughs, Augusten. *A Wolf at the Table* (2007).
9. Cheever, Susan. *Home Before Dark: A Bibliographical Memoir of John Cheever* (1985).
10. Cooper, Bernard. *The Bill From My Father: A Memoir* (2006).
11. Day, Clarence. *Life with Father* (1935).
12. Downing, Lee E. *A Forgotten Horseman: A Son's Weekend Memoir* (2006)
13. Durcan, Paul. *Daddy, Daddy* (1990). Poems.
14. Fiorito, Joe. *The Closer We Are to Dying* (1999).
15. Flynn, Nick: *Another Bullshit Night in Suck City* (2004).
16. Franks, Lucinda. *My Father's Secret War: A Memoir* (2007).
17. Fraser, Sylvia. *My Father's House* (1987).
18 Freadman, Richard. *Shadow of Doubt: My Father and Myself* (2003)
19. Friedman, Bryan. *The Bodybuilder and I* (2007). Film.

20. Funderburg, Lise. *Pig Candy: Taking My Father South, Taking My Father Home: A Memoir* (2008).
21. Gaita, Raimond. *Romulus, My Father* (1988).
22. Gebler, Carlo. *Father and I* (2000).
23. Gordon, Mary. *The Shadow Man: A Daughter's Search for Her Father* (1996).
24. Gosse, Edmund. *Father and Son* (1907).
25. Greer, Germaine. *Daddy We Hardly Knew You* (1990).
26. Harrison, Kathryn. *The Kiss* (1997).
27. Hill, Dan. *I Am My Father's Son: A Memoir of Love and Forgiveness* (2009).
28. Hochschild, Adam. *Half the Way Home: A Memoir of Father and Son* (1986).
29. Holder, Doug. *Wrestling With My Father* (2005)
30. Kahn, Nathaniel. *My Architect* (2003). Documentary film.
31. Imlach, Gary. *My Father and Other Working-Class Football Heroes* (2005).
32. Lagnado, Lucette. *The Man in the White Sharkskin Suit* (2007).
33. Lane, Patrick. *There is a Season* (2004).
34. Lee, Li-Young. *The Winged Seed: A Remembrance* (1995).
35. Lockridge, Larry. *Shade of the Raintree: The Life and Death of Ross Lockridge, Jr.* (1994).
36. Martin, Sandra, ed. *The First Man in My Life: Daughters Write About Their Fathers* (2007). Of particular interest to readers of *Fathers: A Literary Anthology* are the introduction by Margaret Atwood and a piece about Mordecai Richler by his daughter, Emma.
37. Moore, Honor. *The Bishop's Daughter: A Memoir* (2008).
38. Morrison, Blake. *And When Did You Last See Your Father?* (1993).
39. Mortimer, John. *A Voyage Round My Father* (1963). Play.
40. Naipaul, VS. *Between Father and Son: Family Letters* (1991). Letters
41. Offit, Sidney. *Memoir of the Bookie's Son* (2003)

42. Olds, Sharon. *The Father* (1993). Poetry.

43. Orlove, Benjamin S. *In My Father's Study* (1995).

44. Ondaatje, Christopher. *The Man-Eater of Punanai: A Journey of Discovery to the Jungles of Old Ceylon* (1992).

45. Ondaatje, Michael. *Running in the Family* (1996).

46. Owen, Ursula, ed. *Fathers: Reflections by Daughters* (1985).

47. Roth, Philip. *Patrimony: A True Story* (1991).

48. Sabar, Ariel. *My Father's Paradise: A Son's Search for His Jewish Past in Kurdish Iraq* (2008).

49. Saro-Wiwa, Jr., Ken. *In the Shadow of a Saint* (2000).

50. Spiegelman, Art. *Maus I and II* (1986).

51. Silverman, Sue. *Because I Remember Terror, Father, I Remember You* (1996).

52. Trillin, Calvin. *Messages from My Father* (1996).

53. Toews, Miriam. *Swing Low: A Life* (2000).

54. West, Paul. *My Father's War* (2005).

55. Washington-Williams, Essie Mae. *Dear Senator: A Memoir by the Daughter of Strom Thurmond* (2005).

56. Wideman, John Edgar. *Fatheralong: A Meditation on Fathers and Sons, Race and Society* (1994).

57. Wolff, Geoffrey. *The Duke of Deception: Memories of My Father* (1979).

58. Yang, Belle. *Forget Sorrow: An Ancestral Tale* (2010)

THUMBNAIL BIOGRAPHIES

These biographies are impressionistic in nature. Written to give a sense of the writers and their accomplishments, they are also meant to seduce and assist you to read further. Often, too, they provide further information or insights about the writers' relationship to their fathers.

MARGARET ATWOOD

Margaret Atwood, grand matriarch of Canadian Literature, a Virginia Woolf figure, loved, feared, and revered, was born in 1939. It is part of her mythology that she was home-schooled until the age of 14, spent long periods of her childhood in the wilderness of Northern Quebec on field trips with her biologist father and her dietician mother, and later studied under Northrop Frye. Among her many awards are the Governor General's Award, and the Giller and Booker Prizes, for books as various as *The Circle Game* (1964), *The Handmaid's Tale* (1985), and *The Blind Assassin* (2000). *Survival: A Thematic Guide to Canadian Literature* (1972), her seminal work in Canadian literary criticism, helped to establish Canadian Literature as a topic for serious study, as well as positing that the characters in Canadian novels are often survivors with victim mentalities. Perhaps in opposition to this insight, the heroine of *Surfacing* (1972), the brilliant, sinewy novel published in the same year as *Survival*, declares: "This above all, to refuse to be a victim. . . . I have to recant, give up the old belief that I am powerless." Given the subject of this anthology, it must also be noted that the chief plot device of *Surfacing* is the hunt for a missing father.

JAMES BALDWIN

"Each of us, helplessly and forever, contains the other." Black, homo-sexual, and lacking formal education beyond high school, James Baldwin (August 2, 1924–November 30, 1987) believed that as a writer "one is trying to change the consciousness of other people." It is a mea-sure of Baldwin's impact on American consciousness that on May 17th, 1963, he was featured on the cover of *Time Magazine*, and that in 2005, eighteen years after his death, the United States postal service dedicated a postage stamp to him. Harlem-raised, the adoptive son of a poor, storefront preacher—child-preacher himself at the age of 14—Baldwin was the eldest of nine children, and from an early age, he "took care of the kids and dealt with Daddy." After graduating from Dewitt Clinton High School, a predominantly white secondary school for boys in the Bronx, Baldwin found his way to Greenwich Village and from there to Paris. His first novel, *Go Tell It on the Mountain* (1953), centres on a young black boy, struggling to realize himself within the bleak bound-aries of Harlem. His second novel, *Giovanni's Room* (1956), is an anguished, yet tender exploration of the distorting pressures faced by a young American living in Paris and trying to come to terms with his homosexuality. Other important novels and plays include *Another Country* (1962), *If Beale Street Could Talk* (1974), *Blues for Mr. Charlie* (1964), and *The Amen Corner* (1954). While Baldwin also published a volume of poetry, *Jimmy's Blues* (1983), and a collection of highly suc-cessful short stories, *Going to Meet the Man* (1965), his greatest impact was as an essayist, and collections of essays such as *Notes of a Native Son* (1955), *Nobody Knows My Name* (1961), and *The Fire Next Time* (1963) made him an influential voice of the American civil rights movement. According to a Random House publishing blurb, "The Fire Next Time, " an essay first published in *The New Yorker*, "galvanized the nation and continues to reverberate as perhaps the most prophetic and defining statement ever written of the continuing costs of Americans' refusal to face their own history." Mentor and inspiration to writers as important and varied as Maya Angelou, Toni Morrison, Adrienne Rich, and Colm Tóibín, Baldwin certainly continues to effect deep changes in individual and social consciousness.

ALISON BECHDEL
Born Sept 10th, 1960, Alison Bechdel was raised in the small town of Beech Creek, Pennsylvania. Her parents taught high school English, and like his father and grandfather before him, her father also operated the town funeral home. After first attending Simon's Rock College, Bechdel received a BA from Oberlin in 1981. In 1983, while living in New York, she published the first strip of what would become the comic strip "Dykes to Watch Out For." Eventually published by over sixty newspapers, this sharply humorous cartoon mixed empathetic explorations of personal relationships with clear-eyed social criticism. Bechdel produced the strip for twenty-five years, and collections were repeatedly published in award-winning book form, culminating in *The Essential Dykes to Watch Out For* (2008). In 1996, Bechdel published *Fun Home*, a graphic narrative in epic form. On the literary side, comparisons with James Joyce and Annie Dillard are not out of line, especially as Bechdel boldly invokes Joyce as Homer to her Vergil, Vergil to her Dante. On the graphic side, Crumb, Cruse, and Satrapi pale in comparison. The only graphic narrators who approach her are Sacco and Spiegelman, and important as they are, they lack her allusiveness and her subtlety. Just as "Dykes to Watch Out For" fused, explored, and expanded possibilities of community, lesbian identity, and self, *Fun Home* fuses, explores, and expands possibilities of epic, graphic narrative, and memoir.

SAUL BELLOW
Né Solomon Bellows, possibly June 10th, 1915; died Saul Bellow, April 5th, 2005. Like his novels, Saul Bellow looms larger than life. Married

five times, father of five children (the last born when he was 83-years-old), Bellow mythologized the world he lived in. Lachine-born to a poor family of Jewish-Russian immigrants; fluent in French, Hebrew and Yiddish; raised in Prohibition-era Chicago; educated at the University of Chicago and at Northwestern; recipient of numerous awards, including three National Book Awards, a Guggenheim Fellowship, a Pulitzer, and the 1976 Nobel Prize in Literature; friends with Ralph Ellison, Arthur Miller, Delmore Schwartz, Allan Bloom, Phillip Roth, Martin Amis, and John Berryman, Bellow spent his famously Chicago-centered life observing the confusing chaos of modern urban existence, sifting it for signs of soul and meaning, and re-imagining it using a highly colloquial yet erudite style filled with joyful exuberance, high humour, profound insight, and gentle compassion. His novels include masterpieces such as *Seize the Day* (1956), *Henderson the Rain King* (1959), *Herzog* (1964), and *Humboldt's Gift* (1975). Notable, too, is *To Jerusalem and Back: A Personal Account* (1976), musings on the state of Israel in the form of a travel memoir. Though Bellow has rightly been challenged and criticized for philosophical and personal inconsistencies, though he sometimes failed "to imagine life on premises different from [his] own," his greatness is undeniable. His writings repeatedly rescue us from "the humiliations of inconsequence."

ALAN BENNETT

Born in Leeds in 1934, Bennett studied medieval history at Oxford before escaping academia by achieving early fame in 1960 as a member of the comedy stage review *Beyond the Fringe* with Dudley Moore, Jonathan Miller, and Peter Cook. Since then, Bennett, while continuing to work as an actor, has written many radio, television, and screen pieces, most notably *Me-I'm Afraid of Virginia Woolf* (1978), *An Englishman Abroad* (1983), *A Private Function* (1984), and *Talking Heads* (1987). His numerous stage productions include *Habeas Corpus* (1973), *Kafka's Dick* (1986), *The Madness of King George* (1991), and most recently *The*

History Boys (2004), a play which won numerous best play awards in England and the United States. Critic Michael Brooke has described Bennett as "not just a great writer but the definitive chronicler of a certain kind of English ordinariness, whose outwardly placid surface conceals inner turmoil as intense as anything displayed by the more emotionally articulate."

JOHN BERRYMAN

Berryman was born John Smith in 1914, and in 1926 his banker father, also named John Smith, died an apparent suicide. Within ten weeks his mother married John Berryman, another banker, but young John Smith did not legally become John Berryman until 1936. After studying at Columbia, where he was befriended and mentored by Mark Van Doren, Berryman attended Clare College Cambridge on a two-year Kellet scholarship before teaching at Harvard, Princeton and the University of Minnesota. Berryman's life and work was tortured by a sense of loss, and his personal life was a succession of physical and mental breakdowns, financial strains, divorces, and failed battles against alcohol. Berryman owes much of his high reputation to *Homage to Mistress Bradstreet* (1956) and *The Dream Songs* (1969), longer poetic works which earned him numerous awards and prizes, including the Pulitzer Prize, the Bollingen Prize, and the National Book Award. While his poems have been called confessional, he often distances the reader through formal structure, tortured syntax, varied masks, punning playfulness, and stylized theatricality. The impact of his father's supposed suicide on his life and his work is undeniable, but Berryman also recognized that "maybe my long self-pity has been based on an error, and there has been no (hero-)villain (Father) ruling my life, but only an unspeakably powerful possessive adoring MOTHER ." Mother or father, on January 7th, 1962 Berryman killed himself by jumping from the Washington Avenue Bridge in Minneapolis, Minnesota. Of the many influences on his writing, Shakespeare, Yeats, and Crane are perhaps the most significant. Of Yeats he said, "I didn't want to be *like* Yeats; *I* wanted to *be* Yeats." Yeats would seem to be a dangerous poet to emulate.

BLISS BROYARD

Born September 5th, 1966, in Greenwich, Connecticut, daughter of Anatole Paul Broyard and Alexandra Nelson, Bliss Broyard was raised in Fairfield, Connecticut, spent her summers at the family's summer home on Martha's Vineyard, attended Greens Farms Academy, and earned her MFA in creative writing as a Henry Hoyns Fellow at the University of Virginia. Now married and a mother, Broyard has in large part developed her writing life through writings which circle around her father, a noted critic and reviewer for the *New York Times*, and supposedly a model for Coleman Silk, the passing protagonist in Philip Roth's novel *The Human Stain*. The publication of "My Father's Daughter" in 1998 was followed by the collection of short stories, *My Father, Dancing* (1999), and by the patremoir, *One Drop: My Father's Hidden Life—A Story of Race and Family Secrets* (2007). Unlike Essie Mae Washington-Williams, who grew up black only to discover that she was the unacknowledged daughter of a rich, powerful, white man, Bliss Broyard grew up white only to discover that her loving and beloved father was partly black.

ANNE CARSON

While it is possible that her father once said to her, "The letters of your salad are very large," it is certain that Anne Carson was born in Toronto, June 21st, 1950. Because Ann Carson limits the biographical blurb in her books to the short and often false sentence, "Anne Carson lives in Canada," reviewers and critics are quick to talk about her as "notoriously reticent about her personal life." Despite that supposed reticence, she has given interviews to the *U of T Magazine*, *The Guardian*, and *The New York Times*, among others, and it is public knowledge that she grew up Irish Catholic in small-town Ontario, daughter of a banker-father and housewife-mother; that at the age of five she tried to eat an illustrated copy of *The Lives of Saints*; that she was introduced to the study of Greek by a high school teacher and went on to obtain a Ph.D. in classics by studying at University of Toronto and St. Andrews; that she has taught at Princeton, McGill, and the University of Michigan; that she married and divorced; that her highly original and idiosyncratic books blend the essayistic with the poetical, the personal with the classical, the philosophical with the painful; and that she has won numerous prestigious awards including the T. S. Eliot Prize for Poetry, The Griffin Poetry Prize, a MacArthur Fellowship, and a Guggenheim Fellowship. Her work, despite its erudition, complexity, humour, and deep grounding in classical scholarship, often seems highly personal—especially in books such as *Glass, Irony, and God* (1992), *Plainwater* (2002), and *The Beauty of the Husband* (1995). In her book, *Decreation* (2005), Carson signposts the words of Simone Weil: "We participate in the creation of the world by decreating ourselves." Of course, Carson is often disingenuous in her remarks. She has also said that "Loneliness is not an important form of suffering."

ANGELA CARTER

When Angela Carter, aged 51, died of cancer in 1992, she left behind a husband eighteen years younger than herself and an eight-year-old son. She also left behind a body of work that includes several anthologies of fairy tales, nine novels including *The Magic Toyshop* (1967), *The Infernal Desire Machine of Doctor Hoffman* (1972), *Nights at the Circus* (1984), and *Wise Children* (1991), the radical collection of short stories *The Bloody Chamber and Other Stories* (1979), several children's books, an opera libretto, and film scripts for the movies *The Magic Toyshop* and *Company of Wolves*. While a relatively conventional childhood, a storytelling maternal grandmother, anorexia, a stint as a reporter for the Croydon Advertiser, an early failed marriage, English literature studies at the University of Bristol, two years living in Japan, close association with the feminist Virago Press, and teaching at universities such as Brown University and the University of East Anglia might be used to construct a rationale for her life and writing, Carter is best understood as an iconoclast who waged war against the distorting limitations that culture and society try to impose on the self. Folklore, fairy tales, puppets, masks, and mirrors are repeated tropes in her works, tropes which she uses to assault conventionality and repression. If she was, as her friend Salman Rushdie called her, "a benevolent witch-queen, a burlesque artist of genius and antic grace," she was also, as Meja Makinen has said, an "avant-garde literary terrorist of feminism," who was not afraid to explore some of the darker recesses of the human mind. A writer who both invites and resists labelling, she is one of the most original, provocative, and life-affirming writers of the second half of the 20th century.

RAYMOND CARVER

Raymond *Clevie* Carver, Jr., May 25, 1938 – August 2, 1988. "I have to say that the greatest single influence on my life, and on my writing, directly and indirectly, has been my two children. They were born before I was twenty, and from beginning to end of our habitation under the same roof—some nineteen years in all—there wasn't any area of my life where their heavy and often baleful influence didn't reach." The brutality of this Carver statement can only be excused by poverty and alcohol. Carver's parents' marriage was blighted by both, as were the almost twenty five years of Carver's first marriage, and it is a truism of Carver studies that Carver fiction never strays far from the early Carver reality of crap jobs, itinerant poverty, and the ravages of alcohol. Despite this reality Carver did earn a degree from Humboldt State College, attended Iowa State, held a succession of marginal teaching positions, and gradually started getting short stories and poems published. Famously and controversially, Carver's early fiction was heavily edited by Esquire's Gordon Lish, and it attracted labels such as "minimalist" and "Dirty Realism." Free of alcohol and increasingly free of poverty and of Lish, Carver spent the last 10 years of his life living with Tess Gallagher, the woman he married in June of 1988. When he died six weeks later of lung and brain cancer, obituaries hailed him as the American Chekhov. Carver's admiration for Chekhov is well recorded, and certainly in his best stories, stories like *"The Errand,"* *"Elephant," "Cathedral,"* and *"A Small, Good Thing,"* Carver produced Chekhovian masterpieces, "stories that shrive us as well as delight and move us, that lay bare our emotions in ways only true art can accomplish."

BRUCE CHATWIN

Born in 1940 and died in 1989, Chatwin grew up in Birmingham and was educated at Marlborough College. At 18 he joined Sotheby's as a porter and with his brilliance, social gifts, and artistic eye he was a director by 25, before quitting at 26. The word precocious comes to mind. After studying archaeology and working as a writer and reporter for the *London Sunday Times,* in 1976 Chatwin famously resigned with the terse telegram: "Have gone to Patagonia." *In Patagonia* (1977) was the result of this trip, followed by *The Viceroy of Ouidah* (1980), *On the Black Hill* (1982), *The Songlines* (1987), and finally *Utz* (1988). Chatwin was subversively experimental, and his books—written in lyrical, gemlike prose—like Chatwin himself, refuse easy categorization, though *In Patagonia* and *The Songlines* revolutionized the genre of the literary travel book. Chatwin's passions included provocative ideas, the unusual, nomads, travel, art, outlaws, culture, mythological creatures, miracles, and famous people. Deeply influenced by the adventurer, writer, and mythologizer Blaise Cendrars, Chatwin often fictionalized his experience to tell—as his biographer Nicholas Shakespeare so wittily put it—"not a half truth, but a truth and a half."

WINSTON CHURCHILL

"Some chicken! Some neck!" Born 1874, died 1965, Winston Churchill became the pugnacious embodiment of the thick-jowled British bulldog, and much of the humour of his remark made to the Canadian parliament in 1941, a remark intended as a riposte to comments allegedly made by French generals that "In three weeks England will have her neck wrung like a chicken," lies in trying to imagine Churchill's thick, massive neck as that of a scrawny chicken. Descended on his father's side from the 1st Duke of Marlborough and on his mother's side from Leonard Jacobsen, multi-millionaire shareholder of *The New York Times*, Churchill's political career is too lengthy and too well-known to bear repeating. Amateur historians who want to refresh their memories and deepen their knowledge can delve into wonderful biographies by Martin Gilbert and William Manchester. More relevant to this anthology is Churchill's literary career, for which he received the Nobel Prize in Literature in 1953. It was awarded for "his mastery of historical and biographical description, as well as for brilliant oratory in defending exalted human values."

He started his writing career as a daring war correspondent and sometimes soldier, reporting on the Spanish-Cuban conflict for *The Daily Graphic*, the Pathan revolt for *The Daily Telegraph*, and the Sudan conflict, the battle of Omdurman, and the Boer War for *The Morning Post*. These conflicts produced four books, *The Story of the Malakand Field Force* (1898), *The River War* (1899), *London to Ladysmith via Pretoria* (1900), and *Ian Hamilton's March* (1900), to which Churchill added biographies of his father, *Lord Randolph Churchill* (1906), and his four volume biography of his famous ancestor, *Marlborough: His Life and Times* (1933-8). Good as these books are, his Nobel was primarily awarded for his speeches, *Into Battle (Blood, Sweat and Tears)* (1941) and *The Unrelenting Struggle* (1942), to name but two collections, and for his massive histories, *The World Crisis* (six volumes, 1923-1931) and *The Second World War* (six volumes, 1948-1953). Stating the obvious, former Prime Minister Lord Balfour described *The World Crisis* as "Winston's brilliant autobiography, disguised as world history."

JUDITH ORTIZ COFER

"Language," says Judith Ortiz Cofer, "is more powerful than chemistry." Born in Hormigueros, Puerto Rico, in 1952 and, from the age of four, raised in Pattison, New Jersey, Cofer has described herself as "a child caught in that lonely place between two cultures and two languages." Her formal education includes a B.A. from Augusta College, Georgia, and an M.A. from Florida Atlantic University; her informal education includes listening to the *cuentos* of her Puerto Rican *abuela*, or grandmother. Her novels, *The Meaning of Consuelo* (2003) and the Pulitzer nominated *The Line of the Sun* (1989), and her collections of essays, stories and poems, among them *The Latin Deli* (1993), *Women in Front of the Sun: On Becoming a Writer* (2000), and *A Partial Remembrance of a Puerto Rican Childhood* (1990), owe much to that grandmother. In all her work, Cofer follows "the winding path of memory" to recover transformative stories from the gritty particulars of "the examined life." Mother of a daughter, and faculty member at the University of Georgia since 1984, Judith Ortiz Cofer is best described by the following words—words taken from *The Meaning of Consuelo* and words which complete the quotation used to begin this paragraph: "You are what you hear, what you read. And how you remember words, how you tell a story to yourself, makes *you* up. You tell yourself as you live your life."

LEONARD COHEN

"Like a bird on a wire / Like a drunk in a midnight choir / I have tried, in my way, to be free." Whether as lover, poet, novelist, singer, Zen adept, cultural icon, or maker of snow angels and plastic saints, Leonard Cohen is always a nimble-minded ironist who refuses easy categorization. Born September 21st, 1934, into a Jewish middle-class family, he grew up in the affluent Westmount District of Montreal. When his clothier father died in 1943, the nine-year-old Leonard supposedly marked the event by sewing a poem into one of his father's formal bow ties, before burying the tie in the garden. After studying literature at McGill, Cohen flirted briefly with law school at McGill and graduate school at Columbia, before dropping out to become a writer. Montreal, Hydra, New York, and Los Angeles have been among the most influential geographical and psychic landscapes in his cosmopolitan evolution. Critically, Cohen is generally viewed as a flawed and minor early prophet in the church of Canadian Literature, and his current status as cultural icon rests principally on his reputation as songwriter and troubadour of loss and longing. Certainly, his books of poetry, such as *Let Us Compare Mythologies* (1956) and *The Spice-Box of the Earth* (1961), and his two novels, *The Favourite Game* (1963) and *Beautiful Losers* (1966), are unfairly neglected in comparison to the attention and adulation heaped upon songs such as "So Long Marianne," "Suzanne," "Bird on a Wire," "Chelsea Hotel #2," "Hallelujah," and "Democracy." Though Irving Layton once referred to Leonard Cohen "as a narcissist who hates himself," it is more profitable to think of Cohen as a performance artist, an explorer of possible selves, who, as Michael Ondaatje suggested in *Leonard Cohen* (1970), has used the mask of pop-sainthood to bridge the gap "between the serious artist and the public image."

E. E. CUMMINGS

"What are you doing at the other end of fathership?" The son of a Harvard sociologist who later became a Unitarian Minister, Edward Estlin Cummings (1894-1962) was raised in Cambridge, Massachusetts, and educated at Harvard, and his work and life has often been interpreted as both a reaction against and an affirmation of this background. Cummings, though, is far more than the typographical and syntactical iconoclast of popular myth, far more than the Bollingen Prize-winning free spirit of American poetry. Even in his first published book, *The Enormous Room* (1922)—a superb fictionalized account of his three-month imprisonment in a French prisoner of war camp—Cummings declared himself as the champion of the individual and the enemy of the stultifying forces of bureaucracy. Similarily, his poetry—whether intensely lyrical or savagely satirical, experimental or profoundly conventional—while attacking passivity and unthinking conventionality, celebrates love, spontaneity, and courageous individualism. His many poems include such gems as "anyone lived in a pretty how town," "a salesman is an it that stinks Excuse," "i sing of Olaf glad and big," "if i have made, my lady, intricate," "in Just-," "in spite of everything," "pity this busy monster, manunkind," "r-p-o-p-h-e-s-s-a-g-r," and "the Cambridge ladies who live in furnished souls." Well-connected, sociable, loyal, and exceedingly witty, in the course of his life, Cummings was friends with Hart Crane, John Dos Passos, Ford Maddox Ford, Marianne Moore, Ezra Pound, Dylan Thomas, and William Carlos Williams. Sustained by family, patrons, a frugal lifestyle and, eventually, income from his writing, Cummings spent most of his life living in Greenwich Village. Though he had numerous relationships and was married three times, Cummings is only known to have fathered one child. She was 27 before she learned that Cummings was her father, and hers is the question which opens this sketch.

CLARENCE DAY

"Clarence, of violent father reverent son," was born November 18th, 1874, and died December 27th, 1935. The eldest of five boys (though the youngest died at only one year old), for much of his life Day served as a buffer between his blustering, domineering, yet well-intentioned, father and his spirited, resourceful, willful mother. After graduating from Yale in 1896, Day became a partner in his father's stockbroking firm and also joined the Naval Reserves. The onset of crippling arthritis in 1899 left him a lifelong semi-invalid and forced him to retire from his father's firm in 1903 (son and father retired at the same time), even if he did continue to be involved in business affairs throughout his life and was, for several years, owner of the *Yale Alumni Weekly*. Day's arthritis was so severe that he was eventually forced to have his knees fused, and in later years he could only write by suspending his arm over the page with a trolley and sling device. Perceptive, fair-minded, and playful, Day found an outlet for his creative energies in producing essays, stories, and whimsical political cartoons for newspapers and popular magazines such as *Harper's Weekly, Metropolitan Magazine,* and the *Ladies' Home Journal.* Day did not marry until 1928, a year after his father's death, but he had strong friendships with a number of bright women and, not surprisingly, was an active supporter of suffragette and feminist causes. His first book, *This Simian World* (1920), wry, thoughtful speculations on the sociological implications of Darwinian theory, was followed by an equally well-received collection of essays entitled *The Crow's Nest* (1921). However, it wasn't until the last months of his life that Day achieved financial success as a writer. *Life with Father,* a compilation of pieces originally written for *The New Yorker,* was published in 1935 and became an immediate bestseller. Adapted as a play in 1939, *Life with Father* ran for over seven years and is still the longest-running non-musical play ever to run on Broadway. Day's daughter, Wendy Veevers-Carter, has published, in electronic book form, a two-volume biographical compilation of sketches, diaries, and letters which gives intriguing glimpses of this caring, charming, quietly heroic man, this— as he once wrote of W. S. Gilbert—heartening "frontiersman of emotion."

DIANA DER-HOVANESSIAN

While Diana Der-Hovanessian has not revealed her date of birth to the editors of literary encyclopedias, she has said that her father was a soldier-hero who fought for the first Armenian Republic, and that her mother was born in Worcester, Massachusetts, to Armenian parents. Der-Hovanessian grew up in Massachussets and obtained an AB from Boston University. President of the illustrious New England Poetry Club for almost thirty years, she has devoted much of her life to championing poetry and bearing proud witness to Armenian history and culture. Not only do many of her poems reference the life, history and culture of Armenia, she has translated many major Armenian poets into English. Her accomplishments as a translator have been recognized by numerous awards and by two Fulbright scholarships, scholarships which she used to teach and study in Yerevan, Turkey. Although she has published some twenty-three books of poetry, few if any of her poems have achieved the success of "Shifting the Sun."

ANNIE DILLARD

Pittsburgh born in 1945, Annie Dillard was raised in American Standard comfort. A book rat at an early age, she gradually discovered boys, smoking, and drag racing. For her sins she was sent to Hollins College, Virginia, where she earned a B.A. and an M.A. Tellingly, her M.A. thesis was entitled, "Walden Pond and Thoreau." Three times married—the first time, in 1965, to Richard Dillard, eight years her senior and her creative writing instructor at Hollins; the second time to the father of her daughter; and the third to noted biographer and Thoreau scholar Robert Richardson—Dillard was nominally raised Presbyterian, once called herself "spiritually promiscuous," and is now a Roman Catholic. Not surprisingly, her books are infused with a powerful, almost mystical spirituality. Her best books are essayistic in nature. Two, in particular, stand out. The 1974 Pulitzer-Prize-winning *Pilgrim at Tinker Creek* rivals Thoreau's *Walden* as a masterpiece of nature writing and as a "meteorological journal of the mind." Very different, yet equally impressive is *An American Childhood* (1987). Modeled on Twain's *Life On the Mississippi,* this lambent memoir limns a child's awakening to consciousness within a specific historical and cultural matrix. An American original, Dillard at her best uses "an ordinary bit of what is real" to probe "the infinite fabric of time that eternity shoots through."

RITA DOVE

Though Rita Dove was born in 1952, she shares many characteristics with Barack Obama's so-called "Joshua Generation," the generation of idealistic, high achieving, middle class, young, black Americans who, because of the efforts of previous generations, are not defined by skin colour alone and can choose to fight other battles. A Presidential Scholar in 1970, as one of the top 100 undergraduates in the United States, Dove received her undergraduate degree from Miami University, spent a year learning German and studying European Literature at the University of Tübingen on a Fulbright Scholarship, and obtained a MFA from the Iowa Writers' Workshop in 1977. Her first full book of poetry, *The Yellow House on the Corner*, appeared in 1980, her second, *Museum*, (which includes "Grape Sherbet", as well as several other fine father poems), appeared in 1983, and in 1987 she won the Pulitzer Prize for *Thomas and Beulah* (1986), a work in which she conflates and fictionalizes the lives of her aunts, uncles, and grandparents to explore how history intersects with individual lives. In 1993, she became the youngest poet ever to be named Poet Laureate of the United States. Her books include *On the Bus With Rosa Parks* (1999), *American Smooth* (2004), and *Sonata Mulattica* (2009), and her imagination encompasses extremes as disparate as the bloodthirsty madness of General Trujillo and the unassuming heroism of Rosa Parks. While Dove has said that her poetry tends "towards understatement and subtlety," there is often an explosive quality in the fierce restraint of her art. In poem after poem, she offers "a home for all who are dispossessed," celebrating the integrity of the self as it struggles to be accepted on its own terms in the larger world.

MARY GORDON

Mary Gordon was born in Far Rockaway, New York, in 1949, and her work as novelist, biographer, essayist, and short story writer is deeply marked by her fascination with her origins. Her highly successful novels include *Final Payments* (1978), *The Company of Women* (1981) and *Pearl* (2005), and she has won numerous awards (including a Pushcart prize and two O. Henry first prizes) for her short stories. Gordon's most remarkable book is *The Shadow Man: A Daughter's Search for Her Father* (1996), a memoir in which she sketches a passionate portrait of a deeply flawed man, a shabby pornographer with literary pretensions, a convert to Christianity who was so ashamed of his immigrant and Jewish origins that he hid his past and became a nasty anti-Semite and a writer of speeches for Joe McCarthy. Given the depth of the feelings that Gordon shows towards a father who died when she was so young, it is perhaps not surprising that she twice married literary men almost 30 years older than herself. That said, although it is tempting to view Mary Gordon's life solely through the prism of her father, she clearly owes much of her strength and clarity to her mother, a rugged survivor who despite near-incapacitating polio gave birth to Mary when she was 41, and then supported her feckless husband and her baby girl by working as a legal secretary.

EDMUND GOSSE

Born 1849, raised the only child of strict Puritan Plymouth Brethren, motherless at seven, Edmund Gosse had a gift for friendship and for making favourable connections. Thomas Arnold, Robert Browning, and Lord Tennyson provided personal references for him when he applied for a position as Cambridge Clark Lecturer in 1883—a position granted to Leslie Stephen, though Gosse did achieve it the following year when Stephen stepped down—and in the course of his life he developed close, personal friendships with Lawrence Alma-Tadema, Max Beerbohm, Thomas Hardy, Rider Haggard, A.E. Housman, Henry James, Siegfried Sassoon, Robert Louis Stevenson, Algernon Swinburne, and Viscount Haldane, twice Lord Chancellor, to name a few of the more famous. Despite a lack of formal education and, in the words of his close friend Henry James, "a genius for inaccuracy," he became the pre-eminent man of letters of his generation, eventually writing hundreds of critical pieces as chief reviewer for the *Sunday Times*, 1919-1927. He is credited with bringing Henrik Ibsen, André Gide, and Sassoon to the attention of the British public, and with championing the neglected John Donne. Although he became Librarian of the House of Lords (1904-1924) and was knighted in 1925, he had his detractors. Aldous Huxley called him "the bloodiest little old man I have ever seen," and according to Evelyn Waugh, "His eminence sprang from his sedulous pursuit of the eminent. . . . I saw Gosse as Mr Tulkinghorn, the soft-footed, inconspicuous; ill-natured habitué of the great world, and I longed for a demented lady's maid to make an end of him." In point of fact, Gosse died in 1928 while undergoing prostate surgery.

THOMAS HARDY

"Ere be the 'eart, but where be the rest of 'ee?" In her delightful biography, *Thomas Hardy: The Time-Torn Man* (2007), Claire Tomalin describes how in 1866 Hardy, a 26-year-old employee of London architect Arthur Blomfield, oversaw the exhumation of hundreds of bodies from St. Pancras churchyard as part of the preparation for the building of St. Pancras Station. Apart from its Gothic aspect, this incident is of interest in showing how Hardy, a man whose name today is synonymous with a mythical Wessex countryside, was shaped by forces which extended far beyond those of his native Dorset. Hardy was born in Higher Bockhampton, Dorset, on June 2nd, 1840. His father was a mason and village violinist, and his mother, though relatively well-read and ambitious, a servant. At 16 Hardy started articles to become an architect, and in 1862 he moved to London where he spent five years working, studying, and writing poetry. Forced to return to Dorset because of ill health, Hardy gradually turned to novel writing. Though his first novel was never published, Hardy was encouraged and mentored by the likes of George Meredith and Leslie Stephen, and the latter, as editor of *Cornhill Magazine*, published *Far from the Madding Crowd* (1874) and *The Hand of Ethelberta* (1876) in serial form. In all, Hardy wrote some 14 novels, most notably *The Mayor of Castorbridge* (1886), *Tess of the d'Urbervilles* (1891), and *Jude the Obscure* (1895). After the publication of *Jude*, Hardy, now financially secure, stopped writing novels and devoted the next 33 years of his writing life to poetry. "Drummer Hodge," "Heredity," "The Man He Killed," "In Time of 'The Breaking of Nations,'" "The Darkling Thrush," and "The Voice" are but a few of his more notable poems.

Hardy's writings, deeply rooted in Dorset country life, often dramatize aspirations thwarted by constraints of biology, society, history, and accident. Twice married, Hardy never had children, and despite good intentions and loving kindness both marriages were gradually warped and twisted by disillusionment and disappointment. More successful in literature than marriage, Hardy influenced writers as diverse as D. H. Lawrence, Dylan Thomas, and Seamus Heaney. W. H. Auden even went so far as to refer to Hardy as "my poetical father." When he died in 1928, most of his ashes were buried in Westminster Abbey, and Prime Minister Stanley Baldwin, George Bernard Shaw, A. E. Housman, Rudyard Kipling, and Sir Edmund Gosse were among the pallbearers.

ROBERT HAYDEN

"Old Four Eyes fled / to safety in the danger zones." These lines are a biography in miniature. In his writing and his life Hayden is a poet of struggle and transformation. His parents separated before his birth in 1913, and he was raised and supposedly adopted "Robert Hayden" by an unhappily married neighbour couple. His childhood was coloured by coke bottle glasses, books, his stepfather's strong Baptist faith, family tensions, and by growing up poor and black in the Detroit ghetto of "Paradise Valley." Hayden survived the Depression as a student at Detroit City College, did research on African American History for the Federal Writers' Project, and studied under Auden while earning a Masters in English at the University of Michigan. Raised Baptist, Hayden became a Bahá'í in 1943, a year after the birth of his daughter and only child. After twenty-three years as a teacher at Fisk University, Hayden won the Grand Prix de la Poésie at the First World Festival of Negro Arts in Dakar, Senegal, in 1966, an award for which Derek Walcott was runner-up. Ironically, given that some of Hayden's greatest and most moving poems—poems such as "Middle Passage," "Runagate, Runagate" and "The Ballad of Nat Turner"—are painful evocations of slavery and its consequences, in 1966 Hayden was also savagely attacked at the Fisk Black Writers' Conference for being too moderate on racial issues. Despite such attacks, despite relative neglect, and despite bouts of depression, Hayden stayed true to his Bahá'í beliefs, asserting the essential equality of human beings and stubbornly resisting the pressures of prejudice until his death from cancer in 1980. Happily, "Old Four Eyes" did achieve some belated recognition. From 1969 to 1980 Hayden was Professor of English Literature at the

University of Michigan; in 1975 he was elected a fellow of the Academy of American Poets; and from 1976 to 1978 he occupied the poet laureate position of Consultant in Poetry to the Library of Congress.

SEAMUS HEANEY

"History is about as instructive as an abattoir." It is part of Seamus Heaney's history that he was born April 13th, 1939, and grew up at Mossbawn, a small 45-acre cattle farm, thirty miles east of Belfast, in County Derry Ireland. The eldest of nine children, at the age of 12 Heaney won a scholarship to attend St. Colomb's, a Catholic boarding school in Derry, and on graduating he studied English Language and Literature at Queen's University of Belfast before becoming a teacher. *Death of A Naturalist,* Heaney's first book of poetry, was published by Faber and Faber in 1966, the year his first son was born. Since then Heaney has gone on to father two more children, and to write eleven more major volumes of poetry, half a dozen essay collections, two plays, and several translations, including a much-praised version of *Beowulf.* Over the course of his career as academic and poet, Heaney has taught at Queen's University of Belfast, University of California at Berkeley, Carysfort College in County Dublin, Harvard University, and Oxford. The Cholmondeley, the E. C. Gregory, the Somerset Maugham, and the Geoffrey Faber Memorial Prize awards earned by *Death of A Naturalist* were followed by numerous other awards, culminating in the 1995 Nobel Prize in Literature. Tough-minded and tender, deeply informed by the rhythms of nature and country, Heaney's poetry celebrates language and life. It digs deep into past and present, self and society, to create an order "true to the impact of external reality and . . . sensitive to the inner laws of the poet's being." "I rhyme," as he says in "Personal Helicon," "To see myself, to set the darkness echoing." In so doing, he teaches us not to be overwhelmed by the lessons of the abattoir. "Crediting Poetry," his 1995 Nobel lecture, should be compulsory reading for all.

MICHAEL IGNATIEFF

Michael Ignatieff, writer, historian, public intellectual, and now politician, was born May 12th, 1947, to a family of educators and intellectuals. Ignatieff received a Ph.D. from Harvard and held a Senior Research Fellowship at King's College, Cambridge, from 1978 to 1984, as well as being Professor and Director at the Carr Centre for Human Rights Policy, Harvard, from 2000 to 2005. Ignatief is a versatile writer with a wide-ranging intellect: his family memoir, *The Russian Album* (1987), won a Governor General's Award for Non-Fiction; *Isaiah Berlin: A Life* (1998) was short-listed for a James Tait Black Memorial Prize; *Blood and Belonging* (1994), a book on the dangers of ethnic nationalism, received the Lionel Gelber Award; *Scar Tissue* (1993), a deeply moving novel with strong biographical elements, was short-listed for both the Booker prize and the Whitbread Novel Award, and *Virtual War: Kosovo and Beyond* (2000) won the Orwell prize for political non-fiction. At the time of this writing, Michael Ignatieff, M. P. for the Toronto riding of Etobicoke-Lakeshore, is leader of the opposition Liberal Party in Canada.

FRANZ KAFKA

It is titillating, though perhaps not particularly useful, to learn that Kafka was both a reluctant partner in an asbestos factory and—if business guru Peter Drucker is to be believed—the inventor of the civilian safety helmet. Perhaps more useful, though certainly less titillating, is the fact that Kafka was born July 3rd, 1883, the eldest of six children of a German-speaking, middle-class, Jewish family living in the anti-Semitic, largely Catholic, Austro-Hungarian city of Prague. Kafka's two brothers died in infancy before he was seven, and perhaps partly because of their deaths he grew up to be a hypersensitive, neurasthenic, vegetarian practitioner of Fletcherism who, despite several inconclusive love affairs, never completely broke free of his family or of Prague, and whose major works, *The Trial* (1925), *The Castle* (1926) and *Amerika* (1927), were only published after his death, and then only against his last wishes. To summarize Kafka's life in this way is, of course, to caricaturize him and to ignore his charm, his sense of humour, his mastery of German, Czech, French, Yiddish, and Hebrew, his Doctor of Law degree from Charles Ferdinand University in Prague, his work as a highly competent and well respected officer for the Bohemian Workers' Accident Insurance Institute, and the esteem he was held in by various Prague intellectuals for such small masterpieces as *Metamorphosis* (1915) and *In The Penal Colony* (1914). And yet it is certainly true that Kafka spent much of his life using, as Frederick Karl has said, "weakness as a means of asserting strength." Ultimately, the Kafkaesque hero demonstrates his heroism and guilty innocence by struggling resolutely, though ineffectually and with ever-diminishing strength, against the inscrutable, indifferent malignity of the world. On June 3rd, 1924, after more than seven years in and out of sanatoria, Kafka died of tuberculosis.

PATRICK LANE

Born in Nelson, British Columbia in 1933, Patrick Lane is very much a frontier poet, the product of small town British Columbia, a sensitive man raised in a culture of cowboys, miners, and loggers, a man who despite the odds has fought his way to literary success. Among his awards are the Governor General's Award, the Canadian Authors Association Award, and two National Magazine Awards. Lane has published over twenty books of poetry, as well as one novel, *Red Dog* (2008). His memoir, *There is a Season* (2004), is a redemptive masterpiece in which writing and gardening are opposed to the degradations of alcoholism and drug addiction. Published in the United States as *What the Stones Remember*, it is worthy of being read alongside Annie Dillard's *Pilgrim at Tinker Creek* and

Henry David Thoreau's *Walden*. Married to the poet Lorna Crozier, Lane now writes and gardens on Vancouver Island.

DORIS LESSING

Perhaps to suggest a link between her birthplace and her writing career, many biographers and reviewers of Doris Lessing like to point out that she was born in Kermansha, Persia, in 1919. Certainly Lessing has had a very exotic, very unusual writing career. Her first novel, *The Grass is Singing* (1950), and the fearlessness of her subsequent social realist fiction led to her banishment as a prohibited alien from South Africa and Southern Rhodesia in 1956. Her complex, though relatively conventional, explorations of the development of self in the *Children of Violence* series (1952-69) were followed by the highly experimental *The Golden Notebook* (1962), which highlighted the problems women face in trying to establish an autonomous identity. This novel became a feminist classic, though Lessing always resisted attempts to see herself as a high priestess of feminism. Her turning to science fiction in the subsequent Sufi-based *Canopus* novels (1979-1983) was perhaps partly a way to escape categorization as she continued her dissection of the clash between personal ideologies and the social frameworks which call them forth. 2007 Nobel laureate, recipient of a Companion of Honour and of numerous honorary degrees, self-educated, twice-divorced, single mother, communist, mystic, materialist, Cassandra, lover of cats—however she is defined, there is no denying Lessing's determination to break the chains of preconceived cultural notions such as racism, colonialism, sexism, and materialism to achieve spiritual wholeness. Born in Persia, raised in South Africa, based in England, citizen of the world, hers is the exoticism of intellectual courage—a courage and exoticism that shines through in the passion of her brilliant autobiography, *Under My Skin* (1994).

MICHAEL LONGLEY

In 1939 Michael Longley was born a twin to English parents living in Belfast. He has said of himself that "some of the time I feel British, and some of the time I feel Irish." After graduating from the Royal Belfast Academical Institution in 1958, he studied Classics at Trinity College, Dublin, and he worked briefly as a school teacher in Dublin and London, before returning to Belfast. From 1969 to 1981 he championed literature and the traditional arts in his work for the Arts Council of Northern Ireland, and together with his wife, the critic Edna Longley, he has been a major force in helping build a civil society in Northern Ireland. Ever aware of "the importance of walking forward into the past," in his poetry Longley is a painstaking taxidermist of nature and human experience—dissecting, classifying, and reconstituting scraps of existence with loving attention and sharp-eyed affection. Though he is lyric, not epic; though he numbers among his mentors Dickinson and Claire, Yeats and McNeice; Longley's principal voice is Homeric, and his poems—poems such as "Casualty," "Ceasefire," "The Ice-cream Man," "Wreaths," "Mayo Monologue," "An Amish Rug," "The Linen Industry, and "The Wren"—fuse "all we hope with what we know." Honoured by numerous awards, including the Hawthornden Prize, the Whitbread Poetry Award, and the T.S. Eliot Prize, in 2001 Michael Longley also chose to accept the Queen's Gold Medal. The medal was presented at Buckingham Palace, the same place where over 80 years before his father received a Military Cross for bravery. In 2010 Michael Longley was awarded a C.B.E., and part of his biography includes "the deportation of one canary called Pepicek."

ALICE MUNRO

"Pots can show malice, the patterns of linoleum can leer up at you, treachery is the other side of dailiness." Winner of three Governor

General's Awards, two Giller Prizes, a WH Smith Literary Award, a PEN/Malamud Award, an O. Henry Award, a Man Booker International Prize, and numerous other awards and honours, Alice Munro is often compared to short story masters such as Anton Chekhov, James Joyce, Eudora Welty, Flannery O'Connor and Carson McCullers. Significant literary ancestors also include Emily and Charlotte Brontë, the Halldór Laxness of *Independent People*, and James Hogg. Born Alice Laidlaw, July 10, 1931, in Wingham, Ontario, Alice broke free of the hardscrabble existence of small-town, rural Canada with the help of a two-year scholarship to the University of Western Ontario and an early marriage (1951). Marriage was followed by a move to British Columbia and the birth of four children—the second of whom, Catherine, born without kidneys, died within two days. Munro sold her first short story to *Mayfair* magazine in 1953, the year her first daughter was born, and in 1968 her first collection of short stories, *Dance of the Happy Shades*, won a Governor General's Award. As Munro's reputation grew, many of her stories were first published in the *New Yorker*, before being gathered, arranged, and often rewritten in collections such as *Who Do You Think You Are?* (1978), *The Progress of Love* (1986), *The Love of a Good Woman* (1998), and *Too Much Happiness* (2009). Domestic in scale, epic in scope, Munro's short stories use telling detail and clear, crisp prose to perturb reality. They bring out the extraordinary in the ordinary. Again and again, with unsentimental yet loving curiosity—and always with a sense of wonder—Munro tries to make sense of ordinary lives and the way in which such lives are shaped by powerful, often hidden forces of genetics, psyche, culture, history, imagination, character and chance. The shifting depths of her stories roil beneath surfaces "preserved as if under glass, bright as mustard or grimy as charcoal, with every shading in between."

SHARON OLDS

Born in 1942 in San Francisco, educated at Stanford and Columbia, and teacher of creative writing at New York University, Sharon Olds is not a poet for the squeamish. Her excremental vision rivals and possibly exceeds Jonathan Swift's. However, where his poetry contains elements of disgust and self-loathing, her poetry seems more transgressive in its motivations. Perhaps in reaction to a "hellfire Calvinist" childhood, she often seems to write to shock and offend, as if to try and see "if there is anything that shouldn't or can't be written about in a poem." Olds's first book of poetry, *Satan Says* (1980), won the San Francisco Poetry Centre Award, and subsequent books, such as *The Dead and the Living* (1984), *The Gold Cell* (1987), and *The Unswept Room* (2002), have also won numerous awards. Many of her poems painfully probe family life, and her 1993 book, *The Father,* uses the occasion of her father's dying to dissect some of the complexities of the father-daughter relationship. Because Olds explores the visceral and the animal in us—because, too, her poems are often raw and unpolished—her graphic self- exposures, however modulated or controlled, often provoke strong reactions in some readers. Martha Nussbaum, author of *Hiding from Humanity: Disgust, Shame and the Law* (2004), has said that disgust "involves a shrinking from contamination that is associated with a human desire to be non-animal." In her poetry, Sharon Olds tries to help readers overcome such disgust, tries to expand our notions of what it means to be human by acknowledging our animal natures. The best of her poetry is, indeed, "poached game."

MICHAEL ONDAATJE

Michael Ondaatje is a subject worthy of one of his own novels. A cultural hybrid of Dutch-Tamil-Sinhalese-Portuguese ancestry, he was born in Colombo, Ceylon in 1943. The first nine years of his life were spent in Ceylon, the next ten in England, and since 1962 Ondaatje has lived, studied, and written in Canada. While he is now best known for the international success of novels such as *In the Skin of a Lion* (1987), *The English Patient* (1992), *Anil's Ghost* (2000), and *Divisadero* (2007), Ondaatje first achieved recognition with his poetry. Two of his many books of poetry, *The Collected Works of Billy the Kid: Left Handed Poems* (1970) and *There's a Trick with a Knife I'm Learning to Do: Poems 1963-1978* (1979), won a Governor General's award. Ondaatje is a stylistically innovative writer who uses the exotic richness of his language in an attempt to heal wounds of violence and to create wholeness out of fragments. If coming to terms with the past is central to his writing, mythic truths, not facts, are what matter. As he says in "In Another Fashion," we must "build new myths / to wind up the world." Notorious for jealously guarding his privacy (in his introduction to *Leonard Cohen* (1970) he even warns that "nothing is more irritating than to have your work translated by your life"), Ondaatje constantly incites his readers to reconstitute fragments of his past. Part of what makes him great is that he is his own Billy the Kid, his own Buddy Bolden, his own Alice Gull, his own English patient and, most importantly, his own Michael Ondaatje.

SYLVIA PLATH
Born 1932, dead by suicide 1963, Sylvia Plath is arguably one of the best American poets of the 20th century, though much of her accomplishment is often clouded by her connection to her husband, the British poet Ted Hughes, and by her suicide at age 30. Part of the problem, of course, is that she mythologized herself, rooting her powerful, carefully crafted poems so deeply in the raw, emotional substrata of her relatively banal, mid-American upbringing that it is hard to resist a biographical approach to her work. The personal elements of *The Bell Jar* (1963), her harrowing, classic novel of a bright young woman's struggle with society and mental illness, have also fed the tendency to focus excessively on the biographical elements of her writing. Small wonder some feminists have tried to appropriate her

as an icon of feminist martyrdom. Fortunately, her poetry—which manipulates "experiences with an informed and intelligent mind"—transcends her myths and shows how successfully she achieved her youthful ambition of becoming "drunker than Dylan, harder than Hopkins, and younger than Yeats in my saying."

ADRIENNE RICH

"Philoctetes in woman's form," Baltimore born in 1929, Radcliffe- educated, praised by Auden at 21, mother of three sons at 29, widowed by suicide at 41, honoured by numerous awards (including a Bollingen, a MacArthur Fellowship, a National Book Award, and the famously declined National Medal for the Arts), partner of writer Michelle Cliff for almost 35 years, and sufferer of rheumatoid arthritis since her early twenties, Adrienne Rich is a poet, essayist, critic, and revolutionary whose accomplishments are still seriously undervalued. Partly this is because she started as a poet who worked within "the boundaries of perfection" and who, when those boundaries exploded, has sometimes been shrill and polemical in her pursuit of "the truths of outrage and the truths of possibility." It must be remembered, however, that Rich is "a woman with a mission not to win prizes / but to change the laws of history." If some of her later poems lack the polished control of "Aunt Jennifer's Tigers," the metaphysical depths of "Diving," or the biographical symbolism of "Power," many show her to be—as she has said of Karl Marx—"a great geographer of the human condition" and her numerous provocative and insightful essays—essays such as "When We Dead Awaken: Writing as Revision," "If Not With Others, How?," "Compulsory Heterosexuality and Lesbian Existence," and the "Arts of the Possible"—resurvey, remap, and even open up new territory. Equally powerful and transformational are reviews and critical essays such as "Jane Eyre: The Temptations of a Motherless Woman," "Vesuvius at Home: The Power of Emily Dickinson," and "Three Classics for New Readers: Karl Marx, Rosa Luxemburg, Che

Guevera." More Hephaestus than Philoctetes, through her writings Rich has forged tools and instruments with which to probe and "break open lost chambers of possibility."

MORDECAI RICHLER

"World-famous all over Canada" and in Italy, too, Mordecai Richler was born in Montreal, January 27th, 1931, and he died in Montreal, July 3rd, 2001. Grandson of a rabbinical scholar on the maternal side and of a scrap metal dealer on the paternal, Richler grew up poor and Orthodox. His parents' marriage was an unhappy one, and when it ended in 1943 young Mordecai was quick to abandon the Orthodox faith and to rebel against his authoritarian paternal grandfather. An indifferent student, Richler attended Baron Byng High School before dropping out of Sir George William College to go to Paris to become a novelist. His first novel, *The Acrobats*, was published in 1954, but it wasn't until 1959, after two more novels and six years in London, that Richler achieved recognition with *The Apprenticeship of Duddy Kravitz*. Further major novels, written after his return to Montreal, include *St Urbain's Horseman* (1971), *Joshua Then and Now* (1980), *Solomon Gursky Was Here* (1989), and *Barney's Version* (1997). Notable, too, are his children's book, *Jacob Two-Two Meets the Hooded Fang* (1975) and his political travel memoir, *This Year In Jerusalem* (1994). "A rumpled Zorro," blunt, fearless, combative, difficult, hard-drinking, a devoted, happily-married family man, and winner of two Governor General's Awards and a Giller Prize, Mordecai Richler did more than just use satire, parody, and humour to attack the flaws and follies of the world. Not afraid of the coarse, the common, or the vulgar, his rich, riotous novels celebrate his conviction that "In a time when there really is no agreement on values ... you are obliged to work out your own code of honour and system of beliefs and to lead as honourable a life as possible."

THEODORE ROETHKE

"What need for heaven, then, / With that man, and those roses?"
Born in 1908 and raised in Saginaw, Michigan, Roethke was living
and teaching in Washington when he died of a heart attack in 1963.
A brilliant yet troubled man, he struggled with alcohol and manic
depression for most of his life. He studied at the University of Michi-
gan and Harvard Graduate School before the Depression forced
him to support himself by teaching English and coaching tennis. His
first book of poetry, *Open House,* was published in 1941, and it and
his subsequent books earned him a wide readership and many
awards, including a Guggenheim Fellowship, the Bollingen Prize
and the Pulitzer. Superficially confessional, there is a wounded wist-
fulness and puzzled wonder to much of Roethke's artful poetry, as
he, to use Delmore Schwartz's phrase, "uses a variety of devices with
the utmost cunning and craft to bring the unconsciousness to the
surface of articulate expression."

PHILIP ROTH

"Sheer Playfulness and Deadly Seriousness are my closest friends."
Newark born (1933) and Newark-raised, Philip Roth was bar
mitzvahed in 1946 and graduated from Weequahic High School in
1950. In 1959, after prelaw studies at Newark College of Rutgers and
an MA in English from the University of Chicago, Roth achieved
early recognition and notoriety with the publication of "Defender of
the Faith" in *The New Yorker.* Despite two strenuous marriages (the
British actress Claire Bloom gives a bitter version of one of them in
her 1996 memoir, *Leaving a Doll's House*), numerous relationships, a
Halcion-induced nervous breakdown, and a quintuple bypass, Roth
has gone on to write over 28 novels. Out of "a continuing preoccupa-
tion with the relationship between the written and the unwritten
world," Roth constantly rereads, reinterprets, reinvents, and
rewrites the ever-altering self as son, friend, lover, writer,

Newarker, American, and Jew. Much of his writing deliberately confuses and confounds the uncertain boundaries between story and reality so as to achieve an "expansion of moral consciousness." Though Roth has not yet won a Nobel prize, he is, on the strength of *Patrimony* (1991) alone—not to mention a body of work which includes books as varied and ambitious as *Goodbye, Columbus and Five Short Stories* (1959), *Portnoy's Complaint* (1969), *The Ghost Writer* (1979), *The Counterlife* (1987), *Operation Shylock* (1993), *Sabbath's Theatre* (1995), and *The Plot Against America* (2005)—eminently Nobel-worthy. Among his acknowledged patron saints are Sigmund Freud, Henry James, Saul Bellow, and Franz Kafka.

KEN SARO-WIWA, JR.

Born 1968 in Lagos, Nigeria, and educated in England, Ken Saro-Wiwa, Jr. is the son of the writer and activist Ken Saro-Wiwa. Inevitably, for a man who vowed "to make something of my life by trying to save his," Ken Saro-Wiwa, Jr. is still better known as the son of his father than as a person in his own right. As the title of his patremoir *In the Shadow of a Saint* (2000) suggests, this subordinate position is largely of his own choosing. Certainly, he is not lacking in accomplishments. His work as broadcaster for the BBC, the CBC and National Public Radio, and his reporting for *The Guardian* and *The Globe and Mail*, has made him an important commentator on issues relating to globalization. Founder and board member of the Ken Saro-Wiwa Foundation, an organization established to honour the memory of Ken Saro-Wiwa and to continue his mission "to protect the natural environment, to promote the human rights of its defenders and to support grassroots organizations and individuals in furthering the cause of peace, freedom and justice," Ken Saro-Wiwa, Jr.'s preeminent position as social entrepreneur and cultural activist was confirmed by his selection as a Young Global Leader by the World Economic Forum in 2005. Subsequently, he worked as special assistant to two Nigerian presidents. While history and his own efforts may push him even farther onto the Nigerian and global political stage, the deeply perceptive, personal-public postscript to *In the Shadow of a Saint* proves that Ken Saro-Wiwa, Jr. has already moved far beyond his father's shadow. He is ready, as he said in commenting on a $15.5 Shell oil company settlement with the Ogoni, "to stop being the son of my father and be the father to my sons."

ANNE SEXTON

Anne Sexton is to confessional poetry as Al Capone is to sainthood. Born Anne Gray Harvey in 1928, Sexton's life is hard to disentangle from her death by suicide in 1974. Daughter of a Massachusetts wool merchant, at 18 she eloped and married "Kayo" Sexton, a young man who eventually found work in her father's business. Troubled by bipolar disorder and manic breakdowns, Sexton first started writing poetry seriously in 1955, as part of psychotherapy. Her first book of poems, *To Bedlam and Part Way Back*, was published in 1960; *All My Pretty Ones* in 1962; and in 1967, *Live or Die* (1966) won the Pulitzer Prize. Of her writing, Sylvia Plath—friend, fellow poet, and rival in death as well as in life—said, "her poems are wonderfully craftsman-like poems and yet they have a kind of emotional and psychological depth which I think is something perhaps quite new, quite exciting." Intellectual toughness, emotional honesty, control, and craftsmanship are the hallmarks of the best of Sexton's poetry, even if many readers and critics misread her as primarily confessional. Ironically, one of Sexton's best known lines, written for a rather autobiographical piece in *Ms. Magazine,* is usually read metaphysically, instead of literally as intended: "It doesn't matter who my father was, it matters who I remember he was."

DYLAN THOMAS

Dylan Thomas died November 9th, 1953, less than eleven months after the death of his father, and some two years after he wrote "Do

Not Go Gentle into That Good Night." Born in 1914 to Welsh parents who raised their children to be English-speaking, Thomas dropped out of school at the age of 16 to become a reporter. He published his first book of poems, *18 Poems*, in 1934 and his second one, *Twenty-five Poems,* in 1936. The success of those books launched his career as poet, broadcaster, and international celebrity. His private life is legendary for excessive drinking, madcap irresponsible behaviour, and a turbulent marriage that produced three children. His premature, alcohol-induced death, while on his third reading tour of America, also contributes to his romantic image as a *poete maudit*. Dylan's poetry is intensely lyrical. Under the pyrotechnic, often surreal surface of the poems lie carefully crafted and surprisingly varied explorations of life: of art, nature, death, childhood, grief, and joy. Among his most famous works are the radio play *Under Milk Wood* (1954), the short story collection *A Portrait of the Artist as a Young Dog* (1940), and poems such as "In My Craft or Sullen Art," "And Death Shall Have No Dominion," "The Force That Through the Green Fuse Drives the Flower," "Fern Hill," and "Do Not Go Gentle into That Good Night."

MIRIAM TOEWS

Born in 1964, Miriam Toews grew up in the small prairie town of Steinbach, Manitoba, a largely Mennonite community. Toews escaped Steinbach a day after graduating from high school, and after experiences which included "several continents, little money, strange jobs, sporadic university attendance, and two children, each by a different man," she returned to Winnipeg to write and raise a family. If much of her writing is informed by the experience of growing up Mennonite and yearning for a larger world, much too is informed by growing up with a father who suffered from severe depression. Toews' effervescent and often humorous books are -

animated by the tension between self and community, and by an appreciation of the "complicated kindness" which makes that tension almost bearable. While her novels have won numerous awards, including the 2004 Governor General's Award for *A Complicated Kindness* (2004) and the 2008 Writers' Trust Award for *The Flying Troutmans* (2008), Toews' most successful and most original book is her finely modulated, deeply moving patremoir, *Swing Low: A Life* (2000).

DEREK WALCOTT

Winner of the 1992 Nobel Prize for Literature, Derek Walcott was born and raised in the British Colony of St. Lucia, a small Windward Island located some 25 miles from the French colony of Martinique and some 350 miles from Venezuela. In 1930, the year of Walcott's birth, St. Lucia numbered some 80,000 people, mostly black, Creole- speaking Catholics. As befits an island poet, Walcott is a protean figure who assumes many guises and embodies many contradictions in his struggle with class, creed, colour, and colonialism. Biographical scraps include black and white ancestors; a twin brother; a mother who supported three children by taking in sewing and by teaching at the Methodist infant school in Castries; liberal arts studies at the fledgling University College of the West Indies, Kingston, Jamaica; the founding of seminal theatre companies in St. Lucia, Trinidad, and Boston; troubled relationships with women, alcohol, and money; a MacArthur Foundation Fellowship; a teaching position at Boston University; three marriages, and at least three children. Walcott has published many plays, notably *Ti-Jean and His Brothers* (1958), *Dream on Monkey Mountain* (1967) and *Odyssey: A Stage Version* (1993), and about twenty volumes of poems, chief among them *In a Green Night* (1962), *Another Life* (1973), *Omeros* (1990), and *Tiepolo's Hound* (2000). Even if his writing can, on occasion, be pretentious, sententious and sprinkled with unearned puns, Walcott's plays and poetry resonate with dualities of place, race, culture, faith, and identity. Some idea of the richness, power, and complexity of his epic vision is given by the following quotation, a quotation taken from his essay "The Muse of History":

> I accept this Archipelago of the Americas. I say to the ancestor who sold me, and to the ancestor who bought me, I have no father, I want no such father, although I can understand you, black ghost, white ghost, when you both whisper history, for if I attempt to forgive you both I am falling into your idea of history . . .

E.B. WHITE

"I say it's spinach, and I say the hell with it." E. B. White, Pulitzer Prize winner and son of a piano manufacturer, was born in 1899 and died in 1985. Most famous as the author of *Stuart Little* (1945) and *Charlotte's Web* (1952), White was a long-time writer for *The New Yorker* and the best known American essayist of his time. He was a gentle, though tough-minded, humanist writer, whose essays sparkle with quiet wit and humour, as befits a man who counted Dorothy Parker, James Thurber and Stephen Leacock among his friends. White also revised William Strunk's *The Elements of Style*, and to this day "Strunk and White," as the classic style manual is affectionately known, offers invaluable advice to college students and writers.

VIRGINIA WOOLF

Born January 25th, 1882, died by suicide March 28th, 1941. Novelist, critic, essayist, diarist, feminist, pacifist, daughter of the eminent Victorian philosopher and writer Sir Leslie Stephen, wife of the political theorist and writer Leonard Woolf, co-founder with Woolf of the Hogarth Press, and a central member of the Bloomsbury Group which included such artists and intellectuals as Clive Bell, Vanessa Bell, E.M. Forster, David Garnett, Roger Fry, Duncan Grant, John Maynard Keynes, Vita Sackville-West, and Lytton Strachey, Virginia Woolf is one of the major figures of 20th-century literature. Her deep interest in the nature of consciousness, the way in which the mind responds and organizes the varied physical, social, and intellectual stimuli to which it is exposed, helped produce highly lyrical, stylistically bold novels such as *To the Lighthouse* (1927), *Mrs. Dalloway* (1925), and *The Waves* (1931). Her father died when she was twenty-two, and in her diary she later wrote, "If he had lived longer his life would have entirely ended mine. What would have happened? No writing, no books; inconceivable."

ACKNOWLEDGEMENTS

For permission to reprint copyright material the publishers gratefully acknowledge the following:

"Flowers" reproduced with permission of Curtis Brown Group Ltd., London on behalf of Margaret Atwood. Copyright © Margaret Atwood 1995. "Flowers" from *Morning in the Burned House*: Poems / Margaret Atwood © 1995 by O. W. Toad. Published by McClelland and Stewart Ltd. Used with permission of the publisher. "Flowers" from *Morning in the Burned House* by Margaret Atwood. Reprinted by permission of Houghton Mifflin Harcourt Publishing Company. All rights reserved. "Notes of a Native Son" from *Notes of a Native Son* by James Baldwin. Copyright © 1955, renewed 1983, by James Baldwin. Reprinted by permission of Beacon Press, Boston. "Excerpt" from "Old Father, Old Artificer" from *Fun Home: A Family Tragicomedy* by Alison Bechdel. Copyright © 2006 by Alison Bechdel. Reprinted by permission of Houghton Mifflin Harcourt Publishing Company. All rights reserved. "Memoirs of a Bootlegger's Son" by Saul Bellow, originally published in *Granta 41, Autumn 1992*. Copyright © 1992 by Saul Bellow, reprinted by permission of the Wylie Agency LLC. Extract from *Untold Stories* by Alan Bennett. Copyright © 2006. Reprinted with permission by Faber and Faber Ltd. Extract from *Untold Stories* by Alan Bennett (© Forelake Ltd 2005) is used by permission of United Agents (www.unitedagents.co.uk) on behalf of Forelake Ltd. "Dreamsong 384" by John Berryman, from *The Dream Songs*. Copyright © 1982. Reprinted with permission by Faber and Faber Limited. "Dreamsong 384" from *The Dream Songs* by John Berryman. Copyright © 1969 by John Berryman. Copyright renewed 1997 by Kate Donahue Berryman. Reprinted by permission of Farrar, Straus and Giroux LLC. "My Father's Daughter" by Bliss Broyard, copyright © 1998. "Father's Old Blue Cardigan" from *Men in the Off Hours* by Anne Carson, copyright © 2000 by Anne Carson. Used by permission ofn Alfred A Knopf, a division of Random House, Inc. "Father's Old Blue Cardigan" from *Men in the Off Hours* by Anne Carson, published by Jonathan Cape. Reprinted by permission of The Random House Group Ltd. "Sugar Daddy" by Angela Carter, copyright © 1983, reprinted by Permission of the Estate of Angela Carter c/o Rogers, Coleridge & White, 20 Powis Mews, London w11 1jn. "Photograph of my Father in His Twenty-Second Year" from *All of Us: Collected Poems* by Raymond Carver, published by Harvill. Reprinted by permission of The Random House Group. "Photograph of my Father in His Twenty-Second Year" from *All of Us: Collected Poems* by Raymond Carver, copyright © 1996 by Tess

ACKNOWLEDGEMENTS

Peter Senkpiel, for getting me started and more.

Jennifer Bunting of Tilbury House (tilburyhouse.com), and Margaret Reynolds of the Book Publishers of BC (books.bc.ca), for wise counsel and generous encouragement.

Monica Brown and Bill Hesse, for editorial assistance and support. Stuart Houston, role model, inspiration and enthusiastic mentor.